A READER'S GUIDE TO SHAKESPEARE'S PLAYS

A Reader's Guide to Shakespeare's Plays

A Discursive Bibliography

revised edition

RONALD BERMAN
National Endowment for the Humanities

Scott, Foresman and Company
Glenview, Illinois   Brighton, England

Library of Congress Catalog Card Number 73-78189.
ISBN: 0-673-07878-7

Regional offices of Scott, Foresman and Company are located in Dallas,
  Texas; Glenview, Illinois; Oakland, New Jersey; Palo Alto, California;
  Tucker, Georgia; and Brighton, England.

Cover engraving from Wenceslaus Hollar's panorama of London, courtesy of the
Trustees, The British Museum.

FOR MY WIFE, BARBARA

Contents

INTRODUCTION

The Common Reader, whether in the university or simply in the community of the literate, is the primary audience for this book. Its purpose is to reduce the long list of works about Shakespeare's plays to some three thousand entries and to order these so that what is fundamental to each play may easily be known.

Every play has a chapter devoted to it, divided into sections headed text, editions, sources, criticism, and staging. The first section begins in each case with references to the following:
 Peter Alexander, *Shakespeare's Life and Art*
 E. K. Chambers, *William Shakespeare*
 W. W. Greg, *The Shakespeare First Folio*
 The New Arden edition of Shakespeare
 The New Cambridge edition of Shakespeare
 C. J. Sisson, *New Readings in Shakespeare*
Alexander's book gives a brief account of the origin of each play. The works of Chambers and Greg are authoritative for description and analysis of the text itself. The New Arden and New Cambridge are the major ventures of the present in providing critical editions. The volumes of Sisson provide direct explication. No one of these books is accepted in its entirety by all scholars, but they remain, by and large, the best of what is available. The textual sections are completed by references to additional useful studies. Some plays, like *King Lear,* have many such references, and others, like *Twelfth Night,* have very few; the number of additional studies is directly related to the textual problems posed by each play. Not mentioned are more general works on textual research, but Fredson Bowers' *On Editing Shakespeare and the Elizabethan Dramatists,* W. W. Greg's *A Bibliography of the English Printed Drama to the Restoration,* and other well-known works should be consulted automatically.

Under the heading of editions are mentioned the New Arden, the New Cambridge, the New Variorum, and important special editions. The first two have valuable introductions. The New Variorum volumes, begun under H. H. Furness in 1871, are massive storehouses of information on the plays. The Yale and Pelican editions are cited; they are inexpensive and reliable general texts. It should be noted that certain one-volume editions, like those of Peter Alexander, Hardin Craig and David Bevington, and G. L. Kittredge and Irving Ribner, remain among the more distinguished works on Shakespeare.

The sections on sources refer to Kenneth Muir's *Shakespeare's Sources* and Geoffrey Bullough's *Narrative and Dramatic Sources of Shakespeare.*

These are followed by a variety of other studies. Perhaps the most fully developed field of research is that of sources, for which there is almost an *embarras de richesse*. In addition to the specific works cited, others of a more general nature should be consulted, among them Selma Guttman's *The Foreign Sources of Shakespeare's Works.*

The longest and most detailed consideration is given to criticism. I have not been neutral in analyzing critical works. If my judgments are wrong, I am very much at fault, but I believe the duty of the critical bibliographer is to be critical. This is not to say that I take a *parti pris* on any "school" of criticism: where psychologists or mythologers or new critics or historical critics seem to prove their point, they are granted that. Where they have not, I have noted what seem to me to be their errors. Sometimes the same book will be judged differently for different plays: an example might be G. W. Knight's *The Crown of Life,* which is a much less reliable guide to *Cymbeline* than it is to *The Winter's Tale.*

The sections on staging do not refer to the general works of E. K. Chambers, *The Elizabethan Stage,* or G. E. Bentley, *The Jacobean and Caroline Stage,* which I assume are in any case well known. These sections begin with references to six studies:
    H. Craig, *The Complete Works of Shakespeare* (1st edition)
    The New Arden edition of Shakespeare
    The New Cambridge edition of Shakespeare
    G. Odell, *Shakespeare From Betterton to Irving*
    A. C. Sprague, *Shakespeare and the Actors*
    J. C. Trewin, *Shakespeare on the English Stage 1900-1964*
The first three include reliable stage histories. The last three give accounts of specific performances and modes of acting. These works are followed by whatever studies seem best to bring to the reader the sense of participating in a drama. For *The Merchant of Venice* the excellent accounts of J. R. Brown and T. Lelyveld are cited; the great tragedies rely, for example, on the work of Harley Granville-Barker; other plays have reference to reviews of unusual competence.

Needless to say, I am heavily indebted to the bibliographies mentioned. My indebtedness extends to all the works I have covered and to the libraries where I have worked.

BIBLIOGRAPHIES

The standard bibliographies described below present a vast and seemingly unmanageable amount of information. The reader who first encounters them may well imagine, as the saying goes, that wisdom is sorrow. But they are more than reminders of humility; for without them we could hardly realize the kind and quality of work accomplished by our discipline.

The Cambridge Bibliography of English Literature (CBEL) is basic to the study of the Renaissance. It is invaluable for studies of Shakespeare's background, for it offers material on the theater, education, political and philosophical thought, and all other aspects of life. Among the many studies on Shakespeare that it lists are those of the texts, sources, principal editions, and major criticisms. The *CBEL* (1940) has a *Supplement* (1957). W. Jaggard, *Shakespeare Bibliography* (1911), covers the principal early editions. E. K. Chambers, *William Shakespeare* (1930), discusses each play and its textual background. *A Shakespeare Bibliography* (1931) by W. Ebisch and L. Schücking is valuable for its listing of continental scholarship. There is a *Supplement* (1937). G. R. Smith, *A Classified Shakespeare Bibliography 1936-1958* (1963), covers many things, from the problems of Turkish translation of Shakespeare to the acting of Jean-Louis Barrault. Some of the best listings of works on Shakespeare are annual productions of the scholarly quarterlies. Such are the annual bibliographies of *Shakespeare Association Bulletin,* continued after 1948 in *Shakespeare Quarterly.* The latter is itself one of the great sources of scholarship. Other annual listings are in *Studies in Philology, PMLA,* and *Studies in English Literature 1500-1900.* Valuable annotated lists are to be found in *The Year's Work in English Studies* and in the annual volumes of *Shakespeare Survey.* The latter not only discusses current research but reviews a great deal of past work. It is, along with *Shakespeare Quarterly,* one of the few reliable sources for current information on Shakespearean production.

ABBREVIATIONS

SHAKESPEARE'S PLAYS

AC	Antony and Cleopatra
Ado	Much Ado about Nothing
AWW	All's Well that Ends Well
AYL	As You Like It
CE	The Comedy of Errors
Cor	Coriolanus
Cym	Cymbeline
Ham	Hamlet
1H4	Henry the Fourth, Part I
2H4	Henry the Fourth, Part II
H5	Henry the Fifth
1H6	Henry the Sixth, Part I
2H6	Henry the Sixth, Part II
3H6	Henry the Sixth, Part III
H8	Henry the Eighth
JC	Julius Caesar
KJ	King John
Lear	King Lear
LLL	Love's Labour's Lost
Mac	Macbeth
MM	Measure for Measure
MND	A Midsummer Night's Dream
MV	The Merchant of Venice
MWW	The Merry Wives of Windsor
Oth	Othello
Per	Pericles
R2	King Richard the Second
R3	King Richard the Third
RJ	Romeo and Juliet
TA	Titus Andronicus
Tem	The Tempest
TGV	The Two Gentlemen of Verona
Tim	Timon of Athens
TN	Twelfth Night
TrC	Troilus and Cressida
TSh	The Taming of the Shrew
WT	The Winter's Tale

OTHER WORKS CITED

Alexander	P. Alexander, *Shakespeare's Life and Art*
AMS	*Joseph Quincy Adams Memorial Studies*
Archiv	*Archiv für das Studium der neueren Sprachen*
Bullough	G. Bullough, *Narrative and Dramatic Sources of Shakespeare*
BUSE	*Boston University Studies in English*
Camb	The Cambridge edition (New Cambridge) of Shakespeare, ed. A. Quiller-Couch and J. Dover Wilson
CE	*College English*
Chambers	E. K. Chambers, *William Shakespeare,* Vol. I
Clemen	W. Clemen, *The Development of Shakespeare's Imagery*
Coleridge	*Shakespearean Criticism,* ed. T. M. Raysor
CQ	*Critical Quarterly*
Craig	*The Complete Works of Shakespeare* (1st ed.) ed. H. Craig
DUJ	*Durham University Journal*
Ea	*Études anglaises*
EC	*Essays in Criticism*
EIE	*English Institute Essays*
ELH	*Journal of English Literary History*
ES	*English Studies*
E&S	*Essays and Studies*
Evans	B. I. Evans, *The Language of Shakespeare's Plays*
Ex	*Explicator*
Granville-Barker	H. Granville-Barker, *Prefaces to Shakespeare*
Greg	W. W. Greg, *The Shakespeare First Folio*
Hazlitt	*Characters of Shakespeare's Plays,* ed. A. Quiller-Couch
HLQ	*Huntington Library Quarterly*
HR	*Hudson Review*
JEGP	*Journal of English and Germanic Philology*
Johnson	*Samuel Johnson on Shakespeare,* ed. W. K. Wimsatt
KR	*Kenyon Review*
Lib	*The Library*
McManaway	J. G. McManaway, "Recent Studies in Shakespeare's Chronology," *Shakespeare Survey,* III (1950)
MLN	*Modern Language Notes*
MLQ	*Modern Language Quarterly*
MLR	*Modern Language Review*
MP	*Modern Philology*

Muir	K. Muir, *Shakespeare's Sources*
New Arden	The New Arden edition of Shakespeare
NM	*Neuphilologische Mitteilungen*
NQ	*Notes and Queries*
NS	*Die Neueren Sprachen*
NV	*A New Variorum Edition of Shakespeare,* ed. H. H. Furness
Odell	G. Odell, *Shakespeare From Betterton to Irving*
PBA	*Proceedings of the British Academy*
PMLA	*Publications of the Modern Language Association*
PQ	*Philological Quarterly*
QJS	*Quarterly Journal of Speech*
REL	*Review of English Literature*
RES	*Review of English Studies*
RSL	*Royal Society of Literature*
SAB	*Shakespeare Association Bulletin*
SB	*Studies in Bibliography*
SEL	*Studies in English Literature 1500-1900*
Sew	*Sewanee Review*
Sh	Shakespeare
ShJ	*Shakespeare-Jahrbuch* (published in Weimar until 1965, in Heidelburg after 1965)
ShQ	*Shakespeare Quarterly*
ShS	*Shakespeare Survey*
ShStud	*Shakespeare Studies*
Sisson	C. J. Sisson, *New Readings in Shakespeare*
Smith	G. R. Smith, *A Classified Shakespeare Bibliography 1936-1958*
SP	*Studies in Philology*
Sprague	A. C. Sprague, *Shakespeare and the Actors*
Spurgeon	C. Spurgeon, *Shakespeare's Imagery*
TAr	*Theatre Arts*
TDR	*Tulane Drama Review*
TLS	*Times Literary Supplement*
Trewin	J. C. Trewin, *Shakespeare on the English Stage 1900-1964*
TxSE	*Texas Studies in English*
UKCR	*University of Kansas City Review*
UTQ	*University of Toronto Quarterly*
YR	*Yale Review*

THE PLAYS

HENRY THE SIXTH

TEXT Alexander 77-82; Camb (1) vii-l, 102-107, (2) vii-liii, (3) vii-xvi, 117-122; Chambers 277-293; Greg 176-189; New Arden (1) xiii-xxxviii, (2) xi-xlix, (3) xiii-xlv; Sisson II, 68-86.

Textual criticism has considered the plays on Henry VI as revisions, products of collaboration, or Shakespeare's work alone. Malone had doubted the Shakespearean origin of the two quartos; this view has been often asserted. J. Lee's "On the Authorship of 2 and 3H6 and Their Originals," *New Sh Soc. Trans.* (1876), 219-313, assigned parts of the play to Greene, Peele, and Marlowe. C. T. Brooke, "The Authorship of 2 and 3H6," *Trans. Conn. Acad.,* XVII (1912), 141-211, also found Marlowe's hand. Collaboration of various kinds was theorized by H. D. Gray in *PMLA,* XXXII (1917), and A. Gaw in *The Origin and Development of 1H6* (1926). A major change occurred with the publication of M. Doran's *H6, 2 and 3* (1928) and P. Alexander's *Shakespeare's H6 and R3* (1929). Both held for solely Shakespearean authorship and argued that the quartos (known as the *Contention* and the *True Tragedy)* were not the sources for the *H6* plays but only corrupt versions. Alexander's book is indispensable as a review of the text, its problems, and its critics. A major attempt at rebuttal was that of C. T. Prouty, *The Contention and Shakespeare's 2H6* (1954). This has, incidentally, a good comparative and historical analysis of the play's style. J. G. McManaway, *"The Contention and 2H6,"* Weiner Beiträge, LXV (1957), 143-154, is a sound introduction to the textual situation.

See also J. Jordan, "The Reporter of *2H6,"* PMLA, LXIV (1949), 1089-1113; J. Dover Wilson, "Malone and the Upstart Crow," *ShS,* IV (1951), 56-68; L. Kirschbaum, "The Authorship of *1H6,"* PMLA, LXVII (1952), 809-822; G. B. Evans, *"1, 2, 3H6* (New Cambridge Sh)," *ShQ,* IV (1953), 84-92; M. Mincoff, *"3H6* and *The True Tragedy,"* ES, XLII (1961), 273-288 and "The Composition of *1H6,"* ShQ, XVI (1965), 279-287.

EDITIONS The Bankside edition of *2H6,* edited by C. Thomas (1892), has texts of *Contention* and F$_1$. The Bankside edition of *3H6,* edited by A. Morgan (1892), has texts of *The True Tragedie* and F$_1$. See also Camb, ed. J. Dover Wilson (1952); New Arden *(2H6),* ed. A. Cairncross (1957); New Arden *(1H6),* ed. A. Cairncross (1962); New Arden *(3H6),* ed. A. Cairncross (1964); Pelican *(1H6),* ed. David Bevington (1966); *(2H6, 3H6),* ed. Robert Turner, Jr., and George Walton Williams (1967).

SOURCES W. Boswell-Stone, *Shakespere's Holinshed* (1896); C. L. Kingsford, *Prejudice and Promise in Fifteenth Century England* (1925); A. and J. Nicoll, *Holinshed's Chronicle as Used in Shakespeare's Plays* (1927); A. Hart, *Sh and the Homilies* (1934); L. King, "The Use of Hall's *Chronicles* in the Folio and Quarto Texts of *H6*," *PQ*, XIII (1934), 321-332, and "*2* and *3H6*—Which Holinshed?" *PMLA*, L (1935), 745-752; W. G. Zeeveld, "The Influence of Hall on Shakespeare's English Historical Plays," *ELH*, III (1936), 317-353; R. A. Law, "The Chronicles and *1, 2, 3H6*," *TxSE*, XXXIII (1955), 13-32; Bullough (1957–), III, 23-217.

CRITICISM It would be misleading to claim that there is a critical dialectic on these plays, for they have undergone relatively little literary scrutiny. They have, however, been subject to intensive study of their ideological relationship to their times. In 1840 T. P. Courtenay could satisfy himself, in his *Commentaries on the History Plays of Sh,* that the significance of these plays was that they proved the author a bad historian. Like many other nineteenth-century critics he attempted to reconcile them with fact and found them loaded with anachronism. Thereafter R. Simpson, in "The Politics of Shakespeare's Historical Plays," *New Sh Soc. Trans.* (1874), speculated that the histories revealed contemporary problems, and he studied their relationship to specifically Elizabethan ideas. F. Schelling sensed an underlying structure of epic unity in the early histories in his *The English Chronicle Play* (1902). Although he found their dramatic events hopelessly jumbled, he pointed out the great motif of discord. C. T. Brooke's *The Tudor Drama* (1912) asserted a claim that was to gain more influence than it merited: the histories revealed the "Armada" spirit of patriotism and glorified England. J. Marriott in *English History in Sh* (1918) and in a well-known article in *Cornhill,* CXXXVI (1927), 678-690, discussed the themes of national unity, cosmic order reflected in political order, the peculiar immorality of civil war, and the overriding sense of nemesis. He was one of the first to relate the *H6* plays to Hall's chronicle. A series of three articles by German critics began the close study of kingship in Sh: W. Keller, "Shakespeares Königsdramen," *ShJ,* LXIII (1927), 35-53; A. Henneke, "Shakespeares englische Könige," *ShJ,* LXVI (1930), 79-144; W. Clemen, "Sh und das Königtum," *ShJ,* LXVIII (1932), 56-79. The last is of particular interest for its study of the sacred status of kings.

In 1927 W. Lewis yoked together Shakespeare's histories and Frazer's anthropological myths in *The Lion and the Fox.* It is a thought-provoking if not entirely convincing study of the sacrificial nature of kings in the history plays. The publication of E. M. W. Tillyard's *Shakespeare's History Plays* (1944) began a phase of more rigorous research into Elizabethan ideas. Tillyard found the *H6* plays to be something like historical moralities, with the nation itself the hero under God. The first part, although crude, he judged to be filled with admirable dramatic energy; he was sympathetic to the lifelike characters of *2;* the last part he found monotonous in its chaotic violence. L. Campbell, *Shakespeare's Histories: Mirrors of Elizabethan Policy* (1947), is a notable study of the continual relevance of the histories to the history of Elizabethan England itself. In addition she pointed out the moral meaning (for Elizabethan historians) of the York and Lancaster wars: "An usurper seizes the throne; God avenges his sin upon the third heir through the agency of another usurper, whose sin is again avenged upon the third heir."

B. Stirling, *The Populace in Sh* (1949), notes Shakespeare's distortions of the chronicles, in which Jack Cade is a "young man of goodly stature and right pregnant wit   sober in talk, wise in reasoning." He becomes a symbol of the monstrosity of "disorder" in the *H6* plays. Stirling supplies an excellent study of sixteenth-century history. An equally useful book is I. Ribner's *The English History Play in the Age of Sh* (1957), which provides solid coverage of the history play as a genre, the ideological background, and the issues covered by past scholarship. M. M. Reese, *The Cease of Majesty* (1961) unites both historical and literary method, noting how language reinforces "doctrine" in the *H6* plays: "to emphasise their helplessness, the characters are conceived as ships struggling against the tide or carried inertly before the gale, and the storm thus appears as the arbitrary instrument of the chaos which men's actions have created." Information on the political background and the title to the crown and other legal matters will be found in George W. Keeton's *Shakespeare's Legal and Political Background* (1967).

The more purely literary study of the *H6* plays received its impetus from G. W. Knight's *Shakespearian Tempest* (1932), in which the imagery of elemental conflict was examined. R. W. Chambers gives a strong defence of the quality of the plays in *Man's Unconquerable Mind* (1939). They seem to him to reveal, like the plays of Aeschylus, evil in its native element of history. M. Van Doren, *Sh* (1939), writes of the nature of the plays' language, in which he finds thematic clusters of animal imagery. This idea is taken up by A. Yoder in *Animal Analogy in Shakespeare's Character Portrayal* (1947). M. Swayne, "Shakespeare's King Henry VI as a Pacifist," *CE*, III (1941), 143-149, and U. Ellis-Fermor, *The Frontiers of Drama* (1945), consider the idealism for which the king stands. T. Spencer, *Sh and the Nature of Man* (1942), writes of the pattern of the histories: "an existing order is violated, the consequent conflict and turmoil are portrayed, and order is restored by the destruction of the force or forces that originally violated it." H. Craig's "Sh and the History Play," *AMS* (1948), is a first-rate analysis

of the Senecan speeches of the *H6* plays, which are full of "the accumu-
lation of revolting and circumstantial horror, with exclamations, enu-
merations, and epithets." T. M. Parrott, however, in his *Shakespearean
Comedy* (1949), dismisses the language of the first of these plays as
"Marlovian rant." He misses, I think, the *wit* of La Pucelle here and of
Crookback in the later plays.

M. C. Bradbrook, *Sh and Elizabethan Poetry* (1951), writes of the
mirror-scenes in the *H6* plays, in which certain physical attitudes and
rhetorical patterns reveal allegorical meaning. F. Boas, "Joan of Arc in
Sh, Schiller and Shaw," *ShQ*, II (1951), 35-45, awards the palm to Sh.
Even though Joan is exaggerated and in fact depraved in *1H6*, she remains more of a woman than does the animated idea of Shaw. An
admirable study is that of H. T. Price, *Construction in Sh* (1951). Price
suggests that design rather than plot is the principle of construction in
these plays, and as an example he demonstrates the gradual decomposi-
tion of the English characters in *1* and the unification of their enemies.
Events, he observes, are symbolic rather than historic; they reveal the
"controlling moral idea" of the play. He reviews stage effects and figures of speech which intensify dramatic stress. One of the most interesting studies of the language is in Clemen (1951). Many images are
used as "embroidery," and many speeches demonstrate digression
almost as if it were a creative principle. The language, Clemen believes,
has very little relation to the character of those who utter it. Style is
also the concern of the Camb editor, who writes of *2* that it displays
Greene's and Nashe's "ostentatious displays of classical scholarship"
and of *3* that it is written in an exuberant and uncontrollable style. It
should be noted that the editor of the Camb edition holds for divided
authorship. Evans (1952) finds in *H6* the language of high emotional
intensity at its best—and a ranting "riot of words" at its worst.

W. Clemen, "Anticipation and Foreboding in Shakespeare's Early
Histories," *ShS*, VI (1953), 25-35, writes of prophecies, omens, and
dreams. A good essay on style is in C. T. Prouty's *The Contention and
Shakespeare's 2H6* (1954). A. Kernan, "A Comparison of the Imagery
in *3H6* and *Richard, Duke of York*," *SP*, LI (1954), 431-442, takes into
account the work of Clemen and Spurgeon. He examines in particular
the metaphor of sea, wind, and tide, which intensifies the sense of disorder in nature. There are long and valuable critical introductions in the
New Arden editions (1957-1964) by A. S. Cairncross. These editions
have a wealth of material on text, sources, and style; taken as a whole
they equal a long monograph. Although textual discussion predom-
inates, these volumes are clearly the necessary point for beginning the
study of the trilogy's literary meaning. G. W. Knight, *The Sovereign
Flower* (1958), has a sensitive analysis of the language. The characters,
he writes, "cannot open their mouths at a passionate moment without

loading their speech with vivid analogies from nature." In these speeches there is a genuinely tragic mingling of beauty and agony. There is a ponderous study of structure in T. W. Baldwin's *On the Literary Genetics of Shakspere's Plays 1592-1594* (1959). C. M. Quinn, "Providence in Shakespeare's Yorkist Plays," *ShQ,* X (1959), 45-52, writes of irony in these early histories. Each of the dramatic agents finds the opposite of what he expects from his deeds—the overriding scheme is that of ironic retribution.

One of the best recent studies is J. P. Brockbank's "The Frame of Disorder," *Early Sh* (1961). He calls *1H6* the "pageantry of dissension." The savagery is to some extent controlled by a kind of ceremony which, expressed in stage spectacle, allows insight into its symbolic meaning. The second play is more mature in the use of such "staged metaphor," showing, for example, the death of Gloucester as a picture of Virtue literally "choked with foul ambition." The third play shows dissolution into anarchy; with the advent of Richard Crookback "unnatural energies" break free to destroy the tenuous frame of order. R. Berman's "Fathers and Sons in the *H6* Plays," *ShQ,* XIII (1962), 487-497 discusses loyalty and inheritance, and their transvaluations. An excellent study of these plays by H. M. Richmond *(Shakespeare's Political Plays,* 1965) emphasizes that they are to be judged as productions of medieval art. Both politics and style are discussed.

Further reading: K. Schmidt, *Margareta von Anjou vor und bei Sh* (1906); W. Raleigh, *Sh and England* (1918); J. W. Allen, *A History of Political Thought in the Sixteenth Century* (1928); P. Messiaen, "La Trilogie de *H6,*" *Revue des Cours et Conferences,* XXXIX (1938), 137-156; M. B. Smith, *Marlowe's Imagery* (1940); E. M. W. Tillyard, *The Elizabethan World Picture* (1943); J. Palmer, *Political Characters of Sh* (1945); A. Harbage, *As They Liked It* (1947); H. Craig, *An Interpretation of Sh* (1948); H. T. Price, "Mirror-Scenes in Sh," *AMS* (1948); J. Danby, *Shakespeare's Doctrine of Nature* (1949); C. Scott-Giles, *Shakespeare's Heraldry* (1950); H. Jenkins, "Shakespeare's History Plays: 1900-1951," *ShS,* VI (1953), 1-15; A. Richardson, "The Early Historical Plays," *Sh: Of an Age and for All Time* (1954); C. Leech, "The Two-Part Play," *ShJ,* XCIV (1958), 90-106; T. H. McNeal, "Margaret of Anjou," *ShQ,* IX (1958), 1-10; R. Stevenson, *Shakespeare's Religious Frontier* (1958); H. Mathews, *Character and Symbol in Shakespeare's Plays* (1962); Samuel Pratt, "Sh and Humphrey Duke of Gloucester: A Study in Myth," *ShQ,* XVI (1965), 201-216; A. C. Hamilton, *The Early Sh* (1967); K. Muir, "Image and Symbol in Shakespeare's Histories," *Bulletin of the John Rylands Library,* L (1967), 103-123; F. P. Wilson, *Shakespearian and Other Studies* (1969), pp. 4-18.

STAGING   Camb (1) Ii-Iv, (3) xxxix-xlv; Craig 210; Odell *passim;*
Sprague 125-126; Trewin *passim.*

See also R. Watkins, *On Producing Sh* (1950); Price (above); B. L.
Joseph, *Elizabethan Acting* (1951); B. Jackson, "On Producing *H6,"*
ShS, VI (1953), 49-52; J. Sandoe, *"2H6:* Notes During Production,"
Theatre Annual, XIII (1955), 32-48; A. C. Sprague, *Shakespeare's
Histories: Plays for the Stage* (1964); G. Rogoff, "Sh With Tears,"
TDR (Spring 1964), 176-179; J. L. Styan, *Shakespeare's Staging*
(1967), *passim.*

KING RICHARD THE THIRD

TEXT Alexander 83-85; Camb vii-xxxvi, 140-160; Chambers 294-305; Greg 190-199; Sisson II, 87-97.

See also P. Alexander, *Shakespeare's H6 and R3* (1929); D. Patrick, *The Textual History of R3* (1936); R. A. Law, *"R3:* A Study in Shakespeare's Composition," *PMLA,* LX (1945), 689-696; J. Dover Wilson, "Shakespeare's *R3* and *The True Tragedy of Richard the Third,* 1594," *ShQ,* III (1952), 299-307; A. Walker, *Textual Problems of the First Folio* (1953); J. Walton, *The Copy for the Folio Text of R3* (1955) — see the reviews of this book by F. Bowers in *ShQ,* X (1959), 91-96 and 541-544. See also A. Cairncross, "The Quartos and the Folio Text of *R3,*" *RES,* VIII (1957), 225-233; Kristian Smidt, *Iniurious Imposters and R3* (1964) and *The Tragedy of R3* (1969); E. A. J. Honigmann, "The Text of R3," *Theatre Research,* VII (1965), 48-55.

EDITIONS Bankside, ed. E. Calkins (1891); Arden, ed. A. Thompson (1907); *NV,* ed. H. H. Furness, Jr. (1908); Yale, ed. J. Crawford (1927); Camb, ed. J. Dover Wilson (1954); Pelican, ed. G. Blakemore Evans (1959).

SOURCES The most thorough study of sources is G. B. Churchill's *R3 up to Sh* (1900). This indispensable book has a full account of research on the historical background to the year of its publication. See also W. G. Boswell-Stone, *Shakespere's Holinshed* (1896); E. Koeppel, "Shakespeares *R3* und Senecas *Troades,*" *ShJ,* XLVII (1911), 188-190; F. Wilhelm, "Zu Seneca und Sh," *Archiv,* CXXIX (1912), 69-73; R. A. Law, *"R3,* Act I Scene 4," *PMLA,* XXVII (1912), 117-141; A. and J. Nicoll, *Holinshed's Chronicle as Used in Shakespeare's Plays* (1927); E. Begg, "Shakespeare's Debt to Hall and to Holinshed in *R3,*" *SP,* XXXII (1935), 189-196; W. G. Zeeveld, "The Influence of Hall on Shakespeare's English Historical Plays," *ELH,* III (1936), 317-353. The historical authenticity of vat-drowning is discussed by J. Spargo in "Clarence in the Malmsey-Butt," *MLN,* LI (1936), 166-173. See also P. Williams, *"R3:* The Battle Orations," *English Studies in Honor of J. S. Wilson* (1951); Bullough (1957—), III, 221-349.

CRITICISM An early study of unusual merit is C. V. Boyer's *The Villain as Hero in Elizabethan Tragedy* (1914). This work contains studies of the Machiavellian "lion and the fox" years before Wyndham Lewis; of the "strength of intellect" of the protagonist long before the work of A. P. Rossiter; and of "natural order" a full generation before Tillyard's work. Boyer suggests that the end of Richard is simply power itself. He also gives a good critique of the possible Senecan influences.

A. P. Rossiter's analysis of *R3* in "The Structure of *R3*," *DUJ*, XXXI (1938), 44-75, and in his *Angel with Horns* (1961) remains the most intelligent of speculations on the play. He suggests that Richard is the archetype of the Renaissance aspiring will confronted with the archaic and inert order of the Middle Ages; the play becomes a great opposition of the wit and will of the individual against a cosmic myth of "order." Rossiter suggests in addition that the play works in terms of "movements" rather than in terms of historically realistic actions; many of its scenes, he points out, are really rituals rather than credible events. For M. Van Doren, *Sh* (1939), Richard exemplifies a new kind of consciousness: "he is the first character in Sh to achieve his own form, to have sinuous and purposeful movement controlled from within." Rather different is A. Goll in his simplistic "Richard III as the Criminal Type," *Jour. Crim. Law*, XXX (1939), 22-35, who finds that Richard is a form of monstrosity.

S. Thomas, *The Antic Hamlet and R3* (1943), argues that Richard is a forerunner of Hamlet and represents the Vice Dissimulation of the morality plays. He has the antic disposition of this comic villain of the old stage. There is a brilliant account of the working of the providential scheme in *R3* in E. M. W. Tillyard's *Shakespeare's History Plays* (1944). For Tillyard the protagonist of this undervalued play is ultimately believable—a great combination of evil, humor, and artistry in crime. The resemblance of *R3* to *Mac* has often been noted; an account is in F. Smith, "The Relation of *Mac* to *R3*," *PMLA*, LX (1945), 1003-1020. One of the best character studies is in J. Palmer's *Political Characters of Sh* (1945). The paradoxical Richard is "brave, witty, resourceful, gay, swift, disarmingly candid with himself, engagingly sly with his enemies." Palmer suggests that the play calls for a suspension of moral judgment— especially when Richmond, the figurehead for virtue, is full of such "pious twaddle." For Palmer, Richard III is the Nietzschean hero *par excellence*. Two articles by W. A. Armstrong—"The Elizabethan Conception of the Tyrant," *RES*, XXII (1946), 161-181, and "The Influence of Seneca and Machiavelli on the Elizabethan Tyrant," *RES*, XXIV (1948), 19-35—outline a basic pattern of political villainy. The Elizabethan tyrant on the stage and in prose is damned spiritually as well as politically; the power struggle becomes that of good and evil. He characteristically feels despair, pain, and the torments of conscience, and he is destroyed with exemplary violence. L. Campbell, *Shakespeare's Histories* (1947), furnishes accounts of the topical meanings of the play, with reference to the career of Leicester. As for the moral of *R3*, "it is the God of the Old Testament that must be supposed to rule in such a moral order as Sh here depicts, but it is a moral order. The justice is that of an eye for an eye. . . . Prayers that are offered as curses by those with hatred in their hearts are answered by a divine justice without pity."

The Senecan dialogue is the subject of H. Craig, "Sh and the History Play," *AMS* (1948). J. Danby, *Shakespeare's Doctrine of Nature* (1949), has this to say: "the earlier plays hold fast to a Christian belief in the primacy of 'pity, love, and fear.' Against this theological background is thrown the figure of the Machiavel—not a melodramatic monster, but the interpreter of an actual society. The Machiavel rejects 'pity, love, and fear' and kills the King who stands for the holy order of these values." The evil of this kind of individualism is examined also by D. Stauffer in *Shakespeare's World of Images* (1949). Quite a contrary view is that of the Camb editor (1954). He quotes Lamb's praise of the Covent Garden performance of *R3,* and in support of it he argues that melodrama, which is the mode of this play, is both legitimate and highly artistic. It may be wise to side with this view in the face of overly metaphysical theories.

A. Arnold, "The Recapitulation Dream in *R3* and *Mac,*" *ShQ,* VI (1955), 51-62, applies to the dream scene the techniques used by W. Clemen (below). I. Ribner, *The English History Play in the Age of Sh* (1957), returns to the view that this play is largely an *exemplum,* or model, of Senecan dramaturgy. In B. Spivack, *Sh and the Allegory of Evil* (1958), the morality element is once again examined. Like Thomas (above), Spivack writes of Richard as an incarnation of the Vice Deceit. A stimulating study is that of T. Driver in *The Sense of History in Greek and Shakespearean Drama* (1960). Driver accepts a theory of "double-time" first proposed by M. Buland in 1912: the play depicts both a delimited sequence of events and a historical pattern in which "this history of Richard is interwoven with the history of the land, generation laced to generation." The end of this passage through time historical and time symbolical is Judgment: "the outgrowth and the culmination of action taken in the historical arena . . . particular, purposeful, redemptive." A valuable study is that of M. M. Reese, *The Cease of Majesty* (1961). It is here noted that "the structure is severely formal, almost ritualistic. In the action each successive blow of fate is the fulfillment of a curse, until at last the bleeding country is rescued by its foreordained deliverer. The language, vituperative and extravagant, seems to be pitched deliberately high in acknowledgement of these solemnities." A. C. Sprague's *Shakespeare's Histories: Plays for the Stage* (1964) is an exceptionally good analysis of the protagonist as seen by actors of the twentieth century. See also H. Richmond, *Shakespeare's Political Plays* (1965) and R. Berman, "Anarchy and Order in *R3* and *KJ,*" *ShS,* XX (1967), 51-60.

The work of W. Clemen, the outstanding student of this play, deserves separate comment. In *The Development of Shakespeare's Imagery* (1951) Clemen writes that the "formalistic and artificial" manner displayed in antithesis, assonance, symmetry, and parallelism is modified by a firm architecture of style. Words are used less for ornament than for the purpose of revealing character and symbolism. In "Anticipation and Foreboding in Shakespeare's Early Histories," *ShS,* VI (1953), 25-35, Clemen established the structural significance of prophecy in *R3.* It creates an atmosphere of evil and fear in which Nemesis acts as the controlling principle of events. It furnishes also a deep sense of dramatic irony, for each of the characters must eventually encounter the realities of retribution from which they had presumed themselves free. In "Tradition and Originality in Shakespeare's *R3," ShQ,* V (1954), 247-257, Clemen writes of the triumph over chronicle formlessness. He finds that the events of this play are deeply symbolic and follow each other necessarily, like links in a chain. There are no interchangeable speeches; each speech is suited to a particular revelation. The language is very natural, especially in the protagonist, and has what Clemen calls a "humanizing and normalizing" effect. Clemen's *A Commentary on Shakespeare's R3* (1968) is a scene-by-scene analysis of the play that incorporates much of the material here described. It remains the most important study on the subject.

Further reading: R. Moulton, *Sh as a Dramatic Artist* (1885); J. Cunliffe, *The Influence of Seneca on Elizabethan Tragedy* (1893); E. Meyer, *Machiavelli and the Elizabethan Drama* (1897); F. Schelling, *The English Chronicle Play* (1902); K. Schmidt, *Margareta von Anjou vor und bei Sh* (1906); M. Buland, *The Presentation of Time in the Elizabethan Drama* (1912); J. Marriott, *English History in Sh* (1918); W. Raleigh, *Sh and England* (1918); E. K. Chambers, *Sh: A Survey* (1925); W. Lewis, *The Lion and the Fox* (1927); W. Keller, "Shakespeares Königsdramen," *ShJ,* LXIII (1927), 35-53; J. W. Allen, *A History of Political Thought in the Sixteenth Century* (1928); A. Henneke, "Shakespeares englische Könige," *ShJ,* LXVI (1930), 79-144; A. Pollard, "The Making of Sir Thomas More's *Richard III," Essays in Honour of James Tait* (1933); L. Dean, "Literary Problems in More's *Richard III," PMLA,* LVIII (1943), 22-41; E. M. W. Tillyard, *The Elizabethan World Picture* (1943); U. Ellis-Fermor, *The Frontiers of Drama* (1945); B. von Wiese, "Gestaltungen des Bösen," *ShJ,* LXXXIX (1953), 51-71; H. Jenkins, "Shakespeare's History Plays: 1900-1951," *ShS,* VI (1953), 1-15; P. M. Kendall, *Richard the Third* (1955); N. Brooke, "Marlowe as Provocative Agent," *ShS,* XIV (1961), 34-44; L. C. Knights, *Sh: The Histories* (1962); N. Brooke, "Reflecting Gems and Dead Bones: Tragedy vs. History in *R3," Critical Quarterly,* VII (1965), 123-134.

STAGING Camb xlvi-lxi; Craig 301; Odell *passim;* Sprague 94-107; Trewin *passim.*

See also A. P. Wood, *The Stage History of Shakespeare's R3* (1909); W. Winter, *Sh on the Stage* (1911); H. Hillebrand, *Edmund Kean* (1933);

H. Spencer, *The Art and Life of William Sh* (1940); T. C. Worsley, *The Fugitive Art* (1952); A. C. Sprague, *Shakespeare's Histories: Plays for the Stage* (1964); Peter Raby, *The Stratford Scene 1958-1968* (1968).

THE COMEDY OF ERRORS

TEXT Alexander 67-69; Camb vii-xiii, 65-85; Chambers 305-312; Greg 200-202; New Arden xi-xvi; Sisson I, 88-98.

See also *CE,* ed. H. Cunningham (1906); A. Gaw, "The Evolution of *CE," PMLA,* XLI (1926), 620-666; *CE,* ed. T. W. Baldwin (1928); Baldwin, *William Shakspere Adapts a Hanging* (1931); S. A. Tannenbaum, "Notes on *CE," ShJ,* LXVIII (1932), 103-124; R. B. McKerrow, "A Suggestion Regarding Shakespeare's Manuscripts," *RES,* XI (1935), 459-465; McManaway, 23-24; S. Thomas, "The Date of *CE," ShQ,* VII (1956), 377-384.

EDITIONS Ed. H. Cunningham (1906); Camb, ed. A. Quiller-Couch and J. Dover Wilson (1922); Yale, ed. R. D. French (1926); ed. T. W. Baldwin (1928); New Arden, ed. R. A. Foakes (1962); Pelican, ed. Paul Jorgensen (1964).

SOURCES Much of the source study is concerned with the origin of *CE* in Roman comedy. See H. Isaac, "Shakespeares *CE* und die Menächmen des Plautus," *Archiv,* LXX (1883), 1-28; K. Roeder, *Menechmi und Amphitruo in Englischen Drama bis zur Restauration* (1904). The text and Elizabethan translation of *The Menaechmi* were edited by W. H. D. Rouse (1912). C. Coulter discussed the stock plot, characters, and dialogue in "The Plautine Tradition in Sh," *JEGP,* XIX (1920), 66-83. Two articles on *CE* and Plautine comedy by E. Gill are "A Comparison of the Characters in *CE* with those in the *Menaechmi,"* *TxSE,* V (1925), 79-95, and "The Plot-Structure of *CE* in Relation to Its Sources," *TxSE,* X (1930), 13-65. See also K. M. Lea, *Italian Popular Comedy* (1934), and R. Bond, *Studia Otiosa* (1938). T. W. Baldwin's *Shakspere's Five-Act Structure* (1947) has a lengthy account of the conceivable sources. See also V. K. Whitaker, *Shakespeare's Use of Learning* (1953); Muir (1957); Bullough (1957–), I, 3-54. There is a good interpretative essay with texts of the sources in Bullough.

CRITICISM E. K. Chambers sardonically notes in *Sh: A Survey* (1925) that Adriana in *CE,* like Kate in *TSh,* has long been fondly regarded as a dramatic portrait of Anne Hathaway. He suggests that it is more advisable to consider the play a didactic farce, a comical lesson in moral issues. G. W. Knight, *The Shakespearian Tempest* (1932), discusses the theme of reunion and the "tragic essences" of *CE.* Of the language Knight remarks that "the play is full of gold and other riches, of merchants, and sea-voyages." There is continual suggestion of the energy of the market place and the power of the sea. H. B. Charlton, *Shakespearian Comedy* (1938), writes of Shakespeare's "recoil from romanticism" in *CE*. Although Charlton finds in the play the temper of realism, he decries the plot as "a sort of mathematical exhibition of the maximum number of erroneous combinations of four people taken in pairs." The bustle "leaves no room for characterisation, the persons in it enduring their lot as in a nightmare." G. R. Elliott, "Weirdness in *CE*," *UTQ*, IX (1939), 95-106, notes the "comic horror" of mistaken identity and describes the play, with its suggestions of sorcery, as a comedy of the grotesque. Mark Van Doren attacks the play as an "unfeeling farce" in his *Sh* (1939). He finds in it much comic machinery but very little poetry. In N. Frye's important article on "The Argument of Comedy," *EIE* (1948), 58-73, *CE* is found to exemplify a theme of New Comedy: "an individual release which is also a social reconciliation."

H. Craig, *An Interpretation of Sh* (1948), offers a sound if somewhat brief discussion of *CE*. T. M. Parrott, *Shakespearean Comedy* (1949), points out that *CE* is on a far more moral plane than were its Plautine originals. He remarks that the play is not to be understood so much in terms of language as in those of pure action. Two essays by A. B. Feldman should either be avoided or approached only by the connoisseur of the intellectual grotesque. They are in *Int. Jour. Psycho-Analysis*, XXXVI (1955), and *Amer. Imago*, XVI (1959); they attempt to prove that *CE* permitted its author—the Earl of Oxford—to sublimate a desire to commit incest. F. Fergusson, *The Human Image in Dramatic Literature* (1957), reprints a useful essay on the farce and sentimentality of *CE*. J. R. Brown, *Sh and His Comedies* (1957), asserts that *CE* deals with "the follies and evils of possessiveness" in love. Brown adds that "its contrasts of love, commerce, and justice" foreshadow *MV*. D. A. Traversi takes a serious view of *CE* as a study of human relationships in *Sh: The Early Comedies* (1960). He observes that the play is quite unlike its cynical sources, which are both more ribald and cruel than Shakespeare's version. C. Brooks, "Shakespeare's Romantic Shrews," *ShQ*, XI (1960), 351-356, suggests that Adriana, like Kate in *TSh*, has a wit to match her temper, which makes a woman out of a stereotype. There is a good chapter in B. Evans' *Shakespeare's Comedies* (1960). Evans writes that *CE* is a comedy of neither language nor character: its "great resource of laughter is the exploitable gulf spread between the participants' understanding and ours."

What I judge to be the best essay on this play is that by H. Brooks, "Themes and Structure in *CE*," *Early Shakespeare* (1961). Brooks finds that the play presents serious issues of disorder, illusion, and rebellion in human relationships as well as the knockabout farce of its sources. Brooks is especially good on handling what he calls the "averted-tragical" elements—the constant flirtation with death and illicit love. He sums up by saying that "at the centre is relationship: relationship between human beings, depending on their right relationship to truth and

universal law: to the cosmic reality behind appearance." The New
Arden edition (1962) of R. A. Foakes has a helpful introductory essay.
It is the best review of criticism of the play and important in its own
right. The play, Foakes admits, has a "slender nature . . . no great characters, little memorable verse, and a great deal of buffoonery." But it
shows, he adds, "a playwright already beginning to generate, out of
clashes between suffering and joy, disorder and order, appearance and
reality, the peculiar character and strength that is found in his mature
work."

It can readily be seen that the play's critical history is slender. There is,
however, a wealth of information on the genre and background. An
indispensable book on dramatic stereotypes and plots is Marvin T.
Herrick's *Comic Theory in the Sixteenth Century* (1964). Much of what
is said in this book may be applied to *CE*. T. W. Baldwin's *On the Com-
positional Genetics of CE* (1965) is a massive and daunting account of
the intellectual background of this play. It is stuffed with information
on Renaissance learning—not all of which is applied accurately to this
play. A witty review is in *Studies in English Literature,* VI (1966),
359-361. For a short, informative review of the Roman comic background see R. Hosley, "The Formal Influence of Plautus and Terence,"
Elizabethan Theatre, ed. Bernard Harris and John Russell Brown
(1966).

Further reading: J. W. Draper, "Mistaken Identity in Shakespeare's
Comedies," *Revue Anglo Amér.,* XI (1933-1934), 289-297; G. Gordon,
Shakespearian Comedy (1944); D. L. Stevenson, *The Love-Game
Comedy* (1946); T. W. Baldwin, "Respice Finem: Respice Funem,"
AMS (1948); E. C. Pettet, *Sh and the Romance Tradition* (1949); N.
Coghill, "The Basis of Shakespearian Comedy," *E&S* (1950), 1-28;
S. Sen Gupta, *Shakespearian Comedy* (1950); M. C. Bradbrook, *Sh and
Elizabethan Poetry* (1951); N. Frye, "Characterization in Shakespearian
Comedy," *ShQ,* IV (1953), 271-277; M. C. Bradbrook, *The Growth and
Structure of Elizabethan Comedy* (1955); J. R. Brown, "The Interpre-
tation of Shakespeare's Comedies: 1900-1953," *ShS,* VIII (1955), 1-13;
G. Bush, *Sh and the Natural Condition* (1956); J. Dover Wilson, *Shake-
speare's Happy Comedies* (1962); T. W. Baldwin, "Three Homilies in
CE," *Essays on Sh . . . in Honor of Hardin Craig* (1962); E. Talbert,
Elizabethan Drama and Shakespeare's Early Plays (1963); G. Williams,
"CE Rescued from Tragedy," *REL,* V (1964), 63-71; E. M. W. Tillyard,
Shakespeare's Early Comedies (1965); P. Phialas, *Shakespeare's Roman-
tic Comedies* (1966).

STAGING Camb xxvi-xxx; Craig 82; New Arden xxxiv-xxxix; Odell
passim; Sprague 70-71; Trewin *passim.*

See also H. Spencer, *The Art and Life of William Sh* (1940); *Shaw on Sh* (1961); M. Langham, "*CE* and *The Rape of Lucrece*," *KR*, XXVI (1964), 556-559. There are valuable remarks on staging in the article by H. Brooks (above).

TITUS ANDRONICUS

TEXT Alexander 74-77; Camb vii-l, 91-97; Chambers 312-322; Greg 203-209; New Arden xv-xxiv; Sisson II, 134-147.

See also A. Pollard, *Sh Folios and Quartos* (1909); T. M. Parrott, "Shakespeare's Revision of *TA,*" *MLR,* XIV (1919), 16-37; J. Bolton, "The Authentic Text of *TA,*" *PMLA,* XLIV (1929), 765-788; R. McKerrow, "A Note on *TA,*" *Lib,* XV (1934), 49-53; A. Sampley, "Plot Structure in Peele's Plays as a Test of Authorship," *PMLA,* LI (1936), 689-701; J. Q. Adams, *Shakespeare's TA: The First Quarto, 1594* (1936); H. T. Price, "The First Quarto of *TA,*" *EIE* (1948), 137-168; T. M. Parrott, "Further Observations on *TA,*" *ShQ,* I (1950), 22-29; McManaway, 24, and "Textual Studies," *ShS,* III (1950), 143-147; P. Cantrell and G. Williams, "Roberts' Compositors in *TA* Q2," *SB,* VIII (1956), 27-38; R. Hill, "The Composition of *TA,*" *ShS,* X (1957), 60-70; John C. Adams, "Shakespeare's Revisions in *TA,*" *ShQ,* XV (1964), 177-190.

EDITIONS Camb, ed. J. Dover Wilson (1948); New Arden, ed. J. C. Maxwell (1953); Pelican, ed. Gustave Cross (1966).

SOURCES H. Fuller, "The Sources of *TA,*" *PMLA,* XVI (1901), 1-65; M. MacCallum, *Shakespeare's Roman Plays and Their Background* (1910); F. Granger and R. W. Bond, *TLS* (1 April 1920 *et. seq.*); R. A. Law, "The Roman Background of *TA,*" *SP,* XL (1943), 145-153; T. W. Baldwin, *William Shakspere's Small Latine and Lesse Greek* (1944); R. Sargent, "The Source of *TA,*" *SP,* XLVI (1949), 167-183 (of special importance); J. C. Maxwell, "Peele and Sh: A Stylometric Test," *JEGP,* XLIX (1950), 557-561; J. A. K. Thomson, *Sh and the Classics* (1952); V. K. Whitaker, *Shakespeare's Use of Learning* (1953); R. Hill (above); Bullough (1957−) VI, 3-79; J. L. Barroll, "Sh and Roman History," *MLR,* LIII (1958), 327-343; H. Oppel, *TA. Studien zur dramenge-schichtlichen Stellung von Shakespeares früher Tragödie* (1961). Oppel's book contains the best survey of source study.

CRITICISM Dr. Johnson spoke for most critics past and present when he described *TA:* "the barbarity of the spectacles, and the general massacre, which are here exhibited, can scarcely be conceived tolerable to any audience." Yet he added something which present critics often neglect: "they were not only borne, but praised." A. Symons, *Studies in the Elizabethan Drama* (1920), adapted the "Tragedy of Blood" conception for this play. Symons called it "loud, coarse, violent, extravagantly hyperbolical, extravagantly realistic." He related it to the strong nerves and rough taste of its audience, "to which no exhibition of horror or cruelty could give anything but a pleasurable shock." J. Bolton, "*TA:* Sh at Thirty," *SP,* XXX (1933), 208-224, praised plotting and incident. *TA* made full use of the conventional types of Marlovian villain, sentimental child, and anguished father. M. C. Bradbrook's study in *Themes and Conventions of Elizabethan Tragedy* (1935) was supplemented by a valuable essay in *Sh and Elizabethan Poetry* (1951). Bradbrook points out the "emblematic or heraldic quality about all the characters": they are constantly in formal groupings, described as if they were figures in a tapestry or pageant acting out "moral heraldry." The use of personification and the learned and grandiose quality of the style are well explained. H. T. Price, "The Language of *TA,*" *Papers Michigan Academy,* XXI (1935), 501-507, notes that character is suggested by language. Shakespeare's Romans are plain, rising in moments of emotion to heights of rhetoric. Price provides useful explications of the language, which he observes is heavily Latinate.

M. Van Doren, *Sh* (1939), is thoroughly disgusted with the play, which he finds to be simply an exercise in butchery. He performs a critical execution of his own on its plot ("which nothing save ingenuity prolongs"), its style ("as coarse as burlap"), and its action ("a series of anticlimaxes"). An important study is H. Baker's *Induction to Tragedy* (1939). *TA* is related to *The Spanish Tragedy* and to the poems of Ovid. Its medieval elements, "pyramidical" structure of rise and fall, and stark opposition of moral qualities are well displayed. Baker is especially acute on the derivative nature of *TA.* F. Bowers, *Elizabethan Revenge Tragedy: 1587-1642* (1940), lists the variations of *TA* from its dramatic models: undeveloped motivation of blood-revenge; increased complexity of villainy; flaws in the revenger's own character; ironic forms of madness; loose dramatic structure. H. Spencer, *The Art and Life of William Sh* (1940), is sympathetic to the play's violence and gore, reminding the reader of *Oedipus Rex* and *King Lear.* W. Hastings, "The Hardboiled Sh," *SAB,* XVII (1942), 114-125, points out the extreme oppositions in *TA* of "whitest chastity and blackest lust, supreme love and supreme hate." He judges that Sh, in terms of the simplistic stage tradition with which he was working, achieved a dramatic and logical success. He at least proved he was a virtuoso of horror.

H. T. Price, "The Authorship of *TA,*" *JEGP,* XLII (1943), 55-81, refers to the native rather than the classical sources Sh pillaged for *TA.* The play's villain, Aaron, is a relic of the medieval Vice. Price makes important comments on the style and language, the "principle of contrast" in theme and character, and the role of music. E. M. W. Tillyard, *Shakespeare's History Plays* (1944), has a sympathetic estimate of the play. His essay is important for its exposition of the political doctrine, the issues of title and succession, and the "cosmic consciousness" for which the play gropes. It is a natural step, Tillyard declares, from *TA* to the history plays. A. Yoder, *Animal Analogy in Shakespeare's Character Portrayal* (1947), comments on images of cruelty and brutality opposed by others of a remarkably pastoral and peaceful nature. J. Dover Wilson's Camb edition (1948) includes a useful short history of criticism. Wilson believes that Peele is responsible for part of the play. *TA*, he suggests, is actually a burlesque in blood and bathos of earlier dramas of revenge. D. Stauffer, *Shakespeare's World of Images* (1949), has a short but useful summation. R. Sargent (above) finds that the play develops a great opposition between civilization and barbarism and notes its "atmosphere of positive evil." He finds the hero to be a patriot as well as a revenger. H. T. Price, *Construction in Sh* (1951), makes an important contribution in his study of the patterns of speech and action of *TA*. He judges Titus himself to be "Shakespeare's typical ironical figure of the good man causing more harm by his perverse notions of the good than ever the bad man could." There is a good analysis of the play's structure and "Gothic exuberance."

A discussion of the language is in Clemen (1951). There is often "absurd contrast between occasion and image." The play's mythological references and metaphors are explained. The exact nature of its classical allusions is the subject of J. A. K. Thomson's *Sh and the Classics* (1952). A useful introduction accompanies J. C. Maxwell's New Arden edition (1953). C. Coe, *Shakespeare's Villains* (1957), has some remarks on Aaron as an antecedent of Iago. He is far from profound. An indispensable study is E. Waith's "The Metamorphosis of Violence in *TA*," *ShS*, X (1957), 39-49. This fine essay compares the play to its Ovidian sources and offers a theory derived from Ovid: transformation, obliterating human characteristics, is an important psychological and spiritual theme in the play. Waith reviews the symbolism, which he finds to center on disorder in both its physical and moral senses. T. J. Spencer, "Sh and the Elizabethan Romans," *ShS*, X (1957), 27-38, states that *TA* may well be a more characteristic piece of Roman history than Shakespeare's greater plays. There is valuable commentary on the play's political meaning. B. Spivack, *Sh and the Allegory of Evil* (1958), studies the "hybrid" image of the villain. Aaron plays the old morality role of Vice who delights the audience with his wit. Spivack clarifies some important complexities of the Moor's character, particularly the interaction of his passions as a person with his actions as a homiletic Vice. A good study of the structure is in T. W. Baldwin's *On the Literary Genetics of Shakspere's Plays 1592-1594* (1959). The "essential conflict . . . between Rome . . . and the barbarism of primitive, original nature" is the subject of E. Sommers in "Wilderness of Tigers: Structure and Symbolism in *TA*," *EC*, X (1960), 275-289. Sommers points out the use of virtue, piety, and justice as both structural vehicles and moral themes. The language is well studied. H. Oppel's recent book (above) is the most comprehensive study of *TA*. Oppel devotes a good deal of space to examining the play's motifs of honor and suffering and its grandiloquent rhetoric. He explores also its relationship to Marlowe's style. There are many useful references to past research in his notes. E. Talbert, *Elizabethan Drama and Shakespeare's Early Plays* (1963), contains a worthwhile critical summation. A. C. Hamilton attempts to revalue the play in *"TA:* the Form of Shakespearian Tragedy," *ShQ,* XIV 1963, 201-213. He observes that Dover Wilson's description of *TA* as a "broken-down cart, laden with bleeding corpses" and T. S. Eliot's comment that it was "one of the stupidest and most uninspired plays ever written" need some rebuttal, and he argues that the play is a legitimate precursor of the greater tragedies. There is a long essay in Bullough's sixth volume (1966) which considers sources and other matters. N. Brooke takes up style and emblematic language in *Shakespeare's Early Tragedies* (1968), 13-48.

Further reading: J. W. Cunliffe, *The Influence of Seneca on Elizabethan Tragedy* (1893); C. Brooke, *"TA,"* *MLN,* XXXIV (1919), 32-36; A. K. Gray, "Sh and *TA,"* *SP,* XXV (1928), 295-311; W. Schirmer, "Sh und die Rhetorik," *ShJ,* LXXI (1935), 11-31; W. Keller, *"TA,"* *ShJ,* LXXIV (1938), 137-162; P. Reyher, *Essai sur les Idées dans l'Oeuvre de Sh* (1947); H. T. Price, "Mirror-Scenes in Sh," *AMS* (1948); H. Craig, *An Interpretation of Sh* (1948); T. M. Parrott, *"TA,"* *SAB,* XXIV (1949), 117-123; A. Venezky, *Pageantry on the Shakespearean Stage* (1951); M. Doran, *Endeavors of Art* (1954); W. Desmonde, "The Ritual Origin of Shakespeare's *TA,"* *Int. Jour. Psycho-Analysis,* XXXVI (1955), 61-65; J. C. Maxwell, "Shakespeare's Roman Plays: 1900-1956," *ShS,* X (1957), 1-11; C. Leech, "Shakespeare's Use of a Five-Act Structure," *NS,* VI (1957), 249-263; B. Harris, "A Portrait of a Moor," *ShS,* XI (1958), 89-97; J. Reese, "The Formalization of Horror in *TA,"* *ShQ,* XXI (1970), 77-84.

STAGING   Camb lxvi-lxxi; Craig 369; Odell *passim;* Trewin *passim.*

See also H. Spencer (above); J. Dover Wilson, *"TA* on the Stage in 1595," *ShS,* I (1948), 17-22; M. St. Clare Byrne, "Two *Titus* Productions," *Theatre Notebook,* X (1956), 44-48; R. David, "Drams of Eale," *ShS,* X (1957), 126-128; M. St. Clare Byrne, "The Sh Season at the Old Vic, 1956-57, and Stratford-upon-Avon, 1957," *ShQ,* VIII (1957), 461-463; G. Ungerer, "An Unrecorded Elizabethan Performance of *TA,"* *ShS,* XIV (1961), 102-109; Nicholas Brooke, *Shakespeare's Early Tragedies* (1968), 13-48.

THE TAMING OF THE SHREW

TEXT Alexander 69-71; Camb vii-xxiv, 97-126; Chambers 322-328; Greg 210-216; Sisson I, 159-167.

The following consider two basic issues, that *TSh* is either the work of Sh or that he shares its authorship: A. H. Tolman, *Shakespeare's Part in TSh* (1891); H. D. Sykes, *The Authorship of TSh* . . . (1919); E. Kuhl, "The Authorship of *TSh*," *PMLA*, XL (1925), 551-618. Kuhl's study is generally accepted as conclusive evidence of Shakespeare's authorship, but see the adverse critique in *MLR*, XXII (1927), 328-330. See also F. Ashton, "The Revision of the Folio Text of *TSh*," *PQ*, VI (1927), 151-160; B. A. P. Van Dam, *"The Taming of A Shrew,"* *ES*, X (1928), 97-106, and *"TSh," ibid.*, 161-177; H. D. Gray, *"The Taming of A Shrew,"* *PQ*, XX (1941), 325-333. Important research by G. I. Duthie and R. Houk has established single authorship beyond reasonable doubt. Duthie wrote *"The Taming of A Shrew* and *TSh*," *RES*, XIX (1943), 337-356, and Houk published the following series of articles: "The Integrity of Shakespeare's *TSh*," *JEGP*, XXXIX (1940), 222-229; "The Evolution of *TSh*," *PMLA*, LVII (1942), 1009-1038; "Strata in *TSh*," *SP*, XXXIX (1942), 291-320; *"Doctor Faustus* and *A Shrew*," *PMLA*, LXII (1947), 950-957. See also McManaway, 24-25, and R. Hosley, "Was There a 'Dramatic Epilogue' to *TSh*?" *Stud. English Lit.*, I (1961), 17-34.

EDITIONS The Bankside edition of A. Frey (1888) has texts of *A Shrew* and F₁. Arden, ed. R. Bond (1904); Camb, ed. A. Quiller-Couch and J. Dover Wilson (1928); Yale, ed. T. Bergin (1954); Pelican, ed. Richard Hosley (1964).

SOURCES G. C. Taylor, "Two Notes on Sh," *PQ*, XX (1941), 371-376; T. M. Parrott, *"The Taming of A Shrew*—A New Study of an Old Play," *Elizabethan Studies . . . in Honor of G. F. Reynolds* (1945); H. Craig, *"TSh* and *A Shrew," ibid.;* R. Houk, "Shakespeare's *TSh* and Greene's *Orlando*," *PMLA*, LXII (1947), 657-671; Bullough (1957—), I, 57-158; J. W. Shroeder, *"The Taming of A Shrew* and *TSh*," *JEGP*, LVII (1958), 424-443, and "A New Analogue and Possible Source for *TSh*," *ShQ*, X (1959), 251-255; R. Hosley, "Sources and Analogues of *TSh*," *HLQ*, XXVII (1964), 289-308; P. Alexander, "A Case of Three Sisters," *TLS*, 8 July 1965, p. 588; E. M. W. Tillyard, *Shakespeare's Early Comedies* (1965); Jan Brunvand, "The Folktale Origin of *TSh*," *ShQ*, XVII (1966), 345-359. There is a brief and lucid review of the work of Hosley and Brunvand in *ShS*, XXI (1968), 150-151, which agrees with their conclusion that *A Shrew* is not a source of this play.

CRITICISM "Brutality, especially in sexual matters, is quite in the tradition of farce," notes E. K. Chambers in *Sh: A Survey* (1925). To bring to it ethical criteria is to mistake both the play and standards of criticism. This reasoning has not often been observed by later critics, who bring to the play rather elaborate philosophical schemes. G. W. Knight, *The Shakespearian Tempest* (1932), examines the imagery of storms in the speeches of Petruchio. Kate and Bianca are contrasted by poetic language as well as by behavior: the former, like Petruchio, is often described in terms of tempests, while the rhetoric of music applies to the latter. H. B. Charlton, *Shakespearian Comedy* (1938), extensively compares *TSh* with Italian comedy. He notes that, unlike most of these comedies, *TSh* treats love rather than lust. It is the kind of love, however, that is dragged out of heaven and very much down to earth. M. Van Doren, *Sh* (1939), thinks that *TSh* is merely a callous situation farce. He undervalues the play but makes some intelligent remarks on its language. J. Draper, "Kate the Curst," *Jour. Nervous and Mental Diseases*, LXXXIX (1939), 757-764, asserts that the heroine exemplifies the incontinent, diabolical, and perverse "humour" of Choler. This view was attacked and, I think, defeated by R. Houk in "Shakespeare's Heroic Shrew," *SAB*, XVIII (1943), 121-132 and 175-186. Houk finds that Kate is abnormal in neither spirit nor sex but is only the traditional shrew of comic literature.

T. King, "*TSh*," *SAB*, XVII (1942), 73-79, writes a parody of critics hostile to the play. H. Craig's *An Interpretation of Sh* (1948) contains a good introductory essay. The limitations imposed upon character by convention are clearly explained by T. M. Parrott in *Shakespearean Comedy* (1949). For E. C. Pettet, *Sh and the Romance Tradition* (1949), the play is a crude but accurate picture of social realities. Love in this play is, he says, an intrigue, a business, or even an education, but never a romance. One may suggest that these elements are often in romances as reminders of reality. In any case, this particular romance is also a comedy; to exempt love from the operations of the comic and present it in the purity Pettet seems to demand would of course change the play and, I think, its intention. S. Sen Gupta, *Shakespearian Comedy* (1950), judges that romance is overwhelmed by intrigue in *TSh*. He believes, as I do not, that no added understanding of human character is supplied. My views are noted more fully under Berman (below). Evans (1952) writes that the poetry of this play is direct, lively, but undistinguished. The coarse and literal reality brought to the play by Christopher Sly is the subject of T. Greenfield's "The Transformation of Christopher Sly," *PQ*, XXXIII (1954), 34-42. K. Wentersdorf, "The Authenticity of *TSh*," *ShQ*, V (1954), 11-32, is a thorough examination of the imagery in an attempt to prove that the play is entirely the work of Sh. It is a useful study, and it establishes many patterns of language for the play, but it may be doubted whether imagery is a conclusive proof of authorship. M. Prior, "Imagery as a Test of Authorship," *ShQ,* VI (1955), 381-386, has a searching examination of the foregoing.

J. R. Brown, *Sh and His Comedies* (1957), discusses the linkage of love and money in *TSh.* There is a helpful essay in Bullough (1957–). M. C. Bradbrook, "Dramatic Role as Social Image," *ShJ,* XCIV (1958), 132-150, argues that the characters ought to be interpreted in the light of their ideal roles in Elizabethan culture and offers a study of psychology and role as it was understood by Sh and his contemporaries. There are some interchanges on the language and its decency in *TLS* for 1958 (pp. 447, 459, 625). The essay of T. R. Waldo and T. W. Herbert, "Musical Terms in *TSh:* Evidence of Single Authorship," *ShQ,* X (1959), 185-199, is a closely argued study of musical metaphor; it includes a catalogue of musical terms employed in *TSh* and in other Shakespearean plays. One assumption of this essay is that the musical terms allude to more than music, as may be seen in the concept of "harmony." T. W. Baldwin's *On the Literary Genetics of Shakspere's Plays 1592-1594* (1959) studies structure and possible relationships to Marlowe. B. Evans, *Shakespeare's Comedies* (1960), tends to interpret the play solely in terms of its multiple deceptions. While his work is limited to the geometry of the action, it must be admitted that this does in fact throw considerable light on the plot and pace of the play. D. Traversi, *Sh: The Early Comedies* (1960), suggests that *TSh* brings the "relationships of society" under the "rules of 'nature.'" The interplay of love, illusion, and transformation is treated by C. Seronsy in "'Supposes' as the Unifying Theme in *TSh,*" *ShQ,* XIV (1963), 15-30. Seronsy believes that the shrew plot is not the heart of the play but that its ultimate meaning is generated by the change in identity that its characters undergo. R. Berman, "Shakespearean Comedy and the Uses of Reason," *South Atlantic Quar.,* LXIII (1964), 1-9, suggests that Petruchio exemplifies Erasmian folly. He sees the play as a skillful comic blow at reason and reasonableness. For the farcical aspects of this play see R. Heilman, "*The Taming* Untamed, or the Return of The Shrew," *MLQ,* XXVII (1966), 147-161. The long essay in *Shakespeare's Romantic Comedies* (1966) by Peter Phialas is mildly interesting.

Further reading: G. Gordon, *Shakespearian Comedy* (1944); D. L. Stevenson, *The Love-Game Comedy* (1946); N. Frye, "The Argument of Comedy," *EIE* (1948), 58-73; D. Stauffer, *Shakespeare's World of Images* (1949); N. Coghill, "The Basis of Shakespearian Comedy," *E&S* (1950), 1-28; N. Frye, "Characterization in Shakespearian Comedy," *ShQ,* IV (1953), 271-277; J. R. Brown, "The Interpretation of Shakespeare's Comedies: 1900-1953," *ShS,* VIII (1955), 1-13; G. Bush, *Sh and the Natural Condition* (1956); E. Sehrt, *Wandlungen der Shakespeareschen Komödie* (1961); J. Dover Wilson, *Shakespeare's Happy*

Comedies (1962); E. Talbert, *Elizabethan Drama and Shakespeare's Early Plays* (1963); N. Sanders, "Imagery and Themes in *TSh*," *Renaissance Papers 1963* (Southeastern Renaissance Conference, 1964), 63-72; G. R. Hibbard, "*TSh:* A Social Comedy," *Shakespearean Essays,* ed. A. Thaler and N. Sanders (1964), 15-28.

STAGING Camb 181-186; Craig 156; Odell *passim;* Sprague 55-60; Trewin *passim.*

H. Spencer, *The Art and Life of William Sh* (1940); M. Clarke and R. Wood, *Sh at the Old Vic* (1954); C. J. Sisson, "*TSh,*" *Drama,* XXXVIII (1955), 25-27; ed. F. Fergusson and C. J. Sisson (1958); ed. Folio Society (1960). The above editions have useful essays on staging. Sears Jayne, "The Dreaming of *The Shrew,*" *ShQ,* XVII (1966), 41-56.

THE TWO GENTLEMEN OF VERONA

TEXT Alexander 71-74; Camb vii-xix, 77-82; Chambers 329-331; Greg 217-218; New Arden xiii-xxxv (best general survey of the text); Sisson I, 53-61.

See also G. B. Parks, "The Development of *TGV*," *Huntington Lib. Bulletin*, XI (1937), 1-11; S. A. Tannenbaum, "The New Cambridge Sh and *TGV*," *SAB*, XIII (1938), 151-172 and 208-223; C. S. Lewis, "Text Corruptions," *TLS* (3 March 1950), 137.

EDITIONS Arden, ed. R. Bond (1906); Camb, ed. A. Quiller-Couch and J. Dover Wilson (1921); Yale, ed. K. Young (1924); Penguin, ed. G. B. Harrison (1956); Pelican, ed. Berners Jackson (1964); New Arden, ed. Clifford Leech (1969).

SOURCES J. Tynan, "The Influence of Greene on Shakespeare's Early Romance," *PMLA*, XXVII (1912), 246-264. A useful survey of the sources is in O. J. Campbell's *Studies in Sh, Milton and Donne* (1925). Campbell finds that *TGV* has the typically *Commedia dell'Arte* machinery of disguise and pursuit, yet he reminds us that it is more concerned with love than with intrigue. He suggests that it is in fact seminal to the English drama of romance. A variety of sources are examined by the following: T. P. Harrison, "Concerning *TGV* and Montemayor's *Diana*," *MLN*, XLI (1926), 251-252, and "Sh and Montemayor's *Diana*," *TxSE*, VI (1926), 72-120; J. Wales, "Shakespeare's Use of English and Foreign Elements in the Setting of *TGV*," *Trans. Wisc. Academy*, XXVII (1932), 85-125; M. S. Allen, "Brooke's *Romeus and Juliet* as a Source for the Valentine-Sylvia Plot," *TxSE*, XVIII (1938), 25-46; J. Guinn, "The Letter Device in the First Act of *TGV*," *TxSE*, XX (1940), 72-81; D. Atkinson, "The Source of *TGV*," *SP*, XLI (1944), 223-234; T. W. Baldwin, *Shakspere's Five-Act Structure* (1947). Baldwin comments at length on the play's dramatic and structural formulas. There is a good review of source study and a selection of texts in Bullough (1957–), I, 203-266. See also R. Pruvost, "*TGV* . . . et *Gl'Ingannati*," *Ea*, XIII (1960), 1-9.

CRITICISM E. K. Chambers, *Sh: A Survey* (1925), has not very much good to say of *TGV*. It manifests "sentimental bankruptcy" and rhetorical puerility. G. W. Knight, *The Shakespearian Tempest* (1932), discusses language and theme with perhaps too much seriousness, finding sadness and tragedy implicit in the metaphors of *TGV*. The unrealistic reconciliation is the subject of S. A. Small, "The Ending of *TGV*," *PMLA*, XLVIII (1933), 767-776. An excellent study of the dramatic background is in K. M. Lea's *Italian Popular Comedy* (1934). Spurgeon

(1935) has a short survey of the imagery. H. B. Charlton considers the courtly and medieval ideas which underlie the play in his *Shakespearian Comedy* (1938). He evokes a story of romantic love in a "romantic universe, in which mountain and forest are indispensable, mountains which are brigand-haunted, and forests in the gloom of which are abbeys from whose postern gates friars creep into the encircling woods." Charlton drily adds that in such a work no character is ever to be mistaken for a real human being. M. Van Doren, *Sh* (1939), contains intelligent remarks on the themes of travel, the women, the code of manners, and the poetry. S. A. Tannenbaum (above) denounces the play furiously: "its story is preposterous, its dramatic technique puerile, its characters inconsistent and puppet-like, its dialogue dull, uninteresting, and unnatural, its jesting insipid, long drawn out and superfluous, its ethics pernicious, its philosophy juvenile. . . ." The essay is better than first appears. H. T. Price, "Sh as a Critic," *PQ*, XX (1941), 390-399, finds Valentine a fool and the play a parody of courtly love.

H. Craig, "Shakespeare's Development as a Dramatist," *SP*, XXXIX (1942), 226-238, notes the wide distribution of the plot in Renaissance literature. He states that Sh differs from the analogues in the type and intensity of feeling he brings to the story. S. Sen Gupta, *Shakespearian Comedy* (1950), believes that the clowns alone have imagination—the others merely have roles. An important study is that of R. Sargent, "Sir Thomas Elyot and the Integrity of *TGV*," *PMLA*, LXV (1950), 1166-1180. This article reviews past criticism and revalues the play itself. Sargent believes it is an intelligent application of the conventions of romance to serious ideas about human relationships. K. M. Thompson, "Shakespeare's Romantic Comedies," *PMLA*, LXVII (1952), 1079-1093, interprets *TGV* in terms of courtly love. The code, he finds, explains dramatic inconsistencies and lends to the play its conflict of love and honor. Evans (1952) considers the Spenserian rhetoric and the imagery of secular and religious love.

T. A. Perry, "Proteus, Wry-Transformed Traveller," *ShQ*, V (1954), 33-40, theorizes that travel turns the hero into a polished but decadent Italianate courtier. The more he comes to experience the corruption of *le grande monde,* the more he comes to imitate it. M. C. Bradbrook, *Sh and Elizabethan Poetry* (1951), dismisses the play as a colorless study of manners. Its emotions and conventions both seem to be artificial; Launce alone brings nature to the play. J. R. Brown, *Sh and His Comedies* (1957), is concerned with the theme of the deception of appearances. He believes the heart of the play is the recognition of "inward beauty" by the lovers. Bullough (1957—) notes the good points: "instead of the classical farce and the modern fabliau in which life was treated conventionally from the outside, we have a sympathetic exploration of the difficulties of young people in love and friendship."

J. Danby, "Sh Criticism and *TGV,*" *CQ,* II (1960), 309-321, attempts to revalue the play. He finds in it an integrated world-view and an impressive expression of moral meanings: "love in *TGV* is seen as a discipline, and the lover as an initiate. The object of love may be a woman, but woman as the focus and embodiment of values that impose their own constraint on base affection. By means of love the lover is admitted into the realm of the values and thereby submitted to a life-process the outcome of which he can neither force not [sic] dictate." B. Evans, *Shakespeare's Comedies* (1960), asserts that the meaning of the play may be stated in this form: "not only cannot villainy harm innocence; it is even prevented from doing irreparable harm to itself." E. Sehrt writes of *TGV* as a comedy which is occasionally serious in its depiction of men at the mercy of fortune in his *Wandlungen der Shakespeareschen Komödie* (1961).

The metaphor of deceit in *TGV* is explored by Anne Righter in *Sh and the Idea of the Play* (1962). William Scott's essay on "Proteus in Spenser and Sh" is in the first volume of the annual *Shakespeare Studies* (1965), 283-293. This piece considers Renaissance ideas of love's variety and instability. For the association of forgiveness and romance see the brief comments in Robert Hunter's *Sh and the Comedy of Forgiveness* (1965) and the more elaborate study by Peter Phialas in *Shakespeare's Romantic Comedies* (1966). The play's comic structure is the subject of Robert Weimann, "Laughing with the Audience: *TGV* and the Popular Tradition of Comedy," *ShS,* XXII (1969), 35-42.

Further reading: G. Gordon, *Shakespearian Comedy* (1944); D. L. Stevenson, *The Love-Game Comedy* (1946); P. Reyher, *Essai sur les Idées dans l'Oeuvre de Sh* (1947); N. Frye, "The Argument of Comedy," *EIE* (1948), 58-73; T. M. Parrott, *Shakespearean Comedy* (1949); D. Stauffer, *Shakespeare's World of Images* (1949); E. C. Pettet, *Sh and the Romance Tradition* (1949); N. Coghill, "The Basis of Shakespearian Comedy," *E&S* (1950), 1-28; N. Frye, "Characterization in Shakespearian Comedy," *ShQ,* IV (1953), 271-277; M. Doran, *Endeavors of Art* (1954); M. Praz, "Shakespeare's Italy," *ShS,* VII (1954), 95-106; J. R. Brown, "The Interpretation of Shakespeare's Comedies: 1900-1953," *ShS,* VIII (1955), 1-13; M. C. Bradbrook, *The Growth and Structure of Elizabethan Comedy* (1955); G. Bush, *Sh and the Natural Condition* (1956); J. Vyvyan, *Sh and the Rose of Love* (1960); D. A. Traversi, *Sh: The Early Comedies* (1960); J. Dover Wilson, *Shakespeare's Happy Comedies* (1962); E. Talbert, *Elizabethan Drama and Shakespeare's Early Plays* (1963); H. Brooks, "Two Clowns in a Comedy (to say nothing of the Dog)," *Essays and Studies,* XVI (1963), 91-100; Stanley Wells, "The Failure of *TGV,*" *ShJ,* XCIX (1963), 161-173; E. M. W. Tillyard, *Shakespeare's Early Comedies* (1965); Clifford Leech, *Twelfth Night and Shakespearian Comedy* (1965); A. C.

Hamilton, *The Early Sh* (1967); A. Schlösser, "Betrachtungen über *TGV,*" ShJ, CIII (1967), 145-161.

STAGING Camb 105-106; Craig 132; Odell *passim;* Sprague 71-73; Trewin *passim.*

See also H. Spencer, *The Art and Life of William Sh* (1940); *Shaw on Sh* (1961); J. R. Brown, "Three Directors," *ShS,* XIV (1962), 129-137. The New Arden edition has a stage history, xlv-l.

LOVE'S LABOUR'S LOST

TEXT Alexander 86-91; Camb vii-xlii, 98-135; Chambers 331-338; Greg 219-224; New Arden xvii-xxvi; Sisson I, 104-124.

See also H. B. Charlton, "A Textual Note on *LLL,*" *Lib,* VIII (1917), 355-370, and "A Disputed Passage in *LLL,*" *MLR,* XII (1917), 279-285; H. D. Gray, *The Original Version of LLL* (1918); R. Taylor, *The Date of LLL* (1932); F. A. Yates, *A Study of LLL* (1936); L. Kirschbaum, "Is *The Spanish Tragedy* a Leading Case? Did a Bad Quarto of *LLL* Ever Exist?" *JEGP,* XXXVII (1938), 501-512; E. Strathmann, "The Textual Evidence for 'The School of Night' " *MLN,* LVI (1941), 176-186; McManaway, 25; A. Walker, "*LLL,*" *RES,* III (1952), 380-386; A. Harbage, "*LLL* and the Early Sh," *PQ,* XLI (1962), 18-36.

EDITIONS *NV,* ed. H. H. Furness (1904); Camb, ed. A. Quiller-Couch and J. Dover Wilson (1923); Yale, ed. W. Cross and C. T. Brooke (1925); New Arden, ed. R. David (1951); Pelican, ed. Alfred Harbage (1963).

SOURCES An eccentric but partially worthwhile study is A. Lefranc's *Sous le Masque de Sh* (1918). Worth noting are J. Tynan, "The Influence of Greene on Shakespeare's Early Romance," *PMLA,* XXVII (1912), 246-264; J. Phelps, "Father Parsons in Sh," *Archiv,* CXXXIII (1915), 66-86; H. B. Charlton, "The Date of *LLL,*" *MLR,* XIII (1918), 257-266 and 387-400. The latter discusses possible connections with Essex and other topical matters. See also F. Sorenson, "The Masque of the Muscovites in *LLL,*" *MLN,* L (1935), 499-501. An important study of style and sources is O. J. Campbell's essay in *Studies in Sh, Milton and Donne* (1925). Campbell discusses the possible origins of *LLL* in Italian popular comedy and theorizes that the court of France may have influenced plot and characterization. F. Yates' *A Study of LLL* (1936) is valuable but tied too severely to historical allusions. Of great interest is M. C. Bradbrook's *The School of Night* (1936), which asserts that the play is a parody of the intellectual pretensions of Sir Walter Ralegh and his circle. See also A. Lefranc, "Les Éléments Français de *LLL,*" *Revue Historique,* CLXXVIII (1937), 411-432; J. Phelps, "The Source of *LLL,*" *SAB,* XVII (1942), 97-102; L. Stratton, "The Nine Worthies," *Ashland Studies in Sh,* II (1956), 67-99. W. Schrickx, *Shakespeare's Early Contemporaries* (1956), discusses the controversy of Harvey and Nashe as a possible source. The best review of source studies is Bullough (1957—), I, 425-442. See also Muir (1957).

CRITICISM E. K. Chambers, *Sh: A Survey* (1925), believes that too

much literary archaeology is needed to understand the humor. He
judges *LLL* to be a satire and comedy of manners. G. W. Knight, *The
Shakespearian Tempest* (1932), examines the imagery and music. The
dominating imagery of war and weapons in a "civil war of wits" is the
subject of Spurgeon (1935). Two essays by D. Boughner are well known
for their accurate investigation of Renaissance stock dramatic types of
braggart and bully: "Don Armado as a Gallant," *Revue Anglo-Amer.,*
XIII (1935), 18-28, and "Don Armado and the *Commedia dell'Arte,*"
SP, XXXVII (1940), 201-224. Yates (above) has many critical comments. H. B. Charlton, *Shakespearian Comedy* (1938), writes of *LLL* as
the equivalent of a modern musical comedy. He believes its poverty of
story is compensated by the character of its fools. There is a slight but
appreciative essay in M. Van Doren, *Sh* (1939). O. J. Campbell, *Shakespeare's Satire* (1943), examines *LLL* as an attack on bombast in manner and learning. A first-rate discussion of the play may be found in H.
Granville-Barker (1946). He sees the play as considerably more than
satire or spectacle and contributes fine analyses of character, of the
human values that are exemplified, and of the poetry.

In *Comic Characters of Sh* (1946) J. Palmer writes of Berowne as a type
of the courtier. The contradiction between theories of love and its practice is the subject of D. L. Stevenson, *The Love-Game Comedy* (1946).
It is difficult to find a more solid study of formulas and conventions
than T. W. Baldwin's *Shakspere's Five-Act Structure* (1947). Two
essays of another sort examine the poetry: B. Bronson, "Daisies Pied
and Icicles," *MLN*, LXIII (1948), 35-38, and W. Babcock, "Fools,
Fowls and Perttaunt-Like," *ShQ*, II (1951), 211-219. The latter pursues
double-entendres. T. M. Parrott, *Shakespearean Comedy* (1949), calls
the play a great defense of "youth, pleasure, and beauty." Clemen
(1951) observes that the images of *LLL* are linked as in a game; puns
are elaborated, passed from hand to hand, varied and inverted with a
freedom that is at once comic and artistic.

M. C. Bradbrook, *Sh and Elizabethan Poetry* (1951), concludes that
LLL is "a play about courtship which turns out to be a play about love,
and an attack on fine speech which is consistently full of fine speeches."
The New Arden edition (1951) does not have as full an introduction as
other volumes in the series. It does, however, offer a list of allusions
and (possible) identifications of the characters with actual persons. A
study of courtly love is found in K. M. Thompson's "Shakespeare's
Romantic Comedies," *PMLA*, LXVII (1952), 1079-1093. In *LLL* "the
young men, sinners against the religion of love, attain grace by removing
their errors, by contrition, confession, and satisfaction." Thompson
states that their goddesses grant them first "penance" and then
"mercy." L. Cazamian, *The Development of English Humor* (1952),
believes that "the obvious exaggeration of high-flown language, the

overrefinement of exquisite comparisons . . . the superfluous mental
energy lavished upon simple things" invite a contrast with norms in
which comedy is implicit. There is a detailed study of this language in
Evans (1952). The bravura of its puns and metaphors and the muddled
rhetorical enthusiasms of its butts reveal, Evans suggests, Shakespeare's
early interest in language *per se* and his modifications of Elizabethan
rhetorical principles.

A very good critique is that of B. Roesen, *"LLL," ShQ,* IV (1953), 411-
426. Roesen reveals the thematic structure and notes that the play is
much concerned with serious conceptions of the real and the illusory.
She notes also the forces of death and sexuality, both of which temper
the comedy by their presence. J. R. Brown, *Sh and His Comedies*
(1957), discusses the movement from the artificial order of pedantry
and retirement from the world to the natural order of love and marriage. C. L. Barber, *Shakespeare's Festive Comedy* (1959), writes finely
of the elements of masquerade, dance, and pageant. He rejects the idea
of a comedy of character and asserts that the play celebrates the sensual
power of folly. It is itself a "great feast of languages." Special pleading
may be detected in J. Vyvyan's *Sh and the Rose of Love* (1960). The
author attempts to place *LLL* within a scheme of Platonic allegory. In
Shakespeare's Comedies (1960) B. Evans applies his theory of "discrepant awarenesses." He asserts that the play is in part a comedy of the
exploitation of ignorance. C. Hoy, *"LLL* and the Nature of Comedy,"
ShQ, XIII (1962), 31-40, theorizes that the play enlightens the foolish
and affected without destroying them. He finds in it a salutary hum-
bling of pride. There is intelligent consideration of the subterranean
elements of pain and death in Hoy's essay. In "Sh and the Mask," *ShS,*
XVI (1963), 121-131, Philip Parsons considers the relationship of *LLL*
to *RJ.* He states that the themes of "love, death, and self-realization"
dominate this play. The ethics of *LLL* are discussed by E. Talbert in
Elizabethan Drama and Shakespeare's Early Plays (1963). R. Berman,
"Shakespearean Comedy and the Uses of Reason," *South Atlantic
Quar.,* LXIII (1964), 1-9, suggests that the play ridicules Platonism and
celebrates the passions of reality. Peter Phialas, *Shakespeare's Romantic
Comedies* (1966) argues—I think rightly—that the topical allusions are
merely a backdrop to the comic structure. However, his remarks on
action and language are diffuse.

An important group of recent essays takes up the play's language: R. F.
Hill, "Delight and Laughter: Some Aspects of Shakespeare's Early Ver-
bal Comedy," *Sh Studies* (Japan), III (1964), 1-21; W. Mathews, "Lan-
guage in *LLL,"* *E&S,* XVII (1964), 1-11; J. V. Cunningham, " 'With
That Facility': False Starts and Revisions in *LLL,"* *Essays on Sh,* ed.
Gerald Chapman (1965), 91-115; A. Schlösser, *"LLL.* Shakespeares
Jahrmarkt der Eitelkeit," *Zeitschrift für Anglistik und Amerikanistik,*

XIII (1965), 25-34; James Calderwood, "*LLL*: A Wantoning with Words," *SEL,* V (1965), 317-322; Brian Vickers, *The Artistry of Shakespeare's Prose* (1968); R. Berry, "The Words of Mercury," *ShS,* XXII (1969), 69-77.

Further reading: W. Pater, *Appreciations* (1889); A. Gray, "The Secret of *LLL,*" *PMLA,* XXXIX (1924), 581-611; J. Spens, "Notes on *LLL,*" *RES,* VII (1931), 331-334; E. Clark, *The Satirical Comedy of LLL* (1933); G. Willcock, *Sh as a Critic of Language* (1934); G. Gordon, *Shakespearian Comedy* (1944); N. Frye, "The Argument of Comedy," *EIE* (1948), 58-73; E. C. Pettet, *Sh and the Romance Tradition* (1949); N. Coghill, "The Basis of Shakespearian Comedy," *E&S* (1950), 1-28; S. Sen Gupta, *Shakespearian Comedy* (1950); J. Lever, "Three Notes on Shakespeare's Plays," *RES,* III (1952), 117-129; N. Frye, "Characterization in Shakespearian Comedy," *ShQ,* IV (1953), 271-277; V. K. Whitaker, *Shakespeare's Use of Learning* (1953); S. Greenfield, "Moth's *L'Envoy* and the Courtiers in *LLL,*" *RES,* V (1954), 167-168; J. R. Brown, "The Interpretation of Shakespeare's Comedies: 1900-1953," *ShS,* VIII (1955), 1-13; G. Bush, *Sh and the Natural Condition* (1956); W. Blissett, "Strange Without Heresy," *ES,* XXXVIII (1957), 209-211; R. Browne, "The Satiric Use of 'Popular' Music in *LLL,*" *Southern Folklore Quar.,* XXIII (1959), 137-149; J. Dover Wilson, *Shakespeare's Happy Comedies* (1962); A. C. Hamilton, *The Early Sh* (1967); J. Westlund, "Fancy and Achievement in *LLL,*" *ShQ,* XVIII (1967), 37-46; F. P. Wilson, *Shakespearian and Other Studies* (1969), 64-72.

STAGING Camb lix-lxii; Craig 102; Odell *passim;* Sprague 73-75; Trewin *passim.*

See also H. Spencer, *The Art and Life of William Sh* (1940); H. Granville-Barker (1946); E. J. West, "On the Essential Theatricality of *LLL,*" *CE,* IX (1948), 427-429; L. Hale, *The Old Vic, 1949-50* (1950); R. David, "Shakespeare's Comedies and the Modern Stage," *ShS,* IV (1951), 129-138; H. Hunt, *Old Vic Prefaces* (1954); M. Webster, *Sh Without Tears* (1955); Folio Society edition (1959).

ROMEO AND JULIET

TEXT Alexander 113-116; Camb vii-xvii, 112-118; Chambers 338-347; Greg 225-235; Sisson II, 148-165.

See also A. Pollard, *Sh Folios and Quartos* (1909); W. Greg, *Principles of Emendation in Sh* (1928); H. Hoppe, *The Bad Quarto of RJ* (1948); S. Thomas, "The Bibliographical Links Between the First Two Quartos of *RJ,*" *RES*, XXV (1949), 110-114; McManaway, 25-26; G. I. Duthie, "The Text of Shakespeare's *RJ,*" *SB*, IV (1951), 3-29; R. Hosley, "The Corrupting Influence of the Bad Quarto on the Received Text of *RJ,*" *ShQ*, IV (1953), 11-33; C. Hinman, "The Proof-Reading of the First Folio Text of *RJ,*" *SB*, VI (1954), 61-70; J. Dover Wilson, "Recent Work on the Text of *RJ,*" *ShS*, VIII (1955), 81-99; P. Cantrell and G. Williams, "The Printing of the Second Quarto of *RJ,*" *SB*, IX (1957), 107-128; R. Hosley, "Quarto Copy for Q2 *RJ,*" *SB*, IX (1957), 129-141; H. Craig, *A New Look at Shakespeare's Quartos* (1961).

EDITIONS *NV*, ed. H. H. Furness (1871); Arden, ed. E. Dowden (1900); ed. G. L. Kittredge (1941); Yale, ed. R. Hosley (1954); Camb, ed. G. I. Duthie and J. Dover Wilson (1955); Pelican, ed. John Hankins (1960). There are important textual notes in George Williams' edition of *The Most Excellent and Lamentable Tragedie of Romeo and Juliet* (1964).

SOURCES The texts of Brooke's *Romeus and Iuliet* and Painter's *Rhomeo and Iulietta* are accompanied by a useful introduction in P. A. Daniel's edition of 1875. See also N. Delius, "Brookes episches und Shakespeares dramatisches Gedicht von *RJ,*" *ShJ*, XVI (1881), 213-227; A. J. Roberts, "The Sources of *RJ,*" *MLN*, XVII (1902), 82-87; W. Smith, "A Comic Version of *RJ,*" *MP*, VII (1909), 217-220; O. H. Moore, "Le Rôle de Boaistuau dans le Développement de la Légende de Roméo et Juliette," *Rev. Litt. Comp.*, IX (1929), 637-643; R. A. Law, "On Shakespeare's Changes of His Source Material in *RJ,*" *TxSE*, IX (1929), 87-102; O. H. Moore, "The Origins of the Legend of Romeo and Juliet in Italy," *Speculum*, V (1930), 264-277, and Shakespeare's Deviations from *Romeus and Iuliet,*" *PMLA*, LII (1937), 68-74; H. B. Charlton, "France as Chaperone of Romeo and Juliet," *Studies in French . . . Presented to M. K. Pope* (1939); N. B. Allen, "Sh and Arthur Brooke," *Delaware Notes*, XVII (1944), 91-110; O. H. Moore, *The Legend of Romeo and Juliet* (1950); Muir (1957); Bullough (1957–), I, 269-363; Oscar Villarejo, "Shakespeare's *RJ:* Its Spanish Source," *ShS*, XX (1967), 95-105.

CRITICISM An interesting survey of early criticism of *RJ* is in

H. McArthur's "Romeo's Loquacious Friend," *ShQ,* X (1959), 35-44, which covers Dryden, Coleridge, Taine, Schlegel, Tieck, and Goethe. Other collections of criticism may be found in the *NV* and the New Clarendon (1947) editions.

E. Dowden's essay in *Transcripts and Studies* (1888) is deservedly well known. The language is eminently Victorian, but Dowden has insight into the nature of love in "all animated nature" that is perpetually destroyed by the law that "rings the whole of human desire and delight." One may consider academic the entire issue of whether or not *RJ* is a tragedy. F. Boas goes by certain "rules" in his *Shakspere and His Predecessors* (1896) and concludes that it is not a tragedy because the motivation of the lovers is subsidiary to the workings of Fate. Spoken like a philosopher, but in the real world tragedy defines itself as an experience, not a theorem. We are affected by the event rather than by its cause. C. Williams has some worthwhile remarks in *The English Poetic Mind* (1932). Spurgeon (1935) gives an excellent account of the imagery of light in *RJ.* She points out that "brilliance swiftly quenched" is characteristic of the play's rhetorical and existential atmosphere. This sense of life extinguished is supplied by language involving stars, fire, sunlight, and radiance. E. E. Stoll, *Shakespeare's Young Lovers* (1937), subjects Romeo and Juliet to strenuous psychological examination and finds them insufficiently motivated. Rather surprisingly for such a literal critic, he finds this deficiency obviated by the play's real attainment—the depiction of the lovers' "storm of passion."

M. Van Doren, *Sh* (1939), clarifies some of the rhetorical conceits. There is a fine essay in Granville-Barker (1946). He concludes that *RJ* is a "tragedy of mischance" but that it is deftly connected to flaws in character. There are useful summations of the major characters and first-rate comments on staging. T. W. Baldwin's ponderous *Shakspere's Five-Act Structure* (1947) is helpful on sources, conventions, and parallels with other early plays of Sh. H. Cain, "*RJ*: A Reinterpretation," *SAB,* XXII (1947), 163-192, provides a long study of sixteenth-century ethics. There is a good account of the passions, especially that of anger, which Cain finds the characteristic flaw of Romeo. He concludes that Romeo's unreasonable passions do in fact overshadow the mechanical operation of Fate and give him the status of tragic hero.

H. B. Charlton's *Shakespearian Tragedy* (1948) reprints an earlier study of the experimental nature of *RJ.* Charlton notes the difficulty of handling the two motives of Fate and Feud; the latter furnishes the immediate and the former the ultimate dramatic inevitability. Yet, for this critic, the play succeeds because of the pathos of its poetry rather than because of its structure, which he believes is incoherent. L. Bowling, "The Thematic Framework of *RJ*," *PMLA,* LXIV (1949),

208-220, finds the central theme "the wholeness and complexity of things." The lovers progress intellectually, Bowling suggests, from simple opinions about the nature of life to complex discoveries. One of the best essays is that of D. Stauffer in *Shakespeare's World of Images* (1949). In no other play, Stauffer states, "does Sh envisage a general moral order operating with such inhuman mechanical severity." His discussion centers not on the issue of whether or not *RJ* is a "tragedy" but on the more pertinent issue of how it achieves its effects. Stauffer believes that the intensity of ideal love is in fact the principal significance of the play. Language and premonition are examined by E. C. Pettet in "The Imagery of *RJ*," *English,* VIII (1950), 121-126. G. Bonnard, "*RJ*: A Possible Significance," *RES,* II (1951), 319-327, notes that, in contrast to the sources, Shakespeare's story endows the lovers with moral superiority. The sense of impending catastrophe and of love and hatred opposed in the larger scene of Verona is, he notes, also Shakespeare's own contribution.

An intelligent discussion of the relative weights of "real" emotion and emotion expressed in formal rhetoric is in M. C. Bradbrook's *Sh and Elizabethan Poetry* (1951). The importance of *RJ,* she finds, is that it marks Shakespeare's departure from the customary Renaissance apparatus of tragedy, the turgid and ponderous apostrophes to fate, hell, and vengeance that graced the earlier stage. Instead of dealing with the fall of princes and the monuments of time he wrote a profoundly simple and human story of love. J. Nosworthy, "The Two Angry Families of Verona," *ShQ,* III (1952), 219-226, observes that the play is not a theoretical success as a tragedy: it is not well executed, the feud is not sufficiently developed, there is too much comedy. I do not wish to beat a dead horse, but it strains human endurance to witness such an observable dramatic success being judged by rules alien to its nature. About the notion of this being a tragedy, I would humbly urge that there are only two positions: No, it is not equal to the great tragedies, and yes, it is excellent after its own kind.

An interesting study of "Sex and the Sonnet" by G. M. Mathews is in *EC,* II (1952), 119-137. The separation of love and marriage among the Elizabethans leads Mathews to suspect that the tragedy of the play is caused neither by Fate nor by the character of the protagonists, but by the coldly economical marital arrangements that reflected real social conditions. "The unguarded haste of youth" is the subject of B. Stirling's *Unity in Shakespearian Tragedy* (1956). The author demonstrates that dramatic emphasis on the reckless haste, the "headlong quality" of youth in Romeo and Juliet, lends to the play its particularity of meaning. F. Dickey, *Not Wisely But Too Well* (1957), devotes three long chapters to *RJ,* its sources and analogues, and Renaissance attitudes toward love. Dickey concludes that the play balances hatred against love and makes fortune the agent of divine justice. Some valuable comment is in H. S. Wilson's *On the Design of Shakespearian Tragedy* (1957). Although Wilson concurs with those who find *RJ* an "artificial" tragedy, he believes it is an essentially true "representation of human feelings." It is, he suggests, much more to be admired than the sentimental work of Shakespeare's successors. M. M. Mahood, *Shakespeare's Wordplay* (1957), studies the language extensively. Imagery and action unite, Mahood finds, in picturing the classic *Liebestod:* "certainly nearly all the elements of the *amour-passion* myth as it has been defined by Denis de Rougemont are present in the play. The love of Romeo and Juliet is immediate, violent and final. In the voyage imagery of the play they abandon themselves to a rudderless course that must end in shipwreck." The conventional concepts of love as war, religion, and malady also are analyzed, as well as the variations and ambiguities of the language.

R. F. Hill, "Shakespeare's Early Tragic Mode," *ShQ,* IX (1958), 455-469, asserts that *RJ* is a crucial play in the development of its author. Although it contains vestiges of his earlier manner in its ornate diction, "the seeds of the mature tragic style are present in the mixture of serious and comic elements, in the strong characterization, in verisimilitude of speech and in the deep-searching imagery." H. McArthur, "Romeo's Loquacious Friend," *ShQ,* X (1959), 35-44, reviews the early critical history of *RJ* and offers a substantial study of Mercutio. Perhaps the finest of the many studies on this play is Harry Levin's "Form and Formality in *RJ*," *ShQ,* XI (1960), 1-11. Romance, Levin points out, was a new subject for tragedy. The repudiation of artificial language by the leading characters indicates a repudiation of the superficial codes of love—and of an earlier, less realistic dramatic style. Levin has an excellent account of reduplication of action and rhetoric, which leads to what he calls a "polarity" against which the mutuality of the lovers stands out. Their intensely real feelings are framed continually by a series of formal oppositions conceived in terms of rhetoric and character. J. Lawlor, "*RJ*," *Early Sh* (1961), investigates medieval conceptions of tragedy. He suggests that the triumph of death, the turning of the wheel of the strumpet Fortune, are not central to *RJ*. This play shows instead that out of evil comes a greater good, the regeneration and reintegration of life in Verona. I am not sure that Verona is as much transformed as Mr. Lawlor believes. It may be in fact reintegrated, but of its regeneration I have doubts. This play, like many other plays of Sh, ends on a note of peace but not of apotheosis.

A group of J. Draper's essays on *RJ* has been collected in his *Stratford to Dogberry* (1961). The essay "Shakespeare's 'Star-Crossed Lovers' " is worthwhile. P. N. Siegel, "Christianity and the Religion of Love in *RJ*," *ShQ,* XII (1961), 371-392, surveys Renaissance opinion on sacred and profane love. The "mysterious unfolding of personal destiny" is the subject of P. Parsons, "Sh and the Mask," *ShS,* XVI (1963), 121-131. Conventions and Shakespeare's departure from them are the concern of E. Talbert's *Elizabethan Drama and Shakespeare's Early Plays* (1963). For a recent review of the criticism of this play see Gordon R. Smith's *Essays on Sh* (1965), 15-66. Smith's own solution to its problems is Freudian and he attempts to evaluate the play in terms of its correspondences to the psychological doctrine of the unconscious. There is an important account of the *Liebestod* motif in Inge Leimberg's *Shakespeare's RJ* (1968). This book offers a valuable study of earlier love tragedy and comments on Renaissance doctrines of love. A much slighter performance is Robert Evans, *The Osier Cage* (1966), which attempts to examine the play's rhetoric.

Further reading: A. Cohn, *Sh in Germany* (1865); R. Moulton, *The Moral System of Sh* (1903); A. C. Bradley, *Shakespearean Tragedy* (1904); J. Erskine, *"RJ," Shaksperian Studies,* ed. Mathews and Thorndike (1916); C. H. Herford, *Shakespeare's Treatment of Love and Marriage* (1921); A. Nicoll, *British Drama* (1925); E. K. Chambers, *Sh: A Survey* (1925); W. Farnham, *The Medieval Heritage of Elizabethan Tragedy* (1936); N. Allen, *"RJ* Further Restored," *MLN,* LIV (1939), 85-92; H. Spencer, *The Art and Life of William Sh* (1940); Denis de Rougement, *Love in the Western World* (1940); E. C. Pettet, *Sh and the Romance Tradition* (1949); L. Hotson, *Shakespeare's Sonnets Dated* (1949); I. Ribner, *Patterns in Shakespearian Tragedy* (1960); J. Vyvyan, *Sh and the Rose of Love* (1960).

STAGING   Camb xxxviii-lii; Craig 395; Odell *passim;* Sprague 297-319; Trewin *passim.*

See also J. C. Adams, *"RJ:* As Played on Shakespeare's Stage," *TAr,* XX (1936), 896-904; A. Gaw, "The Impromptu Mask in Sh," *SAB,* XI (1936), 149-160; B. L. Joseph, *Elizabethan Acting* (1951); H. Hunt, *Old Vic Prefaces* (1954); R. Hosley, "The Use of the Upper Stage in *RJ," ShQ,* V (1954), 371-379; J. C. Adams, "Shakespeare's Use of the Upper Stage in *RJ,* III.v," *ShQ,* VII (1956), 145-152; C. Haywood, "William Boyce's 'Solemn Dirge' in Garrick's *RJ* Production of 1750," *ShQ,* XI (1960), 173-188; J. R. Brown, "S. Franco Zeffirelli's *RJ," ShS,* XV (1962), 147-155; A. Downer, "For Jesus' Sake Forbear: Sh vs. the Modern Theater," *ShQ,* XIII (1962), 219-230. For a good account of modern performances see John Russell Brown, *Shakespeare's Plays in Performance* (1966).

BIBLIOGRAPHY   S. A. Tannenbaum, *Shakespeare's RJ: A Concise Bibliography* (1950).

KING RICHARD THE SECOND

TEXT Alexander 116-117; Camb vii-x, lxiv-lxxvi, 107-114; Chambers 348-356; Greg 236-239; New Arden xiii-xxix; Sisson II, 15-27.

See also C. Eidam, "Über die Einleitung in Shakespeares *R2*," *NS,* XIX (1911), 277-295; A. Pollard, *A New Sh Quarto: The Tragedy of King Richard II* (1916); M. Black, "Problems in the Editing of Sh: Interpretation," *EIE* (1947), 117-136, and "The Sources of Shakespeare's *R2*," *AMS* (1948); McManaway, 26. The bibliography of the *NV* is indispensable for textual studies. See also R. Hasker, "The Copy for the First Folio *R2*," *SB,* V (1953), 53-72; Charlton Hinman, "Shakespeare's Text—Then, Now and Tomorrow," *ShS,* XVIII (1965), 23-33.

EDITIONS Camb, ed. J. Dover Wilson (1939); ed. G. L. Kittredge (1941); *NV,* ed. M. Black (1955); New Arden, ed. P. Ure (1956); Yale, ed. R. Petersson (1957); Pelican, ed. M. Black (1957). See also Charlton Hinman's edition of *R2, 1597* (1966).

SOURCES W. Boswell-Stone, *Shakespere's Holinshed* (1896); F. Moorman, "Shakespeare's History-Plays and Daniel's *Civile Wars,*" *ShJ,* XL (1904), 69-83; R. Reyher, "Notes Sur Les Sources de *R2,*" *Revue de L'Enseignement des Langues Vivantes,* XLI (1924), 158-168. Two articles by E. Albright—"Shakespeare's *R2* and the Essex Conspiracy," *PMLA,* XLII (1927), 686-720, and "Shakespeare's *R2*, Hayward's *History of Henry IV* and the Essex Conspiracy," *PMLA,* XLVI (1931), 694-719—take an extreme and, I believe, fallacious position on the relationship of the play to contemporary events. See also A. and J. Nicoll, *Holinshed's Chronicle as Used in Shakespeare's Plays* (1927); W. Zeeveld, "The Influence of Hall on Shakespeare's English Historical Plays," *ELH,* III (1936), 317-353; A. P. Rossiter, *Woodstock* (1946); M. Black, "Sources" (above); R. A. Law, "Deviations from Holinshed in *R2*," *TxSE,* XXIX (1950), 91-101; L. Michel and C. Seronsy, "Shakespeare's History Plays and Daniel," *SP,* LII (1955), 549-577; Bullough (1957–), III, 353-491; K. Muir, "Source Problems in the Histories," *ShJ,* XCVI (1960), 47-63.

CRITICISM Coleridge's essay is essential. Virtually every modern study of importance has its roots in his insight into the character of the king. E. K. Chambers, *Sh: A Survey* (1925), defines the play's great opposition as that between "the practical and artistic temperaments." In J. Draper's "The Character of Richard II," *PQ,* XXI (1942), 228-236, the "protean instability" of the king is ascribed to his having the "mercurial type" of psychological humour. This is good as far as it goes, but simplistic. A brilliant essay on the representational quality of the play was written by E. M. W. Tillyard in *Shakespeare's History Plays* (1944). Tillyard states that *R2* is the picture of the lost medieval world of order: in the king we see "the full sanction of medieval kingship and the strong pathos of being the last king to possess it." The ritual style reveals a "more exotically ritual world." Hence, Tillyard says, the portentous solemnity, the formal symbols, and the cosmic analogies. A very interesting study on this subject will be found in *The King's Two Bodies* (1957) by E. Kantorowicz. A recent disagreement with Tillyard's position is in P. Phialas, "The Medieval in *R2*," *ShQ,* XII (1961), 305-310.

John Palmer analyzes Richard's character at length in *Political Characters of Sh* (1945). He discusses Richard's exquisite futility *vis-à-vis* the hard realities of politics. An important essay is in L. Campbell's *Shakespeare's Histories* (1947). Campbell notes the play's reflection of the policies—and weaknesses—of Queen Elizabeth: "through the greater part of Elizabeth's reign she was being compared to Richard II . . . malcontents were using the reign of Richard to point the moral." She finds the play a study of the deposition of kings, deriving its particular relevance from the rebellion of Essex. A study of the rise and fall of kings useful in this connection is that of R. Chapman, "The Wheel of Fortune in Shakespeare's Historical Plays," *RES,* I (1950), 1-7. B. Stirling, "Bolingbroke's 'Decision,' " *ShQ,* II (1951), 27-34, comments on the usurper's political intelligence. Deposition, Stirling points out, is not the issue until the confrontation of Richard and Bolingbroke at Flint Castle. Until that time the issues center on reform and legal redress; the usurpation develops inexorably from these points through the accusation of the king's weakness to the final execution. G. Bonnard, "The Actor in Richard II," *ShJ,* LXXXVII (1952), 87-101, writes on a subject often treated only in passing by critics. The king is "a man who goes through life acting instead of living, turning into drama, with himself in the chief part, whatever he has to live through." Bonnard analyzes the various roles Richard plays, from power to pathos. Another interesting article on this matter is L. Dean's "*R2*: the State and the Image of the Theater," *PMLA,* LXVII (1952), 211-218: Dean demonstrates that both Richard and Bolingbroke act out different roles. Richard becomes the eloquent spokesman for the ideal of the "Christian king" only after he has failed to realize that role. The "histrionic" Bolingbroke, however, is similarly unable to fulfill that role; like Richard, he lives in the "theater of the state" and must hide his real feelings to achieve his ends.

A good introductory essay is in the New Arden edition of P. Ure (1956). Ure makes many useful allusions to the criticism of the play. K. Thompson, "Richard II, Martyr," *ShQ,* VIII (1957), 159-166, discusses the themes of death, retribution, and moral order. One of the finest essays on this play is in D. A. Traversi's *Sh from Richard II to Henry V* (1957). Traversi concludes that "one can trace in Sh a process by which literary artifice, expanding in complexity and psychological correspondence, becomes an instrument of self-analysis; and the person of Richard, as revealed here, represents an important stage in this process." Traversi discusses the character of Richard in terms of the "artifice, weakness, and pathos" of his poetry. A helpful study is in I. Ribner's *The English History Play in the Age of Sh* (1957). The play's central conflict is illuminated by a quotation from Tyndale: "it is better to have a tyrant unto thy king: than a shadow. . . . A king that is as soft as silk and effeminate, that is to say, turned into the nature of a woman . . . shall be much more grievous unto the realm than the right tyrant. Read the chronicles, and thou shalt find it ever so."

J. McPeek, "Richard and His Shadow World," *Amer. Imago*, XV (1958), 195-212, writes of the narcissism and possible schizophrenia of the protagonist. M. Quinn, "The King Is Not Himself," *SP*, LVI (1959), 169-186, analyzes duty and honor and their conflict. He believes that it is the isolation of Richard from both of these that ensures his dissolution as a man and his political downfall. R. Dorius, "Prudence and Excess in *R2* and the Histories," *ShQ*, XI (1960), 13-26, writes that there is "a kind of logical or psychological relationship between the stages of a process from health to disease, marked by metaphors depicting carelessness, eating or sleeping, deafness or blindness, rioting, fatness or excess, sickness, waste, barrenness, and death." The well-known essay of W. B. Yeats is reprinted in *Essays and Introductions* (1961). Yeats saw in Richard "the defeat that awaits all, whether they be Artist or Saint, who find themselves where men ask of them a rough energy and have nothing to give but some contemplative virtue." M. M. Reese, *The Cease of Majesty* (1961), calls Richard's political legacy the "buried fear" of his successor. In this phrase, Reese suggests, is embodied the ultimate failure of the usurper. When Richard is reduced to his nadir he in fact creates his last role, that of the "invincible sacredness" of an annointed king. It is this which tempers his rival's political—and very secular—success. In a recent essay R. F. Hill in *Early Sh* (1961) discusses what he considers the triumph of poetry over psychology in this play: *R2* is "rhetorical tragedy." Hill states, however, that "the supreme flowering of the mannered style at emotional peaks may not sound natural but its intensity is the rhetorical projection of psychological intensity." His estimate of the language seems just, but he is weaker on character. To find Richard free from "the hypocritical arts" is perhaps to indulge in some hero-worship.

Some of the best studies of this play have centered on the poetry. One such is that of M. Doran, "Imagery in *R2* and *H4*," *MLR*, XXXVII (1942), 113-122. According to R. Altick's "Symphonic Imagery in

R2," PMLA, LXII (1947), 339-365, the word play introduces ideas that continually coalesce. The complex of "earth" images "emblematizes the foundation of kingly pride and power" and "is also a familiar symbol of the vanity of human life." Altick notes the extraordinary series of blood and growth images, which link homicidal horror with the inheritance of power. He summarizes the four modes of these linked images: repetition, cumulative effect, interweaving, and "reciprocal coloration." S. Kliger, "The Sun Imagery in *R2," SP,* XLV (1948), 196-202, finds a continual suggestion of eclipse. Richard's light and life are first seen in prosperity by means of sun imagery and then threatened with extinction in the same rhetorical mode. Two articles of note are P. Jorgensen, "Vertical Patterns in *R2," SAB,* XXIII (1948), 119-134, and A. Downer, "The Life of Our Design," *HR,* II (1949), 242-263.

Other language studies include that of Clemen (1951). He notes that imagery is a major mode of expression in this play and that language itself is used as a "sort of substitute for reality." A. Suzman, "Imagery and Symbolism in *R2," ShQ,* VII (1956), 355-370, takes his theme of rise-and-fall metaphor from Hazlitt: "the steps by which Bolingbroke mounts the throne are those by which Richard sinks into the grave." Suzman notes many uses of language which oppose the ascent of Bolingbroke to the descent of Richard: they give iterative and literal force to figurative conception. M. Mahood, *Shakespeare's Wordplay* (1957), is an excellent discussion of the verbal patterns. Mahood finds the play to be "about the efficacy of a king's words" and she demonstrates that they eventually have ironic meanings when they are opposed to the actions of his rival. J. Bryant, "The Linked Analogies of *R2," Sew,* LXV (1957), 420-433, examines the allusions to Christ, Adam, and Cain. S. Heninger, "The Sun-King Analogy in *R2," ShQ,* XI (1960), 319-327, considers the imagery of light and its cosmic allusiveness. It tends, he says, to manifest a principle of order against which neither Richard nor Bolingbroke measures up.

Further reading: F. Schelling, *The English Chronicle Play* (1902); J. Marriott, *English History in Sh* (1918); F. Boas, *Sh and the Universities* (1923); C. Kingsford, *Prejudice and Promise in Fifteenth Century England* (1925); W. Lewis, *The Lion and the Fox* (1927); J. W. Allen, *A History of Political Thought in the Sixteenth Century* (1928); G. W. Knight, *The Imperial Theme* (1931); A. Hart, *Sh and the Homilies* (1934); Spurgeon (1935); W. Farnham, *The Medieval Heritage of Elizabethan Tragedy* (1936); K. Muir and S. O'Loughlin, *The Voyage to Illyria* (1937); J. Dover Wilson, "The Political Background of Shakespeare's *R2* and *H4," ShJ,* LXXV (1939), 36-51; M. Van Doren, *Sh* (1939); E. M. W. Tillyard, *The Elizabethan World Picture* (1943); U. Ellis-Fermor, *The Frontiers of Drama* (1945); I. Ribner, "Bolingbroke, a True Machiavellian," *MLQ,* IX (1948), 177-184; J. Danby, *Shake-*

speare's Doctrine of Nature (1949); H. Jenkins, "Shakespeare's History
Plays: 1900-1951," *ShS,* VI (1953), 1-15; P. Goodman, *The Structure
of Literature* (1954); T. Bogard, "Shakespeare's Second Richard,"
PMLA, LXX (1955), 192-204; J. Bennett, "Britain Among the Fortu-
nate Isles," *SP,* LIII (1956), 114-140; F. Provost, "The Sorrows of
Shakespeare's Richard II," *Studies in English Renaissance Literature*
(1962). See also the two important books by E. W. Talbert, *The Prob-
lem of Order* (1962) and *Elizabethan Drama and Shakespeare's Early
Plays* (1963); J. Dorius, *Discussions of Shakespeare's Histories* (1964);
Donald Reiman, "Appearance, Reality, and Moral Order in *R2,*" *MLQ,*
XXV (1964), 34-45; H. Richmond, *Shakespeare's Political Plays* (1967);
Wilbur Sanders, *The Dramatist and the Received Idea* (1968).

STAGING Camb lxxvii-xcii; Craig 646; Odell *passim;* Sprague 121-
125; Trewin *passim.*

See also W. Winter, *Life and Art of Edwin Booth* (1893); W. Allwardt,
Die englischen Bühnenbearbeitungen von Shakespeares R2 (1909); E.
Bentley, "Doing Sh Wrong," *In Search of Theater* (1947); J. Dover
Wilson and T. Worsley, *Shakespeare's Histories at Stratford 1951*
(1952); R. David, "Shakespeare's History Plays Epic or Drama," *ShS,*
VI (1953), 129-139; *NV* (1955); Folio Society edition (1958). There
are two recent theatre studies of importance. Arthur C. Sprague's
Shakespeare's Histories: Plays for the Stage (1964) reviews a variety of
performances and John Russell Brown, in *Shakespeare's Plays in Performance* (1966), writes of narrative and staging.

A MIDSUMMER NIGHT'S DREAM

TEXT Alexander 104-109; Camb vii-xi, 77-100; Chambers 356-363; Greg 240-247; Sisson I, 125-134.

See also W. Greg, "On Certain False Dates in Shakespearian Quartos," *Lib,* IX (1908), 113-131 and 381-409; A. Pollard, *Sh Folios and Quartos* (1909); E. K. Chambers, "The New Sh," *MLR,* XX (1925), 340-345; W. J. Lawrence, "A Plummet for Bottom's Dream," *Shakespeare's Workshop* (1928); H. Spencer, "A Nice Derangement," *MLR,* XXV (1930), 23-31, and "A Note on Cutting and Slashing," *MLR,* XXXI (1936), 393-395; J. Draper, "The Date of *A Midsommer Nights Dreame,*" *MLN,* LIII (1938), 266-268; McManaway, 26; R. Turner, "Printing Methods and Textual Problems in *MND* Q$_1$," *SB,* XV (1962), 33-55.

EDITIONS *NV,* ed. H. H. Furness (1895); ed. E. K. Chambers (1897); Arden, ed. H. Cunningham (1905); Camb, ed. A. Quiller-Couch and J. Dover Wilson (1924); ed. G. L. Kittredge (1939); Pelican, ed. Madeleine Doran (1959).

SOURCES G. Hart, *Die Pyramus-und-Thisbe Saga* (1889-1891); G. Sarrazin, "Die Abfassungszeit des *Sommernachtstraums,*" *Archiv,* XCV (1895), 291-300, and CIV (1900), 67-74; R. Tobler, "Shakespeares *Sommernachtstraum* und Montemayors *Diana,*" *ShJ,* XXXIV (1898), 358-366; F. Sidgwick, *Sources and Analogues of MND* (1908); R. A. Law, "The Pre-Conceived Pattern of *MND,*" *TxSE,* XXIII (1943), 5-14; Sister M. Generosa, "Apuleius and *MND,*" *SP,* XLII (1945), 198-204; M. Poirier, "Sidney's Influence upon *MND,*" *SP,* XLIV (1947), 483-489; A. Davenport, "Weever, Ovid and Sh," *NQ,* CXCIV (1949), 524-525; K. Muir, "Pyramus and Thisbe: A Study in Shakespeare's Method," *ShQ,* V (1954), 141-153, and *Shakespeare's Sources* (1957); H. Braddy, "Shakespeare's Puck and Froissart's Orthon," *ShQ,* VII (1956), 276-280; Bullough (1957–), I, 367-422; M. Doran, "Pyramus and Thisbe Once More," *Essays on Sh . . . In Honor of Hardin Craig* (1962); N. Coghill, *Shakespeare's Professional Skills* (1964), 40-60.

CRITICISM There have been a number of studies of the topical qualities of *MND.* S. B. Hemingway wrote a brief but important article on "The Relation of *MND* to *RJ,*" *MLN,* XXIV (1911), 78-80, suggesting that the later play is a parody of the love tragedy. E. Rickert, "Political Propaganda and Satire in *MND,*" *MP,* XXI (1923), 53-87 and 133-154, discussed topical allusions and claimed that the play satirized King James I. D. Bethurum, "Shakespeare's Comment on Mediaeval Romance in *MND,*" *MLN,* LX (1945), 85-94, states that the play may be a satire of Chaucer's tale of knightly love, which opposes common sense to romance. K. Muir, "Sh as Parodist," *NQ,* CXCIX (1954), 467-468, believes that *MND* is a satire on those Elizabethan playwrights who failed to make any sense at all of either tragedy or comedy.

Coleridge admired the "fancy" of the play, but Hazlitt objected that it could only be appreciated off the stage. "Fancy cannot be embodied," he said in his *Characters* (1817), because an acceptable illusion in the study becomes merely an ass' head in front of an audience. Most nineteenth-century readers and viewers sided with Coleridge, and the play won a huge following. One of the first important modern studies was E. K. Chambers' "The Occasion of *MND*," *A Book of Homage to Sh* (1916). This connected the play to the festivities of an Elizabethan masque and wedding. Chambers has an intelligent appreciation of the play in his *Sh: A Survey* (1925). Spurgeon (1935) observes that the imagery of moonlight functions to enhance the supernatural; the imagery is rich also in connotations of emotion and sensation. H. B. Charlton, *Shakespearian Comedy* (1938), was one of the first to note the serious content of the play: it is about love, but it leads to marriage; it takes place in an evanescent world, but it is brought back to hard reality. M. Van Doren, *Sh* (1939), has an analysis of the style of *MND* and some reminders about the amplitude of the world which the play depicts. There are short studies in H. Craig, *An Interpretation of Sh* (1948), and in D. Stauffer, *Shakespeare's World of Images* (1949). T. M. Parrott, *Shakespearean Comedy* (1949), examines the conflict of reasonable ideals and passionate realities. Parrott argues that *MND* demonstrates the work of a "master playwright." His essay anticipates Kermode (1961, below) in its examination of themes and construction.

E. Schanzer, "The Central Theme of *MND*," *UTQ,* XX (1951), 233-238, sees the play as a burlesque of romance. Reasonable love, "ardent but not sensual, tender but not sentimental, pure but not ascetic," is its goal. There is a study of the background of masque and entertainment in A. Venezky, *Pageantry on the Shakespearean Stage* (1951). M. C. Bradbrook, *Sh and Elizabethan Poetry* (1951), discusses *MND* as a masque of *Natura Naturans:* that aspect of nature "blossoming, ripening, decaying and renewing." She acknowledges the powerful presence of implicitly tragic forces. P. Siegel, "*MND* and the Wedding Guests," *ShQ,* IV (1953), 139-144, writes of the harmonious concord the wedding imposes on the chaos of preceding events. He believes the play is much concerned with the aristocratic ideal of love and with the idea of love as a mystery. H. Nemerov, "The Marriage of Theseus and Hippolyta," *KR,* XVIII (1956), 633-641, examines the question of the nature of art raised by Theseus. As a statement about poetry *MND* rejects both "entertainment" and "mystery"—and perhaps both Plato and Aristotle as literary arbiters. G. Bonnard, "Shakespeare's Purpose

in *MND,*" *ShJ,* XCII (1956), 268-269, has a useful analysis of imagination and illusion. J. R. Brown, *Sh and His Comedies* (1957), summarizes this play as a statement that "lovers, like lunatics, poets, and
actors, have their own 'truth' which is established as they see the beauty of their beloved." His essay on "Love's Truth" discusses this necessary illusion.

P. Olsen, "*MND* and the Meaning of Court Marriage," *ELH,* XXIV
(1957), 95-119, makes a complex study of symbol, metaphor, source,
and allegory. He finds that the play explores the higher reality of love
that in ordinary life is inhibited by necessity. There is a good analysis
of the confrontation of the power of the state and the passions of its
citizens. P. Fisher, "The Argument of *MND,*" *ShQ,* VIII (1957), 307-
310, finds that the play is an allegory of love linking the different
worlds of nature and society, and not simply a fantasy. His own argument is thin, however, because the definition of "nature" is superficial.
One of the best criticisms of the play is in C. L. Barber's *Shakespeare's
Festive Comedy* (1959). Barber takes up many issues and writes with
unique sanity of the rituals that underlie *MND.* Especially to be recom-
mended are his discussions of the language, wit, and occasion of the
play. The play's structure is the subject of T. W. Baldwin, *On the Literary Genetics of Shakspere's Plays 1592-1594* (1959). S. P. Zitner,
"The Worlds of *MND,*" *South Atlantic Quarterly,* LIX (1960), 397-403,
discusses the great range of the play's allusions to the workaday world.
He finds it intensely realistic, if only by the power of such allusion.
B. Evans, *Shakespeare's Comedies* (1960), offers a worthwhile essay on
the complex meanings of "awareness" in *MND.* F. Kermode, "The
Mature Comedies," *Early Sh* (1961), asserts that *MND* is the best of the
comedies and is "thematically serious."

G. K. Hunter's *Sh: The Later Comedies* (1962) effectively discusses the
play's psychological implications. The book-length treatment by David
Young, *Something of Great Constancy* (1966) is enjoyable and informative. There is a useful amount of background material on the rites of
May; a section on the parody involved in the speeches of the mechan-
icals; and an illuminating discussion of style and structure. Young takes
seriously the play's imaginative "doctrine" and succeeds in placing it
within the Renaissance dialogue on poetical epistemology.

Bottom and the fairies have been the objects of affectionate criticism.
Some studies on the Weaver are J. B. Priestly, *The English Comic Char-
acters* (1925); J. Palmer, *Comic Characters of Sh* (1946); G. K.
Chesterton, *The Common Man* (1950); S. Sen Gupta, *Shakespearian
Comedy* (1950); W. Dillingham, "Bottom: the Third Ingredient,"
Emory Univ. Quar., XII (1956), 230-237. On the fairies, see M. Latham,
The Elizabethan Fairies (1930); D. Miller, "Titania and the Changeling,"

ES, XXII (1940), 66-70; E. Schanzer, "The Moon and the Fairies in
MND," UTQ, XXIV (1955), 234-246; K. M. Briggs, *The Anatomy of
Puck* (1959); L. Reynolds and P. Sawyer, "Folk Medicine and the Four
Fairies of *MND," ShQ,* X (1959), 513-521; D. Kersten, "Shakespeares
Puck," *ShJ,* XCVIII (1962), 189-200; R. L. Green, "Sh and the Fair-
ies," *Folklore,* LXXIII (1962), 89-103. The books by Latham and
Briggs are especially valuable.

Further reading: W. Greg, *Pastoral Poetry and Pastoral Drama* (1906);
A. Lefranc, "La Réalité Dans *MND," Mélanges Bernard Bouvier* (1920);
E. Welsford, *The Court Masque* (1927); G. W. Knight, *The Shakespear-
ian Tempest* (1932); E. E. Stoll, *Shakespeare's Young Lovers* (1937); C.
Cambillard, "Le Songe D'Une Nuit D'Été: Thème Astrologique," *Ea,*
III (1939), 118-126; E. Legouis, "La Psychologie Dans Le Songe D'Une
Nuit D'Été," *ibid.,* 113-117; W. de la Mare, *Pleasure and Speculations*
(1940); H. Kökeritz, "Shakespeare's *Night-Rule," Language,* XVIII
(1942), 40-44; G. Gordon, *Shakespearian Comedy* (1944); D. L.
Stevenson, *The Love-Game Comedy* (1946); N. Frye, "The Argument
of Comedy," *EIE* (1948), 58-73; E. C. Pettet, *Sh and the Romance
Tradition* (1949); S. Thomas, "The Bad Weather in *MND," MLN,* LXIV
(1949), 319-322; N. Coghill, "The Basis of Shakespearian Comedy,"
E&S (1950), 1-28; W. Gui, "Bottom's Dream," *Amer. Imago,* IX
(1952), 251-305 (eccentric); Evans (1952); J. R. Brown, "The Interpretation of Shakespeare's Comedies: 1900-1953," *ShS,* VIII (1955), 1-13;
T. M. Pearce, "*MND,* IV:i, 214-215," *Ex,* XVIII:i (1959); J. Dover
Wilson, *Shakespeare's Happy Comedies* (1962); P. Phialas, *Shakespeare's Romantic Comedies* (1966).

STAGING   Camb 160-168; Craig 184; Odell *passim;* Sprague 50-55;
Trewin *passim.*

See also G. Odell, "*MND* on the New York Stage," *Shaksperian Studies,*
ed. Mathews and Thorndike (1916); E. Welsford, *The Court Masque*
(1927); A. Nicoll, *Stuart Masques* (1937); G. W. Stone, "*MND* in the
Hands of Garrick and Colman," *PMLA,* LIV (1939), 467-482; R.
Watkins, *Moonlight at the Globe* (1946); D. MacCarthy, "*MND*: The
Production of Poetic Drama," *Theatre* (1955); Folio Society edition
(1957); J. R. Brown, "Three Adaptations," *ShS,* XIII (1960), 142-145;
ed. F. Fergusson and C. J. Sisson (1960); W. M. Merchant, "*MND*: A
Visual Re-creation," *Early Sh* (1961); Peter Raby, *The Stratford Scene
1958-1968* (1968); Glynne Wickham, *Shakespeare's Dramatic Heritage*
(1969).

KING JOHN

TEXT Alexander 85-86; Camb vii-lvii, 91-94; Chambers 364-367; Greg 248-255; New Arden xxxiii-xliii; Sisson II, 3-14.

See also H. D. Sykes, *Sidelights on Sh* (1919); G. B. Harrison, "Shakespeare's Topical Significances," *TLS,* (13 Nov. 1930), 939; R. Taylor, "A Tentative Chronology of Marlowe's and Some Other Elizabethan Plays," *PMLA,* LI (1936), 643-688; G. R. Price, "Compositors' Methods," *Papers Bibl. Soc. Amer.,* XLIV (1950), 269-274; McManaway, 26; T. M. Parrott, *"King John*: The Arden Edition," *JEGP,* LV (1956), 297-305; R. A. Law, "On the Date of *KJ,*" *SP,* LIV (1957), 119-127.

EDITIONS Ed. G. C. Moore Smith (1900); *NV,* ed. H. H. Furness, Jr. (1919); Camb, ed. J. Dover Wilson (1936); New Arden, ed. E. A. Honigmann (1954); Pelican, ed. Irving Ribner (1962).

SOURCES W. G. Boswell-Stone, *Shakspere's Holinshed* (1896); G. H. Kopplow, *Shakespeares KJ und seine Quellen* (1900); G. C. Moore Smith, "Shakespeare's *KJ* and the *Troublesome Reign,*" *Furnival Misc.* (1901); A. and J. Nicoll, *Holinshed's Chronicle as Used in Shakespeare's Plays* (1927); J. Elson, "Studies in the *KJ* Plays," *AMS* (1948); V. K. Whitaker, *Shakespeare's Use of Learning* (1953); W. Warren, "What Was Wrong with King John?" *History Today,* VII (1957), 806-812; M. McDiarmid, "Concerning *The Troublesome Reign of King John,*" *NQ,* ns, IV (1957), 435-438; Bullough (1957—), IV, 1-151; K. Muir, "Source Problems in the Histories," *ShJ,* XCVI (1960), 47-63.

CRITICISM R. Simpson, *New Sh Soc. Trans.* (1874), pointed out that "the historical quarrel against John as a tyrant is changed into a mythical one against him as a usurper." He thought the play was addressed to the participants in Elizabethan politics. E. Rose, "Sh as an Adapter," *MacMillan's Magazine* (1878), felt that the potential "power, craft, passion, and deviltry" of John was neglected in *KJ.* John Masefield's well-known thesis in his *William Sh* (1911) was that *KJ* "is an intellectual form in which a number of people with obsessions illustrate the idea of treachery." Masefield's remarks on the Bastard—he found him both a great man and something of an animal—underlie much modern criticism and still seem valid. J. Munro, editor of the *Troublesome Raigne* (1913), set the tone for the dissatisfaction of many readers: he thought the play a conglomeration of bombast, spectacle, violence, disputes, and frenzied rebellions. The essays of F. Liebermann on "Sh als Bearbeiter des *KJ,*" *Archiv,* CXLII (1921), 177-202, and CXLIII (1922), 17-46 and 190-203, pay close attention to sources and problems of character and follow the political sophistry in *KJ.*

E. K. Chambers, *Sh: A Survey* (1925), called the play "incoherent patchwork." Spurgeon (1935) investigated the language of *KJ* and wrote of the "wild and ruthless" presence of war in images of blood and violence. The Bastard was the subject of J. M. Murry's praise in *Sh* (1936). Like many others, Murry thought of him as the incarnation of Englishness: "high-spirited, brave, dare-devil, witty, humorous, penetrating, yet capable of a profound depth of feeling." A review of *Shakespeare's Attitude to the Catholic Church in KJ* (1938) was the subject of G. M. Greenewald. His conclusion was that Sh left out of *KJ* a large amount of matter derogatory to the church. The entire matter of Sh and Catholicism is still problematical. There are, at any rate, useful criticisms in Greenewald's book. D. F. Ash, "Anglo-French Relations in *KJ*," *Ea*, III (1939), 349-358, believes that "the futility of war and of peace, broken oaths, compromises, policy and commodity, kings with feet of clay, jeering subjects" are in the play as a series of reflections of the time in which it was written.

M. Van Doren in *Sh* (1939) is especially concerned with the language of *KJ*. The speeches, he thinks, are overladen and bloated; in the case of Constance, passion is borne so long by the audience as to become intolerable. The Bastard adds a touch of the natural world: his speeches are freighted with terms of "eel-skins, riding-rods, three-farthings, Sir Nob, the Absey Book, Joan, George, and Peter." A historical study of value is *Le Roi Jean et Sh* (1944) by C. Petit-Dutaillis. The author sees in the historical John a manic-depressive characterized by fear, violence, and suspicion. He discusses the changes made by Sh to fit this figure into the ambiance created by the opposition between Puritan and Catholic. E. M. W. Tillyard, *Shakespeare's History Plays* (1944), has not many kind words for this play. He thinks it disunified, with very little control over the rhetoric of emotion. At its best the style is a sign of better things to come, a "new burst of vitality" in Sh. J. Palmer, *Political Characters of Sh* (1945), sums up many objections like those of Tillyard: Sh "failed to concentrate his material upon a central figure. The political issues were diverse and refractory; they refused to cohere. The play is accordingly little more than a succession of episodes, some of them brilliantly executed."

Una Ellis-Fermor, *The Frontiers of Drama* (1945), writes intelligently of the failure of kingship in the histories. An interesting comparison of *KJ* and the *Troublesome Reigne* is in J. H. De Groot, *The Shakespeares and the Old Faith* (1946). This book attempts to prove Shakespeare's sympathy to Catholicism and uses *KJ* as a test case. Not enough is known at present to substantiate this theory. The topical allusions are pursued by L. Campbell in *Shakespeare's Histories* (1947). Her thesis is that *KJ* is a paradigm of rebellion and instability that mirrors English and continental relationships in the political sphere. F. M. Salter, "The

Problem of *KJ," Trans. Royal Soc. Canada,* XLIII (1949), 115-136, has
a thesis with which it is difficult to agree: the murder of Arthur is intended to reveal the goodness of Hubert, which in turn engages our
sympathies for the king who is capable of inspiring the loyalty of such
a man. Since the king is the man who orders Hubert to execute Arthur,
this seems to be a logical short-circuit. A useful essay by R. Chapman is
"The Wheel of Fortune in Shakespeare's Historical Plays," *RES,* I
(1950), 1-7. The four states of the king correspond to the four positions on the Wheel of Fortune—rising, ruling, falling, and cast off. What
I judge to be the best essay on the play is A. Bonjour's "The Road to
Swinstead Abbey," *ELH,* XVIII (1951), 253-274. It contains an extended review of the critics who have found *KJ* unsatisfactory and a
well-reasoned defence of the play. Bonjour finds the crime against
Arthur the fulcrum of the play; it changes a story of understandable
political duplicity to one of moral degradation. It is the crime that leads
to the moral abdication of the king. Bonjour's analysis of the design of
KJ divides the play into two geometrical units. He states that "John's
career represents a falling curve, the Bastard's career a rising curve; and
both curves, perfectly contrasted, are linked into a single pattern."

In addition to the comments of Spurgeon (1935), Clemen (1951) and
Evans (1952) discuss the bloodshed imagery and rhetorical energy of
KJ. The introductory essay of E. Honigmann in his New Arden edition
(1954) is informative; the major themes and images are reviewed, as
well as the "perpetual analysis of moral concepts" which are never
resolved. An informative study is E. C. Pettet's "Hot Irons and Fever:
A Note on Some of the Imagery of *KJ," EC,* IV (1954), 128-144.
Pettet points out a recurrent pattern of heat and fire imagery that cul-
minates in scenes of physical violence and mental anguish. The attempted blinding of Arthur is connected through such imagery to the death
of the king, "burned up with inflaming wrath." J. Calderwood, "Commodity and Honour in *KJ," UTQ,* XXIX (1960), 341-356, traces
honesty and opportunism in the play. Those who stand for honor are
destroyed; those who stand for its opposite fare little better. Both
themes are, in Calderwood's formulation, vehicles for the portrayal of
irony. Honor cannot exist in its ideal form, hence the Bastard's worldly
wisdom, which saves the realm where idealism would fail.

An interesting character study is J. Van de Water's "The Bastard in
KJ," ShQ, XI (1960), 137-146. The Bastard's "sudden moral elevation"
develops after the death of Arthur, and he does in fact become the pillar of the kingdom, yet he has no central role or identity. He is a
mélange of "comic relief, general messenger boy, a spur to the king, a
good stout-hearted Englishman, the spirit of loyalty, the origin of
deeply-felt patriotism—and the chorus." A good account of the intellec-

tual history of the political plays is M. M. Reese's *The Cease of Majesty* (1961). The essay on *KJ* itself is cursory, but the book is valuable for the background study of the play. The premise of W. Matchett, "Richard's Divided Heritage in *KJ*," *EC*, XII (1962), 231-253, is that the memory of Coeur de Lion haunts the play as "the mythically heightened image of a good and heroic king." It is a useful study of the politics of usurpation. R. Stevick, "Repentant Ashes," *ShQ*, XIII (1962), 366-370, takes up the imagery of heat, burning, and destruction.

Sigurd Burckhardt's good essay is in *ELH*, XXXIII (1966), 133-153. As the title indicates—"*KJ*: The Ordering of This Present Time"—Burckhardt is concerned with assessing *KJ* against the doctrine of the "Elizabethan world picture." He concludes that the play is about creating order in the modern sense, by an act of restoration or discovery, and that it should not be interpreted as a model of so-called cosmic analogies. For other recent detailed studies see H. M. Richmond, *Shakespeare's Political Plays* (1967) and R. Berman, "Anarchy and Order in *R3* and *KJ*," *ShS*, XX (1967), 51-59.

Further reading: G. H. Needler, *Richard Coeur de Lion in Literature* (1890); B. Warner, *English History in Shakespeare's Plays* (1894); F. Schelling, *The English Chronicle Play* (1902); C. T. Brooke, *The Tudor Drama* (1912); A. Kerrl, *Die metrischen Unterschiede von Shakespeares KJ und JC* (1913); J. Marriott, *English History in Sh* (1918); W. Raleigh, *Sh and England* (1918); A. Henneke, "Shakespeares englische Könige," *ShJ*, LXVI (1930), 79-144; J. W. Allen, *A History of Political Thought in the Sixteenth Century* (1928); W. Clemen, "Sh und das Königtum," *ShJ*, LXVIII (1932), 56-79; W. Spiegelberger, "Shakespeares Caesarbild," *Neuphil. Mschr.*, X (1939), 177-189; E. M. W. Tillyard, *The Elizabethan World Picture* (1943); W. A. Armstrong, "The Elizabethan Conception of the Tyrant," *RES*, XXII (1946), 161-181, and "The Influence of Seneca and Machiavelli on the Elizabethan Tyrant," *RES*, XXIV (1948), 19-35; H. Craig, *An Interpretation of Sh* (1948); J. Danby, *Shakespeare's Doctrine of Nature* (1949); A. Bonjour, "Le Problème du Héros et la Structure du *Roi Jean*," *Études de Lettres*, XXII (1950), 3-15; J. C. Maxwell, "Notes on *KJ*," *NQ*, CXCV (1950), 75-76 and 473-474; H. Goddard, *The Meaning of Sh* (1951); H. Jenkins, "Shakespeare's History Plays: 1900-1951," *ShS*, VI (1953), 1-15; W. Clemen, "Anticipation and Foreboding," *ShS*, VI (1953), 25-35; P. Frankis, "Shakespeare's *KJ* and a Patriotic Slogan," *NQ*, ns, II (1955), 424-425; P. Tyler, "Phaethon," *Accent*, XVI (1956), 29-44; M. McDiarmid, "A Reconsidered Parallel Between Shakespeare's *KJ* and Kyd's *Cornelia*," *NQ*, ns, III (1956), 507-508; I. Ribner, *The English History Play in the Age of Sh* (1957); G. W. Knight, *The Sovereign Flower* (1958).

STAGING   Camb lxiii-lxxix; Craig 341; New Arden lxxiii-lxxv; Odell *passim;* Sprague 108-116; Trewin *passim.*

See also *NV* (1919); H. Spencer, *The Art and Life of William Sh* (1940); M. St. Clare Byrne, "The Sh Season at the Old Vic, 1956-57, and Stratford-upon-Avon, 1957," *ShQ,* VIII (1957), 482-485; *William Charles Macready's King John,* ed. C. Shattuck (1962).

THE MERCHANT OF VENICE

TEXT Alexander 110-113; Camb 91-119; Chambers 368-375; Greg 240-247; New Arden xi-xxi; Sisson I, 135-142.

See also A. Pollard, *Sh Folios and Quartos* (1909); B. A. P. Van Dam, "The Text of *MV*," *Neophilologus,* XIII (1927), 33-51; McManaway, 27; J. R. Brown, "The Compositors of *Hamlet* Q2 and *MV*," *SB,* VII (1955), 17-40; H. Craig, *A New Look at Shakespeare's Quartos* (1961).

EDITIONS *NV,* ed. H. H. Furness (1888); Camb, ed. A. Quiller-Couch and J. Dover Wilson (1926); ed. G. L. Kittredge (1945); New Arden, ed. J. R. Brown (1955); Pelican, ed. Brents Stirling (1959); Yale, ed. A. Richardson (1960).

SOURCES An unbelievable amount of time has been wasted in the attempt to prove that this play has its real origins in Shakespeare's anti-Semitism. I reject this theory not because it would be painful to contemplate but because this form of prejudice was meaningless for the Elizabethans in general and appears in no conceivable form in other Shakespearean plays. The Old Testament itself is harder on most of its Jewish figures than Sh is on Shylock. Most of the studies listed below concern other matters.

Sir Sidney Lee postulated in *Gentleman's Magazine* (1880) that the trial of a Dr. Lopez for treason in 1594 was the original of the trial in *MV.* A. Dimock argued in "The Conspiracy of Dr. Lopez," *English Historical Review,* IX (1894), 440-472, that Sh did in fact use the Lopez case to "incite hatred" against Jews. He was answered most effectively in the same issue by J. W. Hales (pp. 652-661), whose article should have been the last word on this whole unfortunate matter. The story of the flesh bond is ancient and is discussed in T. Niemeyer, *Der Rechtsspruch gegen Shylock* (1912). The tale of the usurer beguiled is also quite old; it is traced in A. B. Stonex, "The Usurer in Elizabethan Drama," *PMLA,* XXXI (1916), 190-210. A scholarly study is J. L. Cardozo's *The Contemporary Jew in the Elizabethan Drama* (1925). Although it errs in assuming that Sh could not have known any Jews, it makes clear the central principle that *MV* is "not reducible to real life." B. D. Brown, "Mediaeval Prototypes of Lorenzo and Jessica," *MLN,* XLIV (1929), 227-232, traces the young lovers in old stories. Also of interest are: B. V. Wenger, "Shylocks Pfund Fleisch," *ShJ,* LXV (1929), 92-174; C. J. Sisson, "A Colony of Jews in Shakespeare's London," *E&S* (1937), 38-51; H. Sinsheimer, *Shylock* (1947). Texts of the sources are reprinted in Bullough (1957–), I, 445-514. A critical discussion is in Muir (1957).

Source study might include the following, selected from the large body of work: K. Elze, "Zum Kaufmann von Venedig," *ShJ,* VI (1871), 129-168; H. Grätz, *Shylock in der Sage, im Drama und in der Geschichte* (1880); M. Schlauch, "The Pound of Flesh Story in the North," *JEGP,* XXX (1931), 348-380; J. Cardozo, "The Background of Shakespeare's *MV," ES,* XIV (1932), 177-186; C. Roth, "The Background of Shylock," *RES,* IX (1933), 148-156.

CRITICISM   There have been two broad streams of criticism of this play. One has been concerned with the figure of Shylock and the social issues he crystallizes—usury, legality, and ethics. The other is thematic and allegorical. The following belong to the first group.

E. E. Stoll, "Shylock," *JEGP,* X (1911), 236-279, is one of the most important studies of this character (reprinted in his *Sh Studies,* 1927). Stoll makes the observation that Shylock, far from having tragic dimensions, is a traditional comic figure. He notes that it was the actors who changed the old figure of the waxen-nosed villain to the martyr favored in the nineteenth century. Stoll warns of imposing our ideas of justice and sentimentality on a play whose protagonist exists only to be foiled. The warning was lost on those who perennially write furious letters to theatrical companies warning of their intention to boycott the play because it offends their sensibilities. I suggest that the equivalent would be noisy demonstrations against *Hamlet* by all those of Danish extraction. G. W. Keeton, *Sh and His Legal Problems* (1930), defends Portia as judge. There is a good corrective in Lord Normand's "Portia's Judgment," *Univ. Edin. Jour.,* X (1939), 43-45, which points out that, if taken seriously, the trial shows not that Shylock is wicked but that the court is quite unfair in leading him on. See also Keeton's *Shakespeare's Legal and Political Background* (1967).

Spurgeon (1935) makes a connection between the kind and intensity of imagery and the emotion of certain scenes. H. B. Charlton, *Shakespearian Comedy* (1938), interprets the play in terms of Elizabethan hostility to Jews. Charlton is reduced to holding two mutually improbable views: Sh wrote consciously of Shylock the Jewish villain, but his "unconscious dramatic instinct" turned Shylock into a more heroic personage. Both views, however unlikely, *may* be true. But the point is that neither is corroborated by evidence. L. Teeter, "Scholarship and the Art of Criticism," *ELH,* V (1938), 173-194, attempts to substantiate the view of Stoll. He believes that our sympathies are in fact raised for Shylock but are intended to be dashed by his villainy. E. C. Pettet, "*MV* and the Problem of Usury," *E&S* (1945), 19-33, notes the strong strain of anticapitalistic feeling in the time of James I. J. Palmer, *Comic Characters of Sh* (1946), follows Heine, who had asserted that Sh intended to write a comedy but was too great a man to do so and turned out a tragedy instead. This is an attractive but mythical supposition. Many unsound interpretations of this play follow from the characteristic error of confusing the life, of which we know almost nothing, with both the works and our ideals.

A first-rate study is that of Granville-Barker (1946). His thesis is the basic unreality of *MV*: "there is no more reality in Shylock's bond and the Lord of Belmont's will than in Jack and the Beanstalk." For Granville-Barker there are two Shylocks—the one of the old story and the one who might have inhabited a greater unwritten play. J. Draper, "Sh and the Doge of Venice," *JEGP*, XLVI (1947), 75-81, takes up usury and law in the historical Venice. Draper's *Stratford to Dogberry* (1961) contains a group of essays on *MV*. N. Nathan, "Three Notes on *MV*," *SAB*, XXIII (1948), 152-173, has a valuable study of modern defensiveness about the play. M. C. Bradbrook, *Sh and Elizabethan Poetry* (1951), asserts that *MV* is the first of the comedies to directly invite real moral judgment. Morris Carnovsky, "Mirror of Shylock," *TDR*, III (1958), 35-45, is written from an actor's point of view. Carnovsky thinks that our sympathy for Shylock depends not on his philosophy but on his dramatic energy. Regardless of moral issues he is one of certain Shakespearean characters "that assert their right to exist from the moment they come into view." J. Smith, "Shylock," *JEGP*, LX (1961), 1-21, notes that Shylock develops in evil and deteriorates; he is not a static character. P. N. Siegel, "Shylock the Puritan," *Columbia Univ. Forum* (1962) 14-19, connects Judaism, Puritanism, and usury.

The following concentrate on theme and allegory: J. D. Rea, "Shylock and the Processus Belial," *PQ*, VIII (1929), 311-313, reviews the folklore of the trial of Mankind before God. It is the devil who pleads for justice at this trial and who is rebuked by the giving of mercy. I. Gollancz, *Allegory and Mysticism in Sh* (1931), offers some important ideas for the thematic interpretation, as does N. Coghill, "The Governing Idea," *ShQ* (London), I (1948), 9-17. Sigmund Freud writes of the myths of choice underlying *Lear* and *MV* in "The Theme of the Three Caskets," *Collected Papers* (1925), IV, 244-256. His is a seminal essay. Coghill's "The Basis of Shakespearian Comedy," *E&S* (1950), 1-28, has an excellent section on *MV* in which it is pointed out that this play, like the mature comedies, moves from realism to visionary happiness. E. Sehrt, *Vergebung und Gnade bei Sh* (1952), has an important study of the theme of forgiveness. A short but noteworthy article is J. W. Lever's "Shylock, Portia, and the Values of Shakespearian Comedy," *ShQ*, III (1952), 383-386. For Lever, love comprehends the generous give-and-take of emotion, the free "spending of nature's bounty." It is opposed to the usurious perversion of both capital and friendship. A useful study in this connection is J. M. Murry's *Sh* (1936). Murry noted in this book that Shylock is much more than comic: he is the embodiment of irrational hatred and a fully credible human being.

C. Graham, "Standards of Value in *MV*," *ShQ,* IV (1953), 145-151, studies the intricate moral issues of *MV*. He points out that every major character is in fact involved in a system of values that must be expressed and enacted. C. L. Barber's *Shakespeare's Festive Comedy* (1959) includes a good essay which makes sense of the Belmont-Venice relationship. Barber concludes that in every way Shylock, "the ogre of money power," intrudes on "the grace of life." G. Midgley, "*MV*: A Reconsideration," *EC,* X (1960), 119-133, believes the play signifies the opposition of love and hatred. He reaches some unlikely conclusions about the effeminate nature of Antonio. These matured, so to speak, in the 1973 version of the play directed by Ellis Rabb, who forced on the text a homosexual version of the relationship of Antonio and Bassanio. A critique of Midgley's essay by M. Deshpande appeared in the succeeding issue of *EC.* F. Kermode, "The Mature Comedies," *Early Sh* (1961), holds that *MV* revolves about the three ideas of judgment, redemption, and mercy. E. M. W. Tillyard, "The Trial Scene in *MV*," *REL,* II (1961), 51-59, states that Portia is trying in this scene to save not only the body of Antonio but the soul of Shylock. S. Burckhardt, "*MV*: The Gentle Bond," *ELH,* XXIX (1962), 239-262, is an interesting study of the metaphor. Burckhardt thinks that all the characters of *MV* are related by a "bond" but that the nature of this bond varies from love to hate. The contract of Shylock is eventually transformed into "the gentle bond," the ring of Portia. A very good essay on "Biblical Allusion and Allegory in *MV*" is in *ShQ,* XIII (1962), 327-343. The author, Barbara Lewalski, believes that there are elements in the play "generally analogous to Dante's four levels of allegorical meaning: a literal or story level; an allegorical significance concerned with truths relating to humanity as a whole and to Christ as head of humanity; a moral or tropological level dealing with factors in the moral development of the individual; and an anagogical significance treating the ultimate reality, the Heavenly City." See also W. H. Auden, *The Dyer's Hand* (1963) and the long essay in Peter Phialas, *Shakespeare's Romantic Comedies* (1966). For collections of some of the materials listed above see Laurence Lerner, *Shakespeare's Comedies* (1967) and Sylvan Barnet, *Twentieth Century Interpretations of MV* (1970).

Further reading: E. K. Chambers, *Sh: A Survey* (1925); T. M. Parrott, *Shakespearean Comedy* (1949); N. Nathan, "Shylock, Jacob, and God's Judgment," *ShQ,* I (1950), 255-259; S. Sen Gupta, *Shakespearian Comedy* (1950); Evans (1952); N. Frye, "Characterization in Shakespearian Comedy," *ShQ,* IV (1953), 271-277; J. R. Brown, "The Interpretation of Shakespeare's Comedies: 1900-1953," *ShS,* VIII (1955), 1-13, and *Sh and His Comedies* (1957); B. Evans, *Shakespeare's Come-*

dies (1960); B. Grebanier, *The Truth About Shylock* (1962). The last has a great assortment of useful facts vitiated by assertive style and method.

STAGING *MV* has a very rich stage-history. There is a wealth of information available about the malevolent Shylock of Macklin, the passionate Shylock of Kean, and the austere Shylock of Irving. Much of this can be absorbed in the standard biographies of the actors. The following offer a good selection on the play's fortunes on the boards.

Camb 178-186; Craig 505; New Arden xxxii-xxxvi; Odell *passim;* Sprague 19-31; Trewin *passim.*

See also W. Winter, *Sh on the Stage* (1911); A. C. Sprague, *Shakespearian Players and Performances* (1953); T. Lelyveld, *Shylock on the Stage* (1960); J. R. Brown, "The Realization of Shylock," *Early Sh* (1961); G. W. Knight, *Shakespeare in Production* (1964).

BIBLIOGRAPHY S. A. Tannenbaum, *Shakespeare's MV: A Concise Bibliography* (1941).

HENRY THE FOURTH

TEXT Alexander 118-124; Camb (1) vii-xiii, 103-108, (2) 115-123; Chambers 375-384; Greg 262-276; New Arden (1) xv-xxi, lxvi-lxxviii; New Arden (2) xi-xxviii, lxviii-lxxxvi; Sisson II, 28-55.

See also T. Lounsbury, *The Text of Sh* (1906); A. E. Morgan, *Some Problems of Shakespeare's H4* (1924); L. Hotson, *Sh vs. Shallow* (1931); A. Hart, *Sh and the Homilies* (1934); M. Shaaber, "Problems in the Editing of Sh: Text," *EIE* (1947), 97-116; W. Dodds, *"1, 2H4,"* *MLR,* XLII (1947), 371-382; McManaway, 27; A. Walker, "Quarto 'Copy' and the 1623 Folio: *2H4,"* *RES,* II (1951), 217-225, and *Textual Problems of the First Folio* (1953); Walker, "The Folio Text of *1H4,"* *SB,* VI (1954), 45-59; Shaaber, "The Folio Text of *2H4,"* *ShQ,* VI (1955), 134-144; R. A. Law, "The Composition of Shakespeare's Lancastrian Trilogy," *TxSE,* III (1961), 321-327. The *NV* editions (below) contain summaries of textual research.

EDITIONS *NV (1H4),* ed. S. B. Hemingway (1936); *NV (2H4),* ed. M. Shaaber (1940); *(1H4),* ed. G. L. Kittredge (1940); Camb *(1 and 2H4),* ed. J. Dover Wilson (1946); *NV* (*1H4,* Supplement), ed. G. B. Evans (1956); Yale *(1H4),* ed. T. Brooke and S. B. Hemingway (1957); Pelican *(1H4),* ed. Shaaber (1957); Pelican *(2H4),* ed. A. Chester (1957); New Arden *(1H4),* ed. A. R. Humphreys (1960); New Arden *(2H4),* ed. A. R. Humphreys (1966).

SOURCES W. G. Boswell-Stone, *Shakespere's Holinshed* (1896); F. Moorman, "Shakespeare's History-Plays and Daniel's *Civile Wars, ShJ,* XL (1904), 69-83; C. L. Kingsford, *The First English Life of Henry V* (1911); H. Ax, *The Relation of Shakespeare's H4 to Holinshed* (1912); A. and J. Nicoll, *Holinshed's Chronicle as Used in Shakespeare's Plays* (1927); J. Elson, "The Non-Shakespearian *R2* and Shakespeare's *1H4,"* *SP,* XXXII (1935), 177-188; J. Dover Wilson, "The Origins and Development of Shakespeare's *H4,"* *Lib,* XXVI (1945), 2-16; L. Oliver, "Sir John Oldcastle: Legend or Literature?" *Lib,* I (1947), 179-183; L. Michel and C. Seronsy, "Shakespeare's History Plays and Daniel," *SP,* LII (1955), 549-577; Bullough (1957–), IV, 155-343; C. Fish, "H4: Sh and Holinshed," *SP,* LXI (1964), 205-218. For the best review of scholarship on the sources see Bullough and A. R. Humphreys' New Arden edition (1966).

CRITICISM So much has been written about Falstaff that he constitutes a subject in himself. The two great eighteenth-century essays by Dr. Johnson and Maurice Morgann began the long argument between those who judged Falstaff by (relatively) objective and subjective standards. Johnson saw Falstaff as a "compound of sense and vice," and while he admired him he also deprecated his faults. Morgann, on the other hand, tried to make a distinction between character and action which is magnanimous, ingenious, and, I think, sophistical. He appealed not to what Falstaff does but to the effect he has on the reader. If the reader has already committed himself to Falstaff worship, then the effect is predictable. Morgann's *Essay on the Dramatic Character of Sir John Falstaff* (1777) remains in any case one of the most admirable of apologetics.

A distinction between the Falstaff of the two parts of *H4* that seems still to be valid was made by Brandes in his *William Sh* (1898). Falstaff is, says Brandes, in the first part "purely comic" and in the second "indefensible." The terms have been modified but not abandoned. The admiration of A. C. Bradley is summed up in his famous essay on "The Rejection of Falstaff" in *Oxford Lectures* (1909): "he is in bliss and we share his glory. . . . The bliss of freedom gained in humour is the essence of Falstaff. . . . He is the enemy of everything respectable and moral. . . . They are all to him absurd; and to reduce a thing *ad absurdum* is to reduce it to nothing and to walk about free and rejoicing." Moderns will find this sentimental; the essay, however, is well worth acquaintance. For John Masefield, *William Sh* (1911), Falstaff is "base because he is wise." Masefield added, in terms that are still utilized, that Falstaff is "the world and the flesh." J. M. Murry, *Sh* (1936), notes the essential cleavage between Falstaff and the world in which he moves—it is that between history and myth. In H. B. Charlton's *Shakespearian Comedy* (1938) there is a bitter comparison of Falstaff with his degenerate form in *MWW.* Charlton bases his admiration of Falstaff on his "unslakeable thirst for life" and his infinite capacity for survival.

Any "inner consciousness" in Falstaff was dismissed, I think too easily, by S. A. Small in "The Reflective Element in Falstaff," *SAB,* XIV (1939), 108-121 and 131-143. While Small noted the element of self-pity in Falstaff, he was willing to categorize him as simply a "clown." The most influential study has been that of J. Dover Wilson, *The Fortunes of Falstaff* (1943). Wilson searches for Falstaff's origins deep in the early Tudor drama: "Hal associates Falstaff in turn with the Devil of the miracle play, the Vice of the morality, and the Riot of the interlude. . . . And, as heir to the Vice, Falstaff inherits by reversion the functions and attributes of the Lord of Misrule, the Fool, the Buffoon, and the Jester, antic figures the origins of which are lost in the dark backward and abysm of folk-custom." He is part of the great "composite myth" of centuries of allegory. Wilson's book, however, is far more complex than these few summary statements indicate, and it gives an excellent analysis of the character and action of Falstaff as they are revealed in the two plays. In short, Wilson goes back to Johnson in giving a highly moral interpretation to this figure. J. Palmer's *Political Characters of Sh* (1945) has a good discussion of Falstaff and politics. Palmer makes an observation not often seen: if Falstaff is corrupt, he is no worse than the characters who surround him, noble and otherwise. A. Harbage, *As They Liked It* (1947), preferred to drop the ancient charges of cowardice in favor of a new one: Falstaff's "is the larger guilt of having no principles." His vices are actually trivial—it is his intellectual emancipation which makes him a danger in the common-wealth. A poet's license expires in prose, and W. H. Auden's essay in *The Dyer's Hand* (1948) may be accused of creating a Falstaff not far short of supernatural. Auden endows him with a theology: "a comic symbol for the supernatural order of charity." In this exaggerated scheme the fat knight's liason with a whore becomes "a symbol for the charity that loves all neighbours without distinction." I suppose that in an age that makes belief difficult we take our gods where we can get them.

A sharp review of the critics that ends in an appeal to symbol and myth of the *Golden Bough* variety is the substance of J. I. M. Stewart's essay in *Character and Motive in Sh* (1949). In connection with this, see P. Williams, "The Birth and Death of Falstaff Reconsidered," *ShQ*, VIII (1957), 359-365. An essay of admiration will be found in J. M. Murry's *John Clare and Other Studies* (1950). A more limited study is that of S. Sen Gupta, *Shakespearian Comedy* (1950). It is marred by a too-serious view of Falstaff as visionary and alcoholic.

A. Sewell, *Character and Society in Sh* (1951), observes that Falstaff has "no interior mode of existence," a contention that is borne out to some degree by L. Cazamian in *The Development of English Humour* (1952). An interesting response to this mode of criticism is that of W. Empson, "Falstaff and Mr. Dover Wilson," *KR*, XV (1953), 213-262. Empson believes that Falstaff has indeed a real personality with an emotional center to it: "I think there is a quick answer to the idea that the old brute had no heart, and therefore could not have died of break-ing it. If he had had no heart he could have had no power, not even to get a drink, and he had a dangerous amount of power."

The Fortunes of Falstaff is much concerned with conventions which may have dictated the nature of its subject, and many other studies have attempted to trace his allegorical and dramatic origins. Among them are J. Monahan, "Falstaff and His Forebears," *SP*, XVIII (1921), 353-361, and E. E. Stoll, *Sh Studies* (1927). The latter carries "tradi-tion" too far when he identifies Falstaff as coward, satyr, lecher, and parasite on the basis of *other* Renaissance stage types who presumably are his sources. Two informative studies by D. Boughner are "Tradition-al Elements in Falstaff," *JEGP*, XLIII (1944), 417-428, and "Vice,

Braggart, and Falstaff," *Anglia,* LXXII (1954), 35-61. J. Shirley's
"Falstaff, an Elizabethan Glutton," *PQ,* XVII (1938), 271-287, examines the morality background.

The following are useful for their summaries of the Falstaff "problem."
S. B. Hemingway, "On Behalf of That Falstaff," *ShQ,* III (1952), 307-
311; A. C. Sprague, "Gadshill Revisited," *ShQ,* IV (1953), 125-137; R.
Langbaum, *The Poetry of Experience* (1957). The latter has a good
analysis of the position developed by Morgann, which he finds origi-
nated in the new spirit of enlightenment: "liberal in politics, humanitar-
ian in sentiment . . . endowed with the new sensibility." Langbaum puts
the case that interpretation of Falstaff, like that of Hamlet, is essentially part of our history of psychology. He quotes Blake to good purpose
in accounting for the fascination of romantics for Falstaff: "the road
of excess leads to the palace of wisdom."

The fortunes of the Prince and the play have been as varied as those of
Falstaff. For Bernard Shaw, *Dramatic Opinions* (1906), Hal was Shakespeare's "jingo hero," a "combination of conventional propriety and
brute masterfulness in his public capacity with a low-lived blackguard-
ism in his private tastes." In 1875 Dowden had written of Hal as
"Shakespeare's ideal of the practical heroic character," and this opinion
was re-asserted by W. Raleigh in his *Sh* (1907): Hal was "valorous,
generous, and high-spirited." One of the great essays is A. C. Bradley's
"The Rejection of Falstaff" in his *Oxford Lectures* (1909). The "hard-
ness" and the "policy" of the Lancastrians are examined, and much
sentiment about heroism is exploded. There is an excellent summation
of the mixed character of the hero, an explanation essential to understanding why the king rejects the knight. Among the essays hostile to
the Prince, that of Masefield, *Sh* (1911), is both extreme and intelligent: "Prince Henry is not a hero, he is not a thinker, he is not even a
friend; he is a common man whose incapacity for feeling enables him
to change his habits whenever interest bids him." It might be pointed
out that to be for Falstaff has meant, for many critics, to be against the
Prince.

The play itself was the subject of E. K. Chambers, *Sh: A Survey* (1925):
"In *H4,* chronicle-history becomes little more than a tapestry hanging,
dimly wrought with horsemen and footmen . . . which serves as a background to groups of living personages conceived in quite another spirit
and belonging to a very different order of reality." I note that much
recent criticism differs and has as its object the exposure of the relationship that appears to obtain between the nature of character and
that of historical event in these plays. L. C. Knights, *Determinations*
(1934), took a dark view of the plays, which he called satires on thieves
and politicians. He found in them little to admire and much to detest.

An interesting short study may be found in W. Empson's *Some Versions of Pastoral* (1935). Empson writes of the ambiguous nature of the plays: "the parts tend to separate. There are three worlds each with its own hero; rebel camp, tavern, and court; chivalric idealism, natural gusto, the cautious politician. The force and irony of the thing depends on making us sympathise with all three sides so that we are baffled when they meet." There is a subtle examination of the language.

J. Dover Wilson, *The Fortunes of Falstaff* (1943), fought the abuse of the hero and pointed out that it was the product of literary and political romanticism. The man, he wrote, was being attacked simply because he stood for what were positive values in the Elizabethan world: "absolute monarchy, the feudal system, the military virtues." Wilson rejected the tempering of Sh with Rousseau and initiated a rediscovery of Elizabethan ethics. E. M. W. Tillyard, *Shakespeare's History Plays* (1944), relates the character of the Prince to certain Renaissance values, particularly the *sprezzatura* praised by Castiglione. It is "a genuine ethical quality of the Aristotelian type: the mean." Tillyard studies the kingly character well; a valuable ancillary essay is in Una Ellis-Fermor's *The Frontiers of Drama* (1945). A sound study of the plays as exemplars of rebellion is in L. Campbell's *Shakespeare's Histories* (1947). Campbell makes a great many meaningful allusions to Tudor doctrines of obedience. H. McLuhan, "*H4*: A Mirror for Magistrates," *UTQ*, XVII (1947), 152-160, supports the case of J. Dover Wilson (above). McLuhan concludes that "to a non-theological age Milton's Satan appeared heroic and to an unphilosophical and unethical age Falstaff can appear as a victim of ingratitude."

The unsentimental Bolingbroke is described in I. Ribner's essay on his Machiavellianism in *MLQ*, IX (1948), 177-184. J. Danby, *Shakespeare's Doctrine of Nature* (1949), describes the world of these plays as one of "pitiless fraud" in which the Machiavellian is necessarily the hero rather than villain. Danby views the plays as a great opposition of Power and Appetite, with the former the instrument of Order. The strain of pessimism is noted by C. Leech in "The Unity of *2H4*," *ShS*, VI (1953), 16-24. He describes "a clash of feelings within the play, an overt morality intention, a preoccupation with the effects of time, and a latent scepticism." One of the best studies is that of D. A. Traversi, *Sh from Richard II to Henry V* (1957). Traversi analyzes the plays scene by scene and is especially interested in the themes of policy, honor, and retribution. He goes deeply into the "sense of impotence" betrayed especially in the later play. In sum, the book is concerned with "all the divisions between age and youth, action and inaction, anarchic folly and cold calculation" that Traversi finds characteristic of late Elizabethan sensibility. The frailty and mutability themes of these plays are related to the sonnets by L. C. Knights in *Some Shakespearean Themes* (1959).

Anthropological concepts of ritual underlie C. L. Barber's treatment in
Shakespeare's Festive Comedy (1959). For the historical background
see M. M. Reese, *The Cease of Majesty* (1961). The interplay of comedy
and politics is well handled by G. L. Evans in *Early Sh*, ed. J. R. Brown
and B. Harris (1961). See also H. Toliver, "Falstaff, the Prince, and the
History Play," *ShQ*, XVI (1965), 63-80; A. R. Humphreys' introduction
to his New Arden edition (1966); and Alvin Kernan's "The Henriad,"
Modern Shakespearean Criticism (1970). There are useful collections of
criticism and other material in *Discussions of Shakespeare's Histories*,
ed. J. Dorius (1964); *Sh: The Histories*, ed. Eugene Waith (1965);
Twentieth Century Interpretations of 2H4, ed. David Young (1968);
1H4, ed. James Sanderson (1969).

The structure and relationship of the two parts has been the subject of
a good deal of research. The following represent only a part of this:
R. A. Law, "Structural Unity in the Two Parts of *H4*," *SP*, XXIV
(1927), 223-242; J. Dover Wilson, *The Fortunes of Falstaff* (1943); M.
Shaaber, "The Unity of *H4*," *AMS* (1948); H. Cain, "Further Light on
the Relation of *1* and *2H4*," *ShQ*, III (1952), 21-38; G. K. Hunter, "*H4*
and the Elizabethan Two-Part Play," *RES*, V (1954), 236-248.

The following study the language: G. W. Knight, *The Shakespearian
Tempest* (1932); Spurgeon (1935); M. Doran, "Imagery in *R2* and *H4*,"
MLR, XXXVII (1942), 113-122; Clemen (1951); M. Crane, *Shake-
speare's Prose* (1951); Evans (1952); Brian Vickers, *The Artistry of
Shakespeare's Prose* (1958).

Further reading: W. Bowling, *The Wild Prince Hal in Legend and Literature* (1926) *Washington University Studies*, Humanistic Series, XIII,
305-334; J. W. Allen, *A History of Political Thought in the Sixteenth
Century* (1928); J. Draper, "Sir John Falstaff," *RES*, VIII (1932), 414-
424; F. Alexander, "A Note on Falstaff," *Psychoanalytical Quar.*, II
(1933), 592-606; E. Welsford, *The Fool* (1935); J. Dover Wilson, "The
Political Background of Shakespeare's *R2* and *H4*," *ShJ*, LXXV (1939),
36-58; M. Van Doren, *Sh* (1939); A. P. Rossiter, *Woodstock* (1946); E.
Kris, "Prince Hal's Conflict," *Psychoanalytical Quar.*, XVII (1948),
487-506; S. L. Bethell, "The Comic Element in Shakespeare's Histories," *Anglia*, LXXI (1952), 82-101; H. Jenkins, "Shakespeare's History
Plays: 1900-1951," *ShS*, VI (1953), 1-15, and *The Structural Problem
in Shakespeare's H4* (1956); I. Ribner, *The English History Play in the
Age of Sh* (1957); B. Spivack, "Falstaff and the Psychomachia," *ShQ*,
VIII (1957), 449-459; R. Reno, "Hotspur: the Integration of Character
and Theme," *Renaissance Papers* (1962), 17-25; U. Knoepflmacher,
"The Humours as Symbolic Nucleus in *1H4*," *CE*, XXIV (1963), 497-
501; H. Richmond, *Shakespeare's Political Plays* (1967); James Winney,
The Player King (1968).

STAGING   Camb (1) xxix-xlvi; Craig 676; Odell *passim;* Sprague
83-94; Trewin *passim.*

The *NV* editions contain full stage histories. See also H. Spencer, *The
Art and Life of William Sh* (1940); J. Dover Wilson and T. Worsley,
Shakespeare's Histories at Stratford 1951 (1952); R. David, "Shake-
speare's History Plays Epic or Drama?" *ShS,* VI (1953), 129-139; M.
Clarke and R. Wood, *Sh at the Old Vic* (1954); Eleanor Prosser, "Colley
Cibber at San Diego," *ShQ,* XIV (1963), 253-261; Arthur Colby
Sprague, *Shakespeare's Histories: Plays for the Stage* (1964).

MUCH ADO ABOUT NOTHING

TEXT Alexander 130-132; Camb vii-xiii, 89-107; Chambers 384-388; Greg 277-281; Sisson I, 99-103.

See also A. Pollard, *Sh Folios and Quartos* (1909); A. Gaw, "Is Shakespeare's *Ado* a Revised Earlier Play?" *PMLA*, L (1935), 715-738; C. T. Prouty, "A Lost Piece of Stage Business in *Ado*," *MLN*, LXV (1950), 207-208; McManaway, 27; H. Craig, *A New Look at Shakespeare's Quartos* (1961); J. H. Smith, "The Composition of the Quarto of *Ado*," *SB*, XVI (1963), 9-26.

EDITIONS *NV*, ed. H. H. Furness (1899); Camb, ed. A. Quiller-Couch and J. Dover Wilson (1923); Arden, ed. G. Trenery (1924); ed. A. G. Newcomer (1929); ed. G. L. Kittredge (1941); Pelican, ed. J. W. Bennett (1958).

SOURCES G. Sarrazin, "Die Abfassungzeit von *Ado*," *ShJ*, XXXV (1899), 127-135; M. Scott, "*The Book of the Courtyer:* A Possible Source of Benedick and Beatrice," *PMLA*, XVI (1901), 475-502; M. Wolff, "Zur Geschichte des Stoffes von *Ado*," *Englische Studien*, XLVIII (1914), 342-348; R. A. Law, "Notes on Shakespeare's *Ado*," *TxSE*, XII (1932), 77-86; J. G. Wales, "Shakespeare's Use of English and Foreign Elements in the Setting of *Ado*," *Trans. Wisc. Acad.*, XXVIII (1933), 363-398; M. Bennett, "Shakespeare's *Ado* and Its Possible Italian Sources," *TxSE*, XVII (1937), 52-74; A. Thaler, "Spenser and *Ado*," *SP*, XXXVII (1940), 225-235; C. T. Prouty, "George Whetstone, Peter Beverly, and the Sources of *Ado*," *SP*, XXXVIII (1941), 211-220; A. F. Potts, "Spenserian 'Courtesy' and 'Temperance' in *Ado*," *SAB*, XVII (1942), 103-111 and 126-133; D. J. Gordon, "*Ado*: A Possible Source for the Hero-Claudio Plot," *SP*, XXXIX (1942), 279-290; D. Evans, "Some Notes on Sh and *The Mirror of Knighthood*," *SAB*, XXI (1946), 161-167, and XXII (1947), 62-68; T. M. Parrott, "Two Late Dramatic Versions of the Slandered Bride Theme," *AMS* (1948). The most important study of the play, its sources and its structure, is C. T. Prouty's *The Sources of Ado* (1950). Intelligent summations are in Muir (1957) and Bullough (1957–), II, 61-139. See also J. O'Connor, "Three Additional *Ado* Sources," *Essays in Lit. Hist. Presented to J. M. French* (1960).

CRITICISM The criticism of *Ado* has tended to consider three issues: dramatic probability, character, and theme. The first of these was treated by Coleridge, who urged that there was very little meaning in the action of the play alone. E. E. Stoll wrote his *Sh Studies* (1927) after a century of criticism hostile both to the probability of the action and to its morality. He asserted that the convention of "the slanderer believed" accounted for the rejection of Hero by Claudio and that Claudio, if not admirable by modern standards, was thoroughly understandable to Elizabethan viewers. N. Page, "The Public Repudiation of Hero," *PMLA*, L (1935), 739-744, did not agree with Stoll but was sympathetic to Claudio and his part in the action. She invoked Elizabethan religious and social views of female weakness to explain that Claudio's rejection was understandable. A later study, *The Love-Game Comedy* of D. L. Stevenson (1946), found that the action of *Ado* was, as in the other comedies, centered about the self-justifying process of courtship. He noted that critics had found the play unsatisfactory because it so plainly mirrors the difficulties and moral collapse found in reality. E. C. Pettet, *Sh and the Romance Tradition* (1949), asserted that potentially tragic romance did not mix with comedy. He thought too that the events of *Ado* impose "a strain and an aggravated sense of incredibility." A valuable essay is that of T. W. Craik, *"Ado," Scrutiny*, XIX (1953), 297-316. Craik argues that the play makes sense, and his analysis goes a long way to prove it. He is particularly acute in accounting for the changes of Claudio, which, in a sense, are the changes of the play itself. An interesting study is W. Meader's *Courtship in Sh* (1954). The symptoms of love and the forms of declamation and spousal throw a good deal of light on this and other comedies of matrimony. Meader also justifies Claudio in terms of Elizabethan expectancies. A. Gilbert, "Two Margarets: The Composition of *Ado*," *PQ*, XLI (1962), 61-71, remarks that inconsistencies (why doesn't Margaret reveal Hero's innocence?) are not important to an audience although they may disturb a reader.

If Coleridge disapproved of the action, he was captivated by the characters of Beatrice, Benedick, and Dogberry, and he set the tone for the writers who followed him. Mrs. Jameson's *Characteristics of Women* (1833) is in general painfully sentimental but in this case quite keen in its insight into the "high intellect and high animal spirits" of Beatrice. The sympathy to Beatrice and Benedick of a hundred years of criticism is summed up in the Camb edition (1923): the "superabundant life" of these two was able to overcome whatever inconsistencies or immorality *Ado* displayed. E. K. Chambers in *Sh: A Survey* (1925) made the famous and pungent remark that Claudio was a worm. His position, like that of many others, was that the plot and hero were unsatisfactory, conventional or not. N. Page, "My Lady Disdain," *MLN*, L (1935), 494-499, theorized that Hero was medieval woman exemplified but that Beatrice was the "free" woman of the Renaissance. There are some shrewd remarks on the mind of Beatrice. G. Gordon, *Shakespearian Comedy* (1944), found the lovers egotists and summed up Dogberry with elegance as "a profound and awful revelation of the official mind." J. Palmer, *Comic Characters of Sh* (1946), has an excellent chapter on

Beatrice and Benedick. He compares *Ado* with Congreve's *Way of the World* and remarks that in both "comedy grows from the incongruity of human passion with its cool, dispassionate and studied expression" in wit. He notes intelligently that "natural" man is scarcely hidden in these comedies by the manners he affects. E. J. West, "Much Ado About an Unpleasant Play," *SAB,* XXII (1947), 30-34, wrote that the play is venomous, brutal, and bawdy. E. Gulick responded in the next issue that it is no more so than the other comedies. He added with force that its characters are led into their predicaments in this play by their ethical commitments. K. Neil, "More Ado About Claudio," *ShQ,* III (1952), 91-107, finds that criticism of this play is often the story of "the slandered groom" and notes the extent to which Claudio is victimized by his friends as well as by his enemies. B. Evans, *Shakespeare's Comedies* (1960), discusses the structure of plot and counterplot.

The allegorical interpretations generally follow the idea of *redintegratio amoris* of Nevill Coghill in "The Basis of Shakespearian Comedy," *E&S* (1950), 1-28. In *Scrutiny,* XIII (1946), 242-257, J. Smith argued that the characters show *hybris;* that they live in a philistine matchmaking society that brings out the worst in men; that the characteristic mode of this milieu is deception. One may argue that he mistakes egotism for arrogance, common-sense for philistinism, and confusion for deception. An intelligent but obscure essay is that by W. Sypher, "Nietzsche and Socrates in Messina," *PR,* XVI (1949), 702-713. The essay is valuable for its sense of the intellectual content of *Ado.* It follows Smith in finding the ambiance one in which weakness is abused as a matter of course and money dominates love. In this setting Beatrice and Benedick assume almost mythological proportions as destroyers of tradition and participants in real love. M. C. Bradbrook, *Sh and Elizabethan Poetry* (1951), has a good essay on the intuitive powers of love in *Ado.* The kindred theme of "love's truth" is elaborated by J. R. Brown in *Sh and His Comedies* (1957). F. Fergusson observes in *The Human Image in Dramatic Literature* (1957) that individual conditions are transcended by the ceremonious occasions of marriage that end *Ado.* He wisely urges that the intrigue not be taken too symbolically.

A. P. Rossiter's essay in *Angel with Horns* (1961) deals competently with the equivocations of the play and its Italianate atmosphere. For a good general introduction and useful remarks on its theatrical quality see J. R. Mulryne, *Sh: Ado* (1965). There are good essays in the two most recent books on the comedies: Robert Hunter, *Sh and the Comedy of Forgiveness* (1965) and Peter Phialas, *Shakespeare's Romantic Comedies* (1966). The first of these is concerned with allegory; the latter with development of character. The allegorical critique can be carried somewhat too far as in B. Lewalski's "Love, Appearance and Reality: Much Ado about Something," *SEL,* VIII (1968), 235-251.

This imposes a structure of religious meanings upon the play that I do not think it can support. For study of the language see Brian Vickers, *The Artistry of Shakespeare's Prose* (1968). Some of the materials discussed above are in *Twentieth Century Interpretations of Ado,* ed. Walter Davis (1969).

Further reading: G. W. Knight, *The Shakespearian Tempest* (1932); Spurgeon (1935); M. Van Doren, *Sh* (1939); T. M. Parrott, *Shakespearean Comedy* (1949); S. Sen Gupta, *Shakespearian Comedy* (1950); P. Jorgensen, "Much Ado About *Nothing,*" *ShQ,* V (1954), 287-295; J. R. Brown, "The Interpretation of Shakespeare's Comedies: 1900-1953," *ShS,* VIII (1955), 1-13; D. Hockey, "Notes, Notes, Forsooth. . . ." *ShQ,* VIII (1957), 353-358; A. Sochatoff, *Sh* (1958); T. Hawkes, "The Old and the New in *Ado,*" *NQ,* CCIII (1958), 524-525; T. McNeal, "Shakespeare's Cruel Queens," *HLQ,* XXII (1958), 41-50; J. McPeek, "The Thief 'Deformed' " *BUSE,* IV (1960), 65-84; J. Wey, "To Grace Harmony: Musical Design in *Ado,*" *BUSE,* IV (1960), 181-188; B. Everett, "*Ado,*" *CQ,* III (1961), 319-335; C. Owen, "Comic Awareness," *BUSE,* V (1961), 193-207; Paul Jorgensen, *Redeeming Shakespeare's Words* (1962); P. and M. Mueschke, "Illusion and Metamorphosis in *Ado,*" *ShQ,* XVIII (1967), 53-65.

STAGING   Camb 159-164; Craig 532; Odell *passim;* Sprague 11-18; Trewin *passim.*

See also H. Spencer, *The Art and Life of William Sh* (1940); J. C. Trewin, *A Play Tonight* (1952); M. Webster, *Sh Without Tears* (1955); ed. F. Fergusson and C. J. Sisson (1960); *Shaw on Sh* (1961).

HENRY THE FIFTH

TEXT Alexander 128-130; Camb 111-118; Chambers 388-396; Greg
282-288; New Arden xxxvii-xlv; Sisson II, 56-67.

See also A. Pollard and J. Dover Wilson, "The 'Stolne and Surreptitious' Shakespearian Texts," *TLS* (1919), 18, 30, 134, 420; H. T. Price,
The Text of H5 (1920); A. E. Morgan, *Some Problems of Shakespeare's
H4* (1924); H. Craig, "The Relation of the First Quarto . . . to the First
Folio," *PQ,* VI (1927), 225-234; B. Simison, "Stage-Directions: A Test
for the Playhouse Origin of the First Quarto *H5," PQ,* XI (1932), 39-
56; H. T. Price, "The Quarto and Folio Texts of H5," *PQ,* XII (1933),
24-32; G. Okerlund, "The Quarto Version of *H5* as a Stage Adapta-
tion," *PMLA,* XLIX (1934), 810-834; P. Cole, "The Text of *H5,*" *NQ,*
CLXXXVII (1944), 200-203; W. D. Smith, "The *H5* Choruses in the
First Folio," *JEGP,* LIII (1954), 38-57; J. H. Walter, "With Sir John in
It," *MLR,* XLI (1946), 237-245; R. A. Law, "The Choruses in *H5,*"
TxSE, XXXV (1956), 11-21; A. Cairncross, "Quarto Copy for Folio
H5," *SB,* VIII (1956), 67-93; A. Walker, "Some Editorial Principles,
With Special Reference to *H5,*" *SB,* VIII (1956), 95-112; G. I. Duthie,
"The Quarto of Shakespeare's *H5,*" *Papers Mainly Shakespearian*
(1964), 106-130.

EDITIONS Ed. G. C. Moore Smith (1896); Arden, ed. H. Evans
(1903); ed. G. L. Kittredge (1945); Camb, ed. J. Dover Wilson (1947);
New Arden, ed. J. H. Walter (1954); Yale, ed. R. Dorius (1955);
Pelican, ed. Alfred Harbage (1966).

SOURCES W. G. Boswell-Stone, *Shakespere's Holinshed* (1896); P.
Kabel, *Die Sage von Heinrich V bis zu Sh* (1908); J. Dover Wilson,
"Martin Marprelate and Shakespeare's Fluellen," *Lib,* III (1912), 113-
151, and 241-276; A. and J. Nicoll, *Holinshed's Chronicle as Used in
Shakespeare's Plays* (1927); E. Albright, "The Folio Version of *H5* in
Relation to Shakespeare's Times," *PMLA,* XLIII (1928), 722-756. The
latter reaches what E. K. Chambers called the "maximum of absurdity"
in its hunt for topical allusions. See also B. Ward, *"The Famous Victo-
ries of Henry V,"* RES, IV (1928), 270-294; M. Radoff, "Influence of
the French Farce in *H5* and *MWW,*" *MLN,* XLVIII (1933), 427-435; J.
Dover Wilson, "The Origins and Development of Shakespeare's *H5,*"
Lib. XXVI (1945), 2-16; J. Lever, "Shakespeare's French Fruits," *ShS,*
VI (1953), 79-90; Bullough (1957—), IV, 347-432; S. Pitcher, *The Case
for Shakespeare's Authorship of the Famous Victories* (1961).

CRITICISM There are essentially three groups of critics: those who
hate the play and its hero; those who admire both; those who attempt

to remain neutral. I will first discuss the "anti's," who have been characterized by M. M. Reese as "pacifists, republicans, anti-clericals, little Englanders, moralists, even . . . arbiters of etiquette." The first of these was Hazlitt, who in his *Characters* (1817) applied the standards of the French Revolution to the Tudor compromise. He found the king's principles to be simply "brute force, glossed over with a little religious hypocrisy." Swinburne added his disapproval in *A Study of Sh* (1880), and Yeats wrote a famous attack in his *Ideas of Good and Evil* (1903). Yeats disparaged Henry, who had "the gross vices, the coarse nerves, of one who is to rule among violent people." He is, Yeats added, "as remorseless and undistinguished as some natural force." Frank Harris added his mite in *The Man Sh* (1909). The reaction of A. C. Bradley, *Oxford Lectures* (1909), was mixed; although he found Henry the thorough man of action, he also thought him superstitious and unscrupulous. E. K. Chambers, *Sh: A Survey* (1925), thought the play occupied with externalities and the "idols of the forum." H. Granville-Barker, *From H5 to Hamlet* (1925), was also hostile. M. Van Doren attacked the play in his *Sh* (1939) as if it were responsible for militarism in the twentieth century. The language he described as bombastic, the hero hollow, the style as a whole fatty and relaxed. His summation of the king was "a hearty undergraduate with enormous initials on his chest." For H. Spencer, *The Mind and Art of William Sh* (1940), the play represented "a semi-Fascist ideal" and betrayed "intellectual poverty." J. Palmer, *Political Characters of Sh* (1945), compared the epic vision and homiletic morality of the hero to his actual ruthlessness and sophistry. Recently, R. Battenhouse in *Essays on Sh . . . In Honor of Hardin Craig* (1962) wrote that *H5* is an ironic satire on those who have power. He asserts that the king's desire to invade France is served by prostituted sanctity; that the expedition is a grandiose form of armed robbery; that war and "heroism" are seen at their most debased. The views of Van Doren, Spencer, and Battenhouse seem to me to misread the text and the sixteenth century.

Perhaps predictably, Thomas Carlyle, *Heroes and Hero-Worship* (1841), saw in this play the fullest evidence of the hero as poet. His short essay on the theme of national destiny glorifies author and protagonist. H. N. Hudson, *Shakespeare's Life* (1872), and E. Dowden, *Sh, A Critical Study* (1875), praised the play. Dowden was much affected by the heroic "splendid achievement" of the king and saw in him a sign of "union with the vital strength of the world." Other affirmations came from R. G. Moulton, *New Sh Soc. Trans.* (1880-1886), and H. Evans in the Arden edition (1903). A. Tolman wrote the "The Epic Character of Henry V" in *MLN*, XXIV (1919), 7-16. J. Cunliffe, *Shaksperian Studies* (1919), concentrated on the plainness and good sense of the hero. A well-known defence is that of Charles Williams, "*H5*," *Sh Criticism: 1919-1935* (1936). The essay gives needed attention to the themes of honor and love in the play and also discusses its intimations of tragedy. J. Dover Wilson's *The Fortunes of Falstaff* (1943) makes a well-reasoned and important defence.

The third group of critics endeavor to explore the poetry and doctrine. In an important study E. E. Stoll, *Poets and Playwrights* (1930), urged that the wars of *H5* be understood as feudal and chivalric. Stoll added some very thoughtful remarks on the elements of morality and piety in the play, which he related to Elizabethan stage conventions and social beliefs. The rights of kings and obligations of subjects were well treated by A. Hart in *Sh and the Homilies* (1934). T. Spencer, *Sh and the Nature of Man* (1942), refers to the Platonic capabilities of the king. E. M. W. Tillyard, *Shakespeare's History Plays* (1944), compares *H5* to the *Aeneid*. Yet he feels that the play aims for mutually impossible objectives; the national epic does not have a hero with a consistent character or morality. The essay of U. Ellis-Fermor in *The Frontiers of Drama* (1945) finds this play to be the culmination of Shakespeare's study of the statesman-king. The author believes, as I do not, that the play is about the insufficiency, moral and intellectual, of hero and theme. L. Campbell, *Shakespeare's Histories* (1947), has a worthwhile discussion of the play's ideological meaning.

A. Gilbert, "Patriotism and Satire in *H5*," *Studies in Sh*, ed. Mathews and Emery (1953), summarizes some oppositions that complicate our response to the play: justice is often subordinated to will; glory gives way to barbarism, conquest is parodied by petty thievery. A useful account of "The Status and Person of Majesty" is furnished by W. Merchant in *ShJ*, XC (1954), 285-289. He writes of the "three-fold power sacramentally entrusted to the monarch: a power of arms, of law and of priesthood." J. C. Maxwell, "Simple or Complex?" *DUJ*, XLVI (1954), 112-115, considers the declaration of war and the killing of the prisoners and finds both prompted by the complex, prudential character of the king. Good general introductions will be found in J. H. Walter's New Arden edition (1954) and in the earlier Camb edition of J. Dover Wilson (1947). For glimpses of the Elizabethan soldier and his expectations see P. Jorgensen's *Shakespeare's Military World* (1956). D. A. Traversi, *Sh from R2 to H5* (1957), says of this play: "just as the state, already in *2H4*, is regarded in its divisions as a diseased body ravaged by a consuming fever, so is the individual seen increasingly as torn between the violence of his passions and the direction of reason; and just as the remedy to political anarchy lies in unquestioned allegiance to an authority divinely constituted, so does personal coherence depend upon the submission to reason of our uncontrolled desires." I. Ribner, *The English History Play in the Age of Sh* (1957), suggests that Marlowe's *Tamburlaine* gave *H5* its structure. The figure of Germanicus in Tacitus, according to G. R. Price's "Henry V and German-

icus," *ShQ*, XII (1961), 57-60, is a source for the integrity and valor of
the king. M. M. Reese, *The Cease of Majesty* (1961), treats the problem
of unity and concludes that with *H5* Sh "brought his historical sequence to an end with a heartening picture of a society cured of its
sickness and united under a prince whose own redemptive experience
corresponded with that of his people." An essay of importance for this
and the other histories is A. P. Rossiter's "Ambivalence: the Dialectic
of the Histories," *Angel with Horns* (1961). Rossiter observes that
order is won at a high cost and that in *H5* particularly its "ultimate
human validity" is doubtful. R. Berman, "Shakespeare's Alexander:
Henry V," *CE*, XXIII (1962), 532-539, writes of the king as the incarnation of Platonic and Stoic principles. His Machiavellian elements are
the subject of an essay in H. Mathews' *Character and Symbol in Shakespeare's Plays* (1962). There is a first-rate introduction to the play in
Bullough (1962). Although of most use for source study this has a good
deal to say about critical interpretation. For a collection that includes
much of the foregoing see R. Berman, *Twentieth Century Interpretations of H5* (1968).

For the language, see Paul Jorgensen, *Redeeming Shakespeare's Words*
(1962); Brian Vickers, *The Artistry of Shakespeare's Prose* (1968);
C. H. Hobday, "Imagery and Irony in *H5*," *ShS*, XXI (1968), 107-113.

The minor characters have received their critical due. R. Newhall discusses "An Historical Bardolph" in *MLN*, XLVIII (1933), 436-437. An
article on "Pistol and the Roaring Boys" by D. Boughner is in *SAB*, XI
(1936), 226-237. Boughner describes Pistol as the type of braggart and
drunkard who made Elizabethan taverns and bordellos places of danger
as well as pleasure. There is an illuminating study of the lower depths
of the Elizabethan world. Boughner notes too that Pistol is not only a
poltroon but a social climber. J. Draper, "The Humor of Corporal
Nym," *SAB*, XIII (1938), 131-138, says "the brevity of Nym's colloquial style is purposefully calculated as an adjunct to his apparent mar-
tial prowess." He too aspires to the gentility of his betters but is handi-
capped by being, instead of the choleric and fiery type he pretends, a
phlegmatic and cowardly poseur. A fine essay on "Ancient Pistol" is in
L. Hotson's *Shakespeare's Sonnets Dated* (1949). There is a lavish
account of Pistol's infamy and his fustian rhetoric. Pistol, Hotson suggests, is a parody of Tamburlaine, with the same *"amour de l'impossible."* The death of Falstaff is only reported in this play but has attracted an altogether amazing amount of speculation. Two interesting articles on this bottomless subject are A. Mendilow's "Falstaff's Death of a
Sweat," *ShQ*, IX (1958), 479-483, and R. Fleissner's "Falstaff's Green
Sickness unto Death," *ibid.* (1961), 47-55. Both are learned, and neither convinces me of their main points: that Falstaff died as a consequence not only of disease but sin and that his death was bathetic. It is

best to declare a moratorium on the death of Falstaff and perhaps on his life as well.

Further reading: F. Schelling, *The English Chronicle Play* (1902); C. Kingsford, *The First English Life of King Henry the Fifth* (1911); C. T. Brooke, *The Tudor Drama* (1912); J. Marriott, *English History in Sh* (1918); W. Lewis, *The Lion and the Fox* (1927); J. W. Allen, *A History of Political Thought in the Sixteenth Century* (1928); J. H. Wylie, *The Reign of Henry the Fifth* (1929); Spurgeon (1935); P. Jorgensen, "Accidental Judgments, Casual Slaughters and Purposes Mistook: Critical Reactions to Shakspere's *H5*," *SAB*, XXII (1947), 51-61; E. Partridge, *Shakespeare's Bawdy* (1947); E. Jacob, *Henry V and the Invasion of France* (1947); J. Danby, *Shakespeare's Doctrine of Nature* (1949); P. Jorgensen, "The Courtship Scene in *H5*," *MLQ*, XI (1950), 180-188; H. Jenkins, "Shakespeare's History Plays: 1900-1951," *ShS*, VI (1953), 1-15; H. Hulme, "Falstaff's Death: Sh or Theobald," *NQ*, ns, III (1956), 283-287; L. C. Knights, *Shakespeare's Politics* (1957); E. Fogel, "A Table of Green Fields," *ShQ*, IX (1958), 485-492; H. Braddy, "Shakespeare's *H5* and the French Nobility," *TxSE*, III (1961), 189-196; R. Dorius, *Discussions of Shakespeare's Histories* (1964).

STAGING Camb xlviii-lvi; Craig 738; Odell *passim;* Sprague 116-121; Trewin *passim.*

See also J. Dover Wilson and T. Worsley, *Shakespeare's Histories at Stratford 1951* (1952); R. David, "Sh in the Waterloo Road," *ShS*, V (1952), 125-128; L. Burns, "Three Views of *H5*," *Drama Survey,* I (1962), 278-300; A. C. Sprague, *Shakespeare's Histories: Plays for the Stage* (1964).

JULIUS CAESAR

TEXT Alexander 148-152; Camb 92-97; Chambers 396-401; Greg 289-292; New Arden xxi-xxvi, lxix-lxxi; Sisson II, 181-191.

See also P. Kannengiesser, "Eine Doppelredaktion in Shakespeares *JC*," *ShJ*, XLIV (1908), 51-64; H. Bartlett, "Quarto Editions of JC," *Lib*, IV (1913), 122-132; A. P. Rossiter, "Line Division in *JC*," *TLS* (July 29, 1939), 453; response by R. B. McKerrow (Aug. 19, 1939), 492; G. B. Evans, "Shakespeare's *JC*, a Seventeenth Century Manuscript." *JEGP*, XLI (1942), 401-417; J. Dover Wilson, "Ben Jonson and *JC*," *ShS*, II (1949), 36-43; W. D. Smith, "The Duplicate Revelation of Portia's Death," *ShQ*, IV (1953), 153-161; J. C. Maxwell, "Shakespeare's Roman Plays: 1900-1956," *ShS*, X (1957), 3-4; B. Stirling, "*JC* in Revision," *ShQ*, XIII (1962), 187-205.

EDITIONS *NV*, ed. H. H. Furness, Jr. (1913); ed. G. L. Kittredge (1939); Camb, ed. J. Dover Wilson (1949); New Arden, ed. T. S. Dorsch (1955); Yale, ed. A. Kernan (1959); Pelican, ed. S. Johnson (1960); ed. William and Barbara Rosen (1963).

SOURCES C. T. Brooke, *Shakespeare's Plutarch* (1909); M. Mac-Callum, *Shakespeare's Roman Plays and Their Background* (1910); H. Ayres, "Shakespeare's *JC* in the Light of Some Other Versions," *PMLA*, XXV (1910), 183-227; W. Warde Fowler, "The Tragic Element in . . . *JC*," *Roman Essays* (1920); M. Shackford, *Plutarch in Renaissance England* (1929); E. Staedler, "Die Klassischen Quellen der Antoniusrede in Shakespeares *JC*," *Neuphilologische Monatsschrift*, X (1939), 235-245; M. Wickert, "Antikes Gedankengut in Shakespeares *JC*," *ShJ*, LXXXII (1949), 11-33; J. A. K. Thomson, *Sh and the Classics* (1952); V. K. Whitaker, *Shakespeare's Use of Learning* (1953); J. Rees, "*JC*—an Earlier Play, and an Interpretation," *MLR*, L (1955), 135-141; E. Schanzer, *Shakespeare's Appian* (1956); J. C. Maxwell, "*JC* and Elyot's *Governour*," *NQ*, ns, III (1956), 147; Muir (1957); Bullough (1957–), V, 3-211; J. Barroll, "Sh and Roman History," *MLR*, LIII (1958), 327-343.

CRITICISM An acute study of form and structure is in R. G. Moulton's *Sh as a Dramatic Artist* (1906). The double pattern of tragedy in *JC* is outlined: the "Passion-Movement" in the climax of the assassination unites both main and subordinate action. There is useful commentary on the emotional atmosphere. G. W. Knight, *The Imperial Theme* (1931), has two essays on language and themes. He notes the simple metaphor but complex pattern of simile and description. There is a paradoxical relationship of "bloody, fiery, and most terrible" events to "the human element . . . of gentle sentiment, melting hearts,

tears, and the soft fire of love." This is one of the most detailed and
useful studies of the play's language. A work of quite another order is
J. Phillips' *The State in Shakespeare's Greek and Roman Plays* (1940).
This sees *JC* as an object lesson in the virtues of absolutism; it contrasts
the prosperity of Caesar's rule with the chaos of "multiple sovereignty."
Granville-Barker (1946) considers character and structure principally
but makes valuable remarks on the staging. He emphasizes the position
of *JC* as the "gateway" to the great tragedies.

B. Stirling, *The Populace in Sh* (1949), writes of the self-interest and
instability of the mob. There are interesting references to the Elizabethan mob as it was seen by contemporaries and to conceivable topical
allusions. L. Kirschbaum, "Shakespeare's Stage-Blood," *PMLA,* LXIV
(1949), 517-529, writes of the spectacle of *JC* and reviews a number of
critics who have treated the murder and the ritual that surrounds it.
There is a good analysis of the shock to ideology when it is found that
men and not ideas must be murdered. H. T. Price writes in his edition
(1950): "there is this love of Brutus for Caesar and of Caesar for
Brutus, the love of Brutus and Cassius, Brutus and Portia, the mutual
love between Brutus and Lucius and all his servants. Brutus is a center
of love wherever he goes. There is the love of Antony for Caesar, which
drives him to destroy the conspirators. There is the ominous absence of
love around Octavius. Love violated and betrayed, the man who lives
for love violating himself, these are among the most moving *motifs* of
the play." R. Walker, "The Northern Star," *ShQ,* II (1951), 287-293,
writes of the destruction of the "divine-natural order" in *JC.* The political impact of the Roman plays is summed up by L. C. Knights in "Sh
and Political Wisdom," *Sew,* LXI (1953), 43-55: "Neither *JC* nor *Cor*
can be summed up in a moral formula. But, taken together, they point
to two related truths of the greatest importance. The first is that human
actuality is more important than *any* political abstraction, though more
difficult to bear. The second is that politics is vitiated and corrupted to
the extent to which, as politicians, we lose our sense of the *person* on
the other side of the dividing line of class or party or nation." B. Breyer,
"A New Look at *JC,*" *Essays in Honor of W. C. Curry* (1954), denies
that the play is a political exemplum: it seems to him to be permeated
with a "profound despair of finding any objective meaning in life."
Breyer is especially concerned to prove the fraudulence of the ideals
maintained by the various characters. A very useful introduction accompanies T. S. Dorsch's New Arden edition (1955).

A fine chapter on *JC* is in B. Stirling's *Unity in Shakespearian Tragedy*
(1956). The symbolic action of the murder, envisaged by Brutus and
the conspirators as a ritual of purgation, contrasts "ceremonial observance" with an act impossible to justify. There is extended analysis of
the blood imagery. H. S. Wilson, *On the Design of Shakespearian*

Tragedy (1957), considers political tragedy and accompanying moral decline. E. Schanzer, "Preface to *JC*," *Oeuvres Complètes de Sh* (1957), IV, 245-260, relates the play to Aristotelian *peripeteia,* the ironic reversal of expectations. I. Ribner, "Political Issues in *JC*," *JEGP*, LVI (1957), 10-22, finds that the true villain is the mob. The moral of the play, Ribner thinks, is the civil chaos that results when a great and noble leader tries to overthrow long-established institutions. Perhaps the finest study of the intellectual effect of the sources is J. Barroll's "Sh and Roman History," *MLR,* LII (1958), 327-343. This is an excellent demonstration of the meaning pagan history had for the Renaissance as a "mirror" of the providential scheme.

An important book devoted entirely to this play is A. Bonjour's *The Structure of JC* (1958). A very good chapter on the structure of the play precedes special studies of its language, motives, and critical history. This book is perhaps most important for its extended and detailed reading of the text. V. Hall, *"JC:* A Play Without Political Bias," *Studies in the English Renaissance Drama* (1959), believes that political analysis does not clarify the play. He suggests instead that it be approached as a study of Roman grandeur. The best of the studies of imagery is M. Charney's *Shakespeare's Roman Plays* (1961). The chief images identified are the "storm and its portents, blood, and fire." Charney, however, goes beyond mere statistics. His study is a model of imaginative relating of language to meaning. D. A. Traversi, *Sh: The Roman Plays* (1963), contains a distinguished essay on conflicts of ideals and character. The spirit of the play expresses the exposure of human contradiction; in the last analysis, Traversi says, the irrational basis of human motivation results in the annihilation of the self and the ideals it has served. E. Schanzer, *The Problem Plays of Sh* (1963), examines our divided response to the play: is it about a tyrant justly killed, or a hideous crime? What makes it a "problem" play is that this question is left unanswered. Schanzer has some useful comment on irony, used in this play in its Aristotelian sense. There is a good essay in Sigurd Burckhardt's *Shakespearean Meanings* (1968) dealing with the expectations of the conspirators as opposed to the political realities they discover. There are two good collections of essays on *JC*: Leonard Dean's *Twentieth Century Interpretations of JC* (1968) and Peter Ure's *Sh: JC* (1969). The former has a selection of modern essays; the latter, in addition, ranges intelligently from special problems like filming to general interpretation.

Most special studies concern themselves with the characters of Caesar and Brutus. The namesake of the play was well studied by E. Dowden in his *Sh: A Critical Study* (1875). He noted, and most modern commentators have agreed, that the figure of Caesar is divided into two parts: the man as he really is, and his "legendary and mythical" component. A rather literal interpretation was offered by L. Schücking in his *Character Problems in Shakespeare's Plays* (1922). In his view, Caesar had very few faults. Schücking underplayed the egocentricity that is observably present. An extreme view of Caesar as Shakespeare's authoritarian *beau idéal* is that of L. Morsbach in *Shakespeares Cäsarbild* (1935). J. Dover Wilson's Camb edition (1949) has an indignant essay on Caesarism, evidently influenced by twentieth-century events. Dover Wilson saw Caesar as a "monstrous tyrant"; D. A. Stauffer, on the contrary, wrote of him as an Elizabethan "ideal governor" in *Shakespeare's World of Images* (1949). Caesar falling under the sway of his own vision of himself is ably depicted in J. I. M. Stewart's *Character and Motive in Sh* (1949). There is excellent comment on the obscure and fearful emotions behind the stoic mask.

M. MacCallum's study of Brutus is in his *Shakespeare's Roman Plays* (1910). Brutus is seen as the creature of "devout imagination" and "unconscious sophistry." G. W. Knight's *The Wheel of Fire* (1930) presents a Brutus who is very like Macbeth. For Knight the play is preeminently the working out of the spiritual destruction of Brutus. A notable study is M. Hunter's "Politics and Character in Shakespeare's *JC*," *RSL, X* (1931), 109-140. Taking issue with the Romantic conception of Brutus as hero, Hunter stated that he is, "for all his studious habits, no profound or subtle thinker, that he has no coherent political philosophy, and is not the 'ideal Republican' Swinburne imagined him to be." Hunter pragmatically demonstrates that while his motives are unblemished his reason is confused and perhaps dishonest. The dishonor of Brutus is the subject of M. Deutschbein, "Die Tragik in Shakespeares *JC*," *Anglia, LXII* (1938), 306 320. J. Palmer, *Political Characters of Sh* (1945), has a fine essay on Brutus, whom he sees as having "precisely the qualities which in every age have rendered the conscientious liberal ineffectual in public life." He has, however, a sensitive account of Brutus' rise to dignity and greatness at the end of the play. D. Brewer's astute study of the meaning of "Brutus' Crime" is in *RES*, III (1952), 51-54. E. Schanzer, "The Tragedy of Shakespeare's Brutus," *ELH, XXII* (1955), 1-15, notes that Brutus is the only person in the play who experiences "any inner conflict." He is, therefore, the tragic consciousness of the play. Two articles of interest are G. R. Smith's "Brutus, Virtue, and Will," *ShQ,* X (1959), 367-379, and A. Paolucci's "The Tragic Hero in *JC*," *ShQ,* XI (1960), 329-333. Norman Rabkin writes in *Sh and the Common Understanding* (1967) that in this play "the conventions [of revenge tragedy] establish a dramatically convincing representation of a universe, governed by inexorable law, in which events are brought about not according to man's idealistic intentions but deterministically by their own logic."

The great speeches in the Forum are well analyzed in the following:

R. Zandvoort, "Brutus' Forum Speech in *JC," RES,* XVI (1940), 62-66;
R. M. Frye, "Rhetoric and Poetry in *JC," QJS,* XXXVII (1952), 41-48;
K. Burke, "Antony in Behalf of the Play," *The Philosophy of Literary
Form* (1957).

Further reading: A. C. Bradley, *Shakespearean Tragedy* (1904); J. M.
Murry, *Countries of the Mind* (1931); F. T. Wood, "Sh and the Plebs,"
E&S (1932), 53-73; J. Draper, "The Realism of Shakespeare's Roman
Plays," *SP,* XXX (1933), 225-242; Spurgeon (1935); T. Spencer, *Death
and Elizabethan Tragedy* (1936); M. Van Doren, *Sh* (1939); A. Thaler,
Sh and Democracy (1941); T. W. Baldwin, *William Shakspere's Small
Latine and Lesse Greeke* (1944); H. B. Charlton, *Shakespearian Tragedy*
(1948); M. Felheim, "The Problem of Time in *JC," HLQ,* XIII (1950),
399-405; H. Brown, "Enter the Shakespearean Tragic Hero," *EC,* III
(1953), 285-302; R. A. Foakes, "An Approach to *JC," ShQ,* V (1954),
259-270; J. C. Maxwell, "Shakespeare's Roman Plays: 1900-1956,"
ShS, X (1957), 1-11; Y. Bonnefoy, "De La Rome Troublée à la Conscience Élisabéthaine," *Cahiers Renaud-Barrault,* XXX (1960), 3-16;
J. Markels, *Shakespeare's JC* (1961); M. Charney, *Discussions of Shakespeare's Roman Plays* (1964). Northrop Frye, *Fools of Time* (1965);
Matthew Proser, *The Heroic Image in Five Shakespearean Tragedies*
(1965); Maynard Mack, *"JC," Modern Shakespearean Criticism,* ed.
Alvin Kernan (1970).

STAGING   Camb xxxiv-xliii; Craig 772; Odell *passim;* Sprague 319-
326; Trewin *passim.*

See also W. Winter, *Life and Art of Edwin Booth* (1893); ed. O. Welles
and R. Hill (1939); J. McDowell, "Analyzing *JC* for Modern Production," *QJS,* XXXI (1945), 303-314; H. Hunt, *Old Vic Prefaces* (1954);
ed. F. Fergusson and C. J. Sisson (1958); R. Walker, "Unto Caesar,"
ShS, XI (1958), 132-134; *Shaw on Sh* (1961); P. Ure, *Sh:JC* (1969).

AS YOU LIKE IT

TEXT Alexander 132-134; Camb 93-108; Chambers 401-404; Greg 293-295; Sisson I, 143-158.

See also J. Wilcox, "Putting Jaques into *AYL*," *MLR*, XXXVI (1941), 388-394.

EDITIONS *NV*, ed. H. H. Furness (1890); Arden, ed. J. W. Holme (1914); Camb, ed. A. Quiller-Couch and J. Dover Wilson (1926); ed. G. L. Kittredge (1939); Yale, ed. S. Burchell (1954); Pelican, ed. R. Sargent (1959).

SOURCES N. Delius, "Lodges *Rosalynde* und Shakespeares *AYL*," *ShJ*, VI (1871); 226-249; W. G. Boswell-Stone, "Shakespeare's *AYL* and *Rosalynde* Compared," *New Sh Soc. Trans.* (1880-1885), 277-293; J. Zupitza, "Die Mittelenglischer Vorstuffe von Shakespeares *AYL*," *ShJ*, XXI (1886), 69-148; A. H. Thorndike, "The Relation of *AYL* to the Robin Hood Plays," *JEGP*, IV (1901), 59-69; A. H. Tolman, "Shakespeare's Manipulation of His Sources in *AYL*," *MLN*, XXXVII (1922), 65-76; E. D. Romig, "Shakespeare's Use of His Source, Lodge's *Rosalynde*," *Univ. Colorado St.*, XVI (1929), 300-322; J. W. Draper, "Jaques' 'Seven Ages,' " *MLN*, LIV (1939), 273-276; A. Thaler, *Sh and Democracy* (1941); C. Seronsy, "The Seven Ages of Man Again," *ShQ*, IV (1953), 364-365; R. Baird, "*AYL* and Its Source," *Essays in Honor of W. C. Curry* (1954); Muir (1957); Bullough (1957–), II, 143-266. An important article is M. Mincoff's "What Sh Did to *Rosalynde*," *ShJ*, XCVI (1960), 78-89, which studies what Sh rejected—the moralizings and structural looseness of Lodge—as well as what he refined. See also William Miller, "All the World's a Stage," *NQ*, X (1963), 99-101.

CRITICISM An excessive amount of critical energy has been lavished on Jaques, who is a minor personage in *AYL*. In "Shakspere, Marston, and the Malcontent Type," *MP*, III (1905), 281-303, E. E. Stoll suggested that Jaques was a form of the cynic made famous by Marston. Z. Fink, "Jaques and the Malcontent Traveller," *PQ*, XIV (1935), 237-252, noted that he had been labelled by critics a melancholiac, misanthrope, cynic, libertine, and even a moralist. Fink offered the alternative of the "Italianated Englishman," sick in mind and body: "a leprous soule and a tainted body." O. J. Campbell, in "Jaques," *Huntington Lib. Bulletin*, VIII (1935), 71-102, wrote a long review of critical theories and suggested that Jaques is both a libertine and cynic—in his phrase an "exhausted roué." He dismisses the possibility that Jaques represents either Marston or Ben Jonson. J. W. Bennett, "Jaques' Seven Ages," *SAB*, XVIII (1943), 168-174, reviews scholarship on the theme of man's ages. Stoll returned to the attack in "Jaques and the Antiquaries," *MLN,* LIV (1939), 79-85. He warned there against an overly simple theory of humours in the interpretation of Jaques or other characters. In O. J. Campbell's *Shakespeare's Satire* (1943) it is suggested that Jaques, himself deeply flawed, satirizes some zealous and venomous Elizabethan satirists.

Dr. Johnson said of *AYL* that "the fable is wild and pleasing." Most critics since have agreed. In "Genial Literary Satire in the Forest of Arden," *SAB,* X (1935), 212-231, P. V. Kreider found *AYL* a self-satirizing comedy impatient with the conventions it relied upon. M. Van Doren, *Sh* (1939), found the triad of intelligence, instinct, and love its exemplary pattern. J. Smith in *Scrutiny,* IX (1940), 9-32, suggested that *AYL* had affinities with the problem comedies. Jaques he saw not as an intruder in the play but as a figure who crystallized the varied forms of "melancholy" so frequently manifested in the other characters. He perhaps takes Jaques and melancholy too seriously; that has been done before. C. L. Barber, "The Use of Comedy in *AYL,*" *PQ,* XXI (1942), 353-367, asserted that the play was a system of themes and variations on "romantic participation in love and humorous detachment from its follies." S. L. Bethell's *Sh and the Popular Dramatic Tradition* (1944) found *AYL* "no more naturalistic than *The Mikado.*" He is convincing in his estimate of Touchstone as wise in spirit and foolish in action—the double nature implies comic conventions, not, as some would have it, schizophrenia.

J. Palmer noted the strong element of realism and common sense that mediate the sentiment of *AYL* in his *Comic Characters of Sh* (1946). He has perhaps the final word on the inflation of Jaques: "the romantic critics saw Jaques through a mist of sorrowful Werthers, itinerant Childe Harolds and mysterious Manfreds. They were making ready for an orgy that culminated in the neo-gothic masterpieces of Victor Hugo and the rosicrucian imbecilities of Lord Lytton." An extremely useful general survey is A. Harbage's *As They Liked It* (1947), which deals with the nature of comedy on the Elizabethan stage. Two worthwhile articles are H. Nearing's "The Penaltie of Adam," *MLN,* LXII (1947), 336-338, and W. Staebler's "Shakespeare's Play of Atonement," *SAB,* XXIV (1949), 91-105. The latter is concerned with the moral equipoise of *AYL;* he finds in it a unique sense of psychological and natural harmony. T. M. Parrott offers a useful study of character in his *Shakespearean Comedy* (1949). N. Coghill's well-known essay "The Basis of Shakespearian Comedy," *E&S* (1950), 1-28, is important for the theme of reconciliation through love, which it applies to the comedies. A rather different theme, that of "melancholy," is offered in L. Babb's *The Elizabethan Malady* (1951). This very good study might be supplemented by the much earlier *Anatomy of Melancholy* of Robert Burton (1621), which remains our best treatise on Renaissance psychology.

An article of importance is J. Shaw's "Fortune and Nature in *AYL,*" *ShQ,* VI (1955), 45-50. Shaw points out that Fortune and Nature oppose each other—the wisdom of the latter must dominate the vagaries of the former. Nature is in this play pictured as inherently noble, while Fortune, as ever, is inherently treacherous. There is a good discussion of the rhetoric involving these terms. H. Jenkins, "*AYL,*" *ShS,* VIII (1955), 40-51, demonstrates how the real often reinforces the ideal in this play, which is a corrective to most criticism. *Wise Fools in Sh* (1955) by R. Goldsmith gives Touchstone a good deal of attention. G. Bush, *Sh and the Natural Condition* (1956), suggests that "Comedy accepts the penalty of Adam into the Forest of Arden." There is a convincing account of the thematic seriousness of the mature comedies. J. R. Brown, *Sh and His Comedies* (1957), sees *AYL* as the story of harmony in love overcoming disorder in society. In politics as in love the experience of "Nature" in Arden allows the *dramatis personae* to learn "service, observance, and faith." Helen Gardner's essay, "*AYL,*" is in *More Talking of Shakespeare,* ed. John Garrett (1959). It is a very good commentary on those elements of comic theory suggested by Suzanne Langer's *Feeling and Form.* C. L. Barber's *Shakespeare's Festive Comedy* (1959) restates much of his earlier essay (above). He remarks intelligently that there is a strange combination of liberty and morality in Arden—ironic wit in this play moderates and intellectualizes *Saturnalia.* The study of B. Evans in *Shakespeare's Comedies* (1960) is of particular interest for the light it casts on the structure of *AYL.* It is perhaps overly confined to the subject of awareness and deception. Two recent studies are F. Kermode's "The Mature Comedies" in *Early Sh* (1961) and G. K. Hunter's *Sh: The Late Comedies* (1962). In "No Clock in the Forest," *SEL,* II (1962), 197-207, Jay Halio discusses the timelessness of Arden and the complexity of the outer world. He has perceptive remarks on the function of Rosalind linking these two dramatic worlds. For a learned account of pastoral vs. civilized manners see Madeleine Doran, "Yet Am I Inland Bred," *Sh 400,* ed. James G. McManaway (1964), 99-114. There is a discussion of the language in Brian Vickers, *The Artistry of Shakespeare's Prose* (1968). For collections of essays on this play see Herbert Weil, Jr., *Discussions of Shakespeare's Romantic Comedy* (1966) and Jay Halio, *Twentieth Century Interpretations of AYL* (1968).

Further reading: J. B. Priestly, *The English Comic Characters* (1925); J. W. Draper, "Orlando, the Younger Brother," *PQ,* XIII (1934), 72-77, and "Shakespeare's Orlando Innamorato," *MLQ,* II (1941), 179-184; H. Kökeritz, "Touchstone in Arden," *MLQ,* VII (1946), 61-63, and

Shakespeare's Pronunciation (1953); N. Frye, "The Argument of
Comedy," *EIE* (1948), 58-73; L. Babb, "On the Nature of Elizabethan
Psychological Literature," *AMS* (1948); T. Spencer, "The Elizabethan
Malcontent," *AMS* (1948); E. C. Pettet, *Sh and the Romance Tradition*
(1949); M. C. Bradbrook, *Sh and Elizabethan Poetry* (1951); W.
Meader, *Courtship in Sh* (1954); J. R. Brown, "The Interpretation of
Shakespeare's Comedies: 1900-1953," *ShS*, VIII (1955), 1-13; P.
Bennett, "The Statistical Measurement of a Stylistic Trait," *ShQ*, VIII
(1957), 33-50; D. Schäfer, "Die Bedeutung des Rollenspiels," *ShJ*,
XCIV (1958), 151-174; R. Draper, "Shakespeare's Pastoral Comedy,"
Ea, XI (1958), 1-17; P. Seng, "The Forester's Song," *ShQ*, X (1959),
246-249; W. Jones, "William Sh as William in *AYL*," *ShQ*, XI (1960),
228-231; E. Sehrt, *Wandlungen der Shakespeareschen Kömodie* (1961).
Samuel Chew's *The Pilgrimage of Life* (1962) is a remarkable compen-
dium and analysis of emblems, stories, sculpture, and paintings on the
virtues and sins of man's "ages." The matter is no longer thought of as
absolutely central to *AYL*, but the book is an elegant diversion. See also
Peter Phialas, *Shakespeare's Romantic Comedies* (1966); Herbert
Howarth, *The Tiger's Heart* (1970).

STAGING Camb 167-171; Craig 589; Odell *passim;* Sprague 31-40;
Trewin *passim.*

See also H. Spencer, *The Art and Life of William Sh* (1940); Jan Simko,
"Sh in Slovakia," *ShS,* IV (1951), 109-116; ed. P. Brook (1953); M.
Clarke and R. Wood, *Sh at the Old Vic* (1955); M. Webster, *Sh Without
Tears* (1955); W. Carson, "*AYL* and the Stars," *QJS,* XLIII (1957); ed.
F. Fergusson and C. J. Sisson (1959).

TWELFTH NIGHT

TEXT Alexander 134-138; Camb 89-101; Chambers 404-407; Greg 296-298; Sisson I, 184-194.

See also S. A. Tannenbaum, *Shaksperian Scraps* (1933), and H. Yamada, "The Textual Problems of *TN,*" *Kenkyu Bulletin,* XXVI (1962), 57-63.

EDITIONS *NV,* ed. H. H. Furness (1901); Arden, ed. M. Luce (1906); Camb, ed. A. Quiller-Couch and J. Dover Wilson (1930); ed. G. L. Kittredge (1941); Yale, ed. W. Holden (1954); Pelican, ed. C. T. Prouty (1958).

SOURCES H. Meissner, *Die Quellen zu Shakespeares Was Ihr Wollt* (1895); H. Conrad, "Zu den Quellen von Shakespeares *TN,*" *Englische Studien,* XLVI (1912), 73-85; M. P. Tilley, "The Organic Unity of *TN,*" *PMLA,* XXIX (1914), 550-566; A. Thaler, "The Original Malvolio?" *SAB,* VII (1932), 57-71; P. Mueschke and J. Fleisher, "Jonsonian Elements in the Comic Underplot of *TN,*" *PMLA,* XLVIII (1933), 722-740; L. B. Wright, "A Conduct Book for Malvolio," *SP,* XXXI (1934), 115-132; H. A. Kaufman, "Nicolò Secchi as a Source of *TN,*" *ShQ,* V (1954), 271-280; Muir (1957); Bullough (1957–), II, 269-372.

CRITICISM Charles Lamb generated a long tradition of sentimental defensiveness about Malvolio, whom he found more sinned against than sinning. His essay may be conveniently found in the *NV.* An interesting article on his reaction is S. Barnet's "Charles Lamb and the Tragic Malvolio," *PQ,* XXXIII (1954), 177-188. P. Mueschke and J. Fleisher in "Jonsonian Elements in the Comic Underplot of *TN,*" *PMLA,* XLVIII (1933), 722-740, discuss the victims and gulls of Jonsonian comedy. They judge that in Malvolio and Sir Andrew the types of humours satirized by Jonson are given renewed expression. An important and most revealing book is E. Welsford's *The Fool* (1935). It tells the history of Misrule and the traditional revels of folly on Twelfth Night. J. W. Draper's *The Twelfth Night of Shakespeare's Audience* (1950) attempts to analyze *TN* purely as a product of Elizabethan social codes. It imposes an unrealistic amount of history and humour theory on the play. N. A. Brittin, "The *Twelfth Night* of Sh and of Professor Draper," *ShQ,* VII (1956), 211-216, is a corrective. A. Downer, "Feste's Night," *CE,* XIII (1952), 258-265, is in praise of the fool. Downer finds him to be more than Misrule incarnate—it is Feste who causes the other characters to cease their folly. L. Hotson, *The First Night of Twelfth Night* (1954), speculates about the first staging of the play before the court of the Queen. It is an elaborate study and, although not conclusive in its history, has much to say about the aristocratic mores common to the play and the court. There are a number of responses to this book listed in Smith, 663.

R. Goldsmith, *Wise Fools in Sh* (1955), centers on Feste and concludes that his language exhibits more than "verbal felicity." He stands for an entire "ethical system" of the wise and moderate experiencing of what life has to offer. An important essay is that of J. H. Summers, "The Masks of *TN*," *UKCR*, XXII (1955), 25-32. Summers has an excellent treatment of the dualities intimated by disguise and of the freedom which is inhibited by bondage self-imposed. J. Hollander, "Musica Mundana and *TN*," *EIE* (1956), 55-82, believes that music and its metaphor is fundamental to the play. He uses the term "musica humana" to describe its origins—the revels and the life of the appetite. It is connected to the themes of indulgence and surfeit. In *"TN* and the Morality of Indulgence," *Sew*, LXVII (1959), 220-238, Hollander discusses connections to the humours of Jonson. The humours of *TN* are "kinetic," revealing character rather than burlesquing it. The moral for Hollander is that "Lechery, trickery, dissembling and drunkenness, inevitable . . . in mundane existence . . . are just those activities which, mingled together in a world of feasting, serve to purge Man of the desire for them." A valuable essay is L. G. Salingar's "The Design of *TN*," *ShQ*, IX (1958), 117-139. It attempts to account for the inconsistencies remarked by Dr. Johnson, explaining that the play is emotionally if not logically coherent. There are good critiques of the protean power of love, of "uncivil rule," and of the conflicting aristocratic impulses of order and pleasure. This essay is a first-rate introduction to *TN*.

S. Nagarajan, "What You Will," *ShQ*, X (1959), 61-67, finds that the comedy depends for its point on the great difference between what we desire and what we are. He traces the rhetoric of "appetite" and "will," their operation, and their continual imbalance in the *dramatis personae*. C. L. Barber, *Shakespeare's Festive Comedy* (1959), makes a good deal of sense out of the reversals of sexual role. His conclusion in general is that liberty—achieved through disguise, delusion, and festivity—allows the expression of natural nobility. H. Jenkins, "Shakespeare's *TN*," *Rice Inst. Pamphlet*, XLV (1959), 19-42, relates *TN* to the early comedies. Perhaps its greatest success, according to Jenkins, is its ability to put across the "feeling of wonder" about love in which the characters participate. B. Evans, *Shakespeare's Comedies* (1960), analyzes the structure at length but may emphasize masquerade and "practice" to the exclusion of other things. M. Seiden, "Malvolio Reconsidered," *UKCR*, XXVIII (1961), 105-114, finds the steward a form of scapegoat who undergoes sacrificial comic death so that comedy itself may live. His Malvolio is not entirely a Puritan but the kind of person who exempts himself from the prohibitions he imposes on others. Seiden deals intelligently with the social-climbing issue. P. Williams, "Mistakes in *TN* and Their Resolution," *PMLA,* LXXVI (1961), 193-199, proposes that the deceptions are superficially like those of Italian comedy; they are, however, subtle and thematic to a degree unapproached by their sources, for they reveal character and the nature of reality itself.

In "Thematic Patterns in *TN,*" *Sh Studies,* ed. J. Leeds Barroll (1965), Barbara Lewalski writes that "the central themes and motifs of this play contain something of the religious significance associated with Epiphany." The theme of love and indulgence is discussed by Peter Phialas in *Shakespeare's Romantic Comedies* (1966). For collections of essays on this play see Herbert Weil, Jr., *Discussions of Shakespeare's Romantic Comedy* (1966); Laurence Lerner, *Shakespeare's Comedies* (1967); Walter N. King, *Twentieth Century Interpretations of TN* (1968).

Further reading: G. W. Knight, *The Shakespearian Tempest* (1932); H. B. Charlton, *Shakespearian Comedy* (1938); M. Van Doren, *Sh* (1939); G. Gordon, *Shakespearian Comedy* (1944); E. West, "Bradleyan Reprise: On the Fool in *TN,*" *SAB,* XXIV (1949), 264-274; T. M. Parrott, *Shakespearean Comedy* (1949); E. C. Pettet, *Sh and the Romance Tradition* (1949); N. Coghill, "The Basis of Shakespearian Comedy," *E&S* (1950), 1-28; S. Sen Gupta, *Shakespearian Comedy* (1950); M. C. Bradbrook, *Sh and Elizabethan Poetry* (1951); K. M. Thompson, "Shakespeare's Romantic Comedies," *PMLA,* LXVII (1952), 1079-1093; M. Crane, "*TN* and Shakespearian Comedy," *ShQ,* VI (1955), 1-8; J. R. Brown, "The Interpretation of Shakespeare's Comedies: 1900-1953," *ShS,* VIII (1955), 1-13; G. Bush, *Sh and the Natural Condition* (1956); J. R. Brown, *Sh and His Comedies* (1957); F. Kermode, "The Mature Comedies," *Early Sh* (1961); B. Hardy, *TN* (1962); Brian Vickers, *The Artistry of Shakespeare's Prose* (1968); Walter King, "Sh and Parmenides: the Metaphysics of *TN,*" *SEL,* VIII (1968), 284-306.

STAGING Camb 173-179; Craig 618; Odell *passim;* Sprague 3-11; Trewin *passim.*

See also E. Welsford, *The Court Masque* (1927); R. David, "Sh in the Waterloo Road," *ShS,* V (1952), 121-124; L. Hotson, *The First Night of Twelfth Night* (1954); N. Marsh, "A Note on a Production of *TN,*" *ShS,* VIII (1955), 69-73; R. Walker, "The Whirligig of Time," *ShS,* XII (1959), 122-130; J. R. Brown, "Directions for *TN,*" *TDR,* (1961), 77-88; L. Forbes, "What You Will?" *ShQ,* XIII (1962), 475-485; A. Downer, "For Jesus' Sake Forbear: Sh vs. the Modern Theater," *ShQ,* XIII (1962), 219-230; Clifford Leech, *TN and Shakespearian Comedy* (1965); John Russell Brown, *Shakespeare's Plays in Performance* (1966); Gareth L. Evans, "Interpretation or Experience? Sh at Stratford," *ShS,* XXIII (1970), 134-135.

HAMLET

TEXT Alexander 152-162; Camb vii-lix; Chambers 408-425; Greg 299-333; Sisson II, 206-229.

See also J. Dover Wilson, *The Manuscript of Shakespeare's Hamlet and the Problems of its Transmission* (1934; there is a revised edition, 1963); G. I. Duthie, *The 'Bad' Quarto of Hamlet* (1941); P. Alexander, *Shakespeare's Punctuation* (1945); J. M. Nosworthy, "*Hamlet* and the Player Who Could Not Keep Counsel," *ShS,* III (1950), 74-82 and *Shakespeare's Occasional Plays: Their Origin and Transmission* (1965); A. Walker, "The Textual Problem of *Hamlet,*" *RES,* II (1951), 328-338, and *Textual Problems of the First Folio* (1953); articles by J. R. Brown, F. Bowers, H. Jenkins, and A. Walker in *SB* (1955-56); C. Leech, "Studies in *Hamlet,* 1901-1955," *ShS,* IX (1956), 4-7. Chambers and Greg are authoritative; Duthie and Leech offer surveys of research on the text.

EDITIONS *NV,* ed. H. H. Furness (1877); ed. J. Q. Adams (1929); Camb, ed. J. Dover Wilson (1934); ed. G. L. Kittredge (1939); Yale, ed. T. Brooke and J. R. Crawford (1957); Pelican, ed. W. Farnham (1957).

SOURCES J. Schick, *Das Corpus Hamleticum. Hamlet in Sage und Dichtung, Kunst und Musik* (1912-1938); G. Murray, *Hamlet and Orestes* (1914); V. Østerberg, *Studier over Hamlet-teksterne* (1920); K. Malone, *The Literary History of Hamlet* (1923); I. Gollancz, *The Sources of Hamlet* (1926); ed. J. Q. Adams (1929); J. Dover Wilson, *What Happens in Hamlet* (1935), and Camb edition; F. Bowers, *Elizabethan Revenge Tragedy* (1940); R. A. Law, "Belleforest, Sh, and Kyd," *AMS* (1948); Muir (1957); Bullough (1957—), forthcoming volume.

CRITICISM C. Williamson's *Readings on the Character of Ham* (1950) is an extensive and indiscriminate anthology of criticism. *ShS* for 1956 is devoted entirely to studies of *Ham.* Other useful collections are those of C. Sacks and W. Whan, *Ham: Enter Critic* (1960); J. C. Levenson, *Discussions of Ham* (1960); R. Leavenworth, *Interpreting Ham* (1960); ed. C. Hoy (1963); J. R. Brown and B. Harris, *Ham* (1964); David Bevington, *Twentieth Century Interpretations of Ham* (1968). The best collection of earlier studies is in the *NV.*

See also Dr. Johnson's *Notes,* edited either by W. Raleigh (1908) or W. Wimsatt (1960). Goethe's *Wilhelm Meister* (1795) has a famous description of the protagonist: "a lovely, pure, noble, and most moral nature, without the strength of nerve which forms a hero, sinks beneath a burden which it cannot bear and must not cast away." Schlegel's study is in *Lectures on Dramatic Art and Literature* (1808). Coleridge's essay, which has had enormous influence, is reprinted in *Shakespearean Criticism,* ed. T. Raysor (1930). Coleridge created the Hamlet of "great, enormous intellectual activity, and a consequent proportionate aversion to real action." Lamb's "On the Tragedies of Sh," published in 1811, is still worth knowing. Hazlitt's essay in *Characters* (1817) is about the "prince of philosophical speculators." The effect of Hamlet on the Continent is touched on in O. LeWinter's critical anthology, *Sh in Europe* (1963). P. Conklin, *A History of Ham Criticism: 1601-1821* (1957), analyzes these responses to the play. R. Wellek's *A History of Modern Criticism: 1750-1950* (1955–) is extremely useful.

E. Dowden's *Sh: A Critical Study* (1875) and his Arden edition (1899) have important comments. A. C. Bradley, *Shakespearean Tragedy* (1904), has two excellent lectures. The Hamlet of Bradley changed earlier views drastically: he was not constitutionally unable to act; he was not the spiritual giant that Goethe had made of him; his melancholy was a consequence of his misfortunes. Bradley's analysis of character may not be wholly satisfying, but it remains the best thing we have of this nature. He made an important distinction between Hamlet as we see him and as he might be in other circumstances. W. Trench, *Shakespeare's Ham: a New Commentary* (1913), is worth reading. Two studies appearing in 1919 and the year following asserted that the play had failed to assimilate the materials upon which it was based. J. M. Robertson, in *The Problem of Ham,* stated that Kyd's source play endowed Sh with theatrical mechanisms he could not utilize. T. S. Eliot, "Hamlet and His Problems," *The Sacred Wood* (1920), made the famous observation that Hamlet's emotion was in excess of the facts offered to account for it. His disgust can be neither understood nor objectified. E. E. Stoll, *Ham: An Historical and Comparative Study* (1919), reminds the modern reader of Elizabethan stage practices and writes of the play's theatrical qualities. Stoll considers a good deal of previous criticism which, according to his habit, he rejects.

L. Schücking discusses the melancholy psychological type in *Character Problems in Shakespeare's Plays* (1922). Many details of interpretation are offered by J. Q. Adams in his edition (1929). L. Campbell, *Shakespeare's Tragic Heroes: Slaves of Passion* (1930), opines that the Prince allows his reason to be submerged by excessive passion. G. W. Knight has two essays in *The Wheel of Fire* (1930) and another in *The Imperial Theme* (1931). The first discusses the "shadow of death" over the play; the second is essentially about the dualism of passivity and action. The last examines language and "life-themes." A. J. Waldock's reliable *Ham: A Study in Critical Method* (1931) reviews much past criticism. E. E. Stoll's *Art and Artifice in Sh* (1933) contrasts character and dramatic structure; Stoll urges that we dismiss the idea that the play serves as a psychological case history. Hamlet's madness is feigned: "though less

psychological, it is much more dramatic." Perhaps the best-known interpretation is J. Dover Wilson's *What Happens in Ham* (1935). There is a
wealth of detail in the reading of individual scenes; large conceptions
are generally avoided, and valuable contributions are made to our knowledge of the particulars of the action.

One of the most important studies is in Granville-Barker (1946). The summation of this book-length essay is that Hamlet does not pluck the heart
out of the mystery, nor does the reader. The "tragedy of thwarted thought
and tortured spirit" accompanies the tragic action itself. The hero's
scepticism and cruelty, his madness and pretence are well covered. C. S.
Lewis, *Ham: The Prince or the Poem?* (1942), attempts to ignore the
problems of the play and to reach its meaning in "the poetry and the
situation." The substance of the play, Lewis argues, is the language itself. R. Walker, *The Time Is Out of Joint* (1948), has a good running
commentary. S. de Madariaga, *On Ham* (1948, rev. ed. 1965), is a realistic study of the hero's egocentricity. H. B. Charlton, *Shakespearian
Tragedy* (1948), has some sentimental remarks about the protagonist
but offers a good account of Elizabethan ethics revealed by the play.
Charlton usefully contrasts the barbarism of the action and the idealism
of the rhetoric. F. Fergusson, *The Idea of a Theater* (1949), describes
the main action of *Ham* as "the attempt to find and destroy the hidden
'imposthume' which is poisoning the life of Claudius' Denmark. All of
the characters—from Polonius with his 'windlasses' and 'assays of bias,'
to Hamlet with his parables and symbolic shows—realize this action, in
comic, or evil, or inspired ways." There is a fine account of the ritual
content of the play. G. R. Elliott, *Scourge and Minister* (1951), is a
very close analysis of speech and scene, based on certain themes (principally pride) which are found to underlie each revolution of the plot.
The best study of the scepticism of *Ham* is in D. G. James, *The Dream
of Learning* (1951). James has an excellent discussion of the collisions
of Christianity and scepticism, scientific optimism and spiritual doubt.

M. Mack has two distinguished articles on this play: "The World of
Ham," *Yale Review*, XLI (1952), 502-523, and "The Jacobean Sh,"
Jacobean Theatre (1960). The first treats the mystery of Hamlet's
world and the second the nature of the tragic hero. Two worthwhile
books are B. Joseph's *Conscience and the King* (1953) and P. Alexander's *Hamlet, Father and Son* (1955). The first is written from the
theatrical viewpoint; the latter brings to bear Aristotelian ideas of tragedy. Alexander has a very good historical summation; he is convinced
that the hero is indeed that—an "ideal type" who dramatizes the struggle of civilization itself to survive. H. D. Kitto, *Form and Meaning in
Drama* (1956), compares *Ham* and Greek tragedy: "we may say that
both in the Greek trilogy and in Shakespeare's play the Tragic Hero,

ultimately, is humanity itself; and what humanity is suffering from, in *Ham* is not a specific evil, but Evil itself." H. Levin's *The Question of Ham* (1959) is essential to understanding style and structure. Levin discusses the nature of interrogation, doubt, and irony; his study of madness ("the antic disposition") is reinforced by the evidence of Renaissance doctrines. L. C. Knights, *An Approach to Ham* (1960), explores the atmosphere of corruption and the sense of the failure of the rational in *Ham*. J. Holloway, *The Story of the Night* (1961), covers the alienation of the central figure and the role of chance in the drama. Holloway finds that what is superficially a drama dominated by accident is in reality a display of the workings of an inexorable retributive scheme.

For study of the theatrical metaphor see Anne Righter, *Sh and the Idea of the Play* (1962). This book's biographical ascription, however, should be disregarded. There are two important recent books: Morris Weitz has covered the major critical theories of interpreting this play in *Ham and the Philosophy of Literary Criticism* (1964). This is a very lucid and detailed view of the play's critical history, and it serves principally to undermine our confidence in previous literary guides. Maurice Charney's *Style in Ham* (1969) is a close and complete reading of the scenes. It offers intense and sensitive coverage of action and language.

The number of special studies is infinite. As far as psychology is concerned, one might begin with Freud's *The Interpretation of Dreams* in *Complete Works,* IV (1953). Ernest Jones' *Ham and Oedipus* (1949) is a Freudian interpretation of Ham which centers on the sublimation of incest. While it may or may not be true, it takes a great deal of mind and energy to grapple with. K. Muir has written "Some Freudian Interpretations of Sh," *Proc. Leeds Philo. Soc.,* VII (1952), 43-52. C. Leech has a short summary of psychological investigations in "Studies in Hamlet," *ShS,* IX (1956), 12-13. See also Nigel Alexander, "Critical Disagreement About Oedipus and Hamlet," *ShS,* XX (1967), 33-39; the important accounts of Norman Holland in *Psychoanalysis and Sh* (1964) and of Morris Weitz in *Ham and the Philosophy of Literary Criticism* (1964). Holland is generally convinced of the value of such criticism; Weitz devotes his efforts to demonstrating its flaws.

The language of *Ham* is well studied in the following: Johnson; Spurgeon (1935); M. Morozev, "The Individualization of Shakespeare's Characters Through Imagery," *ShS,* II (1949), 93-106; Clemen (1951); Evans (1952); M. Mahood, *Shakespeare's Wordplay* (1957). See also Paul Jorgensen, *Redeeming Shakespeare's Words* (1962); M. Doran, "The Language of Ham," *HLQ,* XXVII (1964), 259-278; Brian Vickers, *The Artistry of Shakespeare's Prose* (1968); Maurice Charney, *Style in Ham* (1969).

Further reading: A. Tolman, *The Views About Ham* (1904); G.

Santayana, *Life and Letters* (1928); J. M. Murry, *Sh* (1936); J. Draper, *The Ham of Shakespeare's Audience* (1938); L. Schücking, *The Baroque Character of the Elizabethan Tragic Hero* (1938); T. Spencer, "Hamlet and the Nature of Reality," *ELH*, V (1938), 253-277; L. C. Knights, *Explorations* (1946); F. Wertham, *Dark Legend* (1947); R. Flatter, *Hamlet's Father* (1949); E. M. W. Tillyard, *Shakespeare's Problem Plays* (1949); A. Jack, *Young Hamlet* (1950); F. Bowers, "Hamlet as Minister and Scourge," *PMLA*, LXX (1950), 740-747; S. F. Johnson, "The Regeneration of Hamlet," *ShQ*, III (1952), 187-207; W. Empson, "*Ham* When New," *Sew*, LXI (1953), 15-42 and 185-205; A. Bonjour, "Hamlet and the Phantom Clue," *ES*, XXXV (1954), 1-6; R. Altick, "*Ham* and the Odor of Mortality," *ShQ*, V (1954), 167-176; B. Stirling, *Unity in Shakespearian Tragedy* (1956); L. Kirschbaum, "Hamlet and Ophelia," *PQ*, XXXV (1956), 376-393; R. West, *The Court and the Castle* (1957); H. S. Wilson, *On the Design of Shakespearian Tragedy* (1957); C. Heilbrun, "The Character of Hamlet's Mother," *ShQ*, VIII (1957), 201-206; Robert Ornstein, *The Moral Vision of Jacobean Tragedy* (1960); J. Lawlor, *The Tragic Sense in Sh* (1960); W. Rosen, *Sh and the Craft of Tragedy* (1960); Sister M. Joseph, "*Ham*, A Christian Tragedy," *SP*, LIX (1962), 119-140; Terence Hawkes, *Sh and The Reason* (1964); Roger Cox, "Hamlet's *Hamartia*: Aristotle or St. Paul," *YR*, LV (1965-66), 347-364; Eleanor Prosser, *Ham and Revenge* (1967).

STAGING Camb lxix-xcvii; Craig 902-903; Odell *passim;* Sprague 127-184; Trewin *passim.*

See also H. Spencer, *Sh Improved* (1927); G. W. Stone, "Garrick's Long Lost Alteration of *Ham*," *PMLA*, XLIX (1934), 890-921; R. Gilder, *John Gielgud's Hamlet* (1937); J. M. Brown, *Broadway in Review* (1940); A. C. Ward, *Specimens of English Dramatic Criticism* (1945); R. Mander and J. Mitchenson, *Hamlet Through the Ages* (1952); A. C. Sprague, *Shakespearian Players and Performances* (1953); Folio Society edition (1954); G. Reynolds, "*Ham* at the Globe," *ShS*, IX (1956), 49-53; E. Browne, "English Hamlets of the Twentieth Century," *ShS*, IX (1956), 16-23; P. Conklin, *A History of Ham Criticism: 1601-1821* (1957); B. Joseph, *The Tragic Actor* (1959); R. Leavenworth, *Interpreting Ham* (1960); Martin Holmes, *The Guns of Elsinore* (1964); Norman Sanders, "Metamorphoses of the Prince: Some Critical and Theatrical Interpretations of *Ham* 1864-1964," *Shakespearean Essays,* ed. Sanders and Alwin Thaler (1964); Carol Carlisle, *Sh from the Greenroom* (1969).

BIBLIOGRAPHY *NV* (1877); A. Raven, *A Ham Bibliography and Reference Guide: 1877-1935* (1936); C. Leech, "Studies in *Ham*: 1901-1955," *ShS*, IX (1956), 1-15; P. Conklin (above); S. Wells, "A Reader's Guide to *Ham*," *Ham,* ed. J. R. Brown and B. Harris (1964).

THE MERRY WIVES OF WINDSOR

TEXT   Alexander 124-127; Camb vii-xxxix, 93-101; Chambers 425-438; Greg 334-337; Sisson I, 62-73.

See also A. Pollard, *Sh Folios and Quartos* (1909); Pollard and J. Dover Wilson, "The 'Stolne and Surreptitious' Shakespearian Texts," *TLS* (1919), 18, 30, 134, 420; L. Schücking, "The Fairy Scene in *MWW* in Folio and Quarto," *MLR,* XIX (1924), 338-340. L. Hotson's *Sh Versus Shallow* (1931) is an attempt to link new documentary information about Sh with *MWW*. Hotson believes that Shallow and Slender satirize the unpleasant Sir William Gardiner and his nephew, who were ill-disposed to Sh and his company. He fixes the date of the play—and hence of the *H4* plays—as no later than 1597. There is a wealth of conjecture, by no means all of it accepted. See the review by J. Hannigan, *SAB,* VII (1932), 174-182. J. Crofts, *Sh and the Post Horses* (1937), examines contemporary events to which the play may allude. It is generally an obscure and unconvincing book. V. Ogburn, "*MWW* Quarto, A Farce Interlude," *PMLA,* LVII (1942), 654-660, discusses the denuded language and character of the 1602 quarto. It is not convincing when it intrudes weakly aesthetic terms like "refinement," "good taste," and "fine idealism" in judging this text. See also McManaway, 28-29; W. Bracy, *MWW: The History and Transmission of Shakespeare's Text* (1952); the review by W. W. Greg in *ShQ,* IV (1953), 77-79; Hardin Craig, *A New Look at Shakespeare's Quartos* (1961); William Green, *Shakespeare's MWW* (1962); J. M. Nosworthy, *Shakespeare's Occasional Plays: Their Origin and Transmission* (1965). Green discusses text, date, and occasion in detail.

EDITIONS   Arden, ed. H. Hart (1904); Camb, ed. A. Quiller-Couch and J. Dover Wilson (1921); Arden, ed. B. White (1956); Pelican, ed. Fredson Bowers (1963).

SOURCES   R. S. Forsythe, "A Plautine Source of *MWW,*" *MP,* XVIII (1920), 401-421, and "*MWW*: Two New Analogues," *PQ,* VII (1928), 390-398; O. J. Campbell, "The Italianate Background of *MWW,*" *Essays and Studies in English and Comp. Lit.* (1932), 81-117; M. Radoff, "Influence of the French Farce in *H5* and *MWW,*" *MLN,* XLVIII (1933), 427-435; D. Bruce, "*MWW* and *Two Brethren,*" *SP,* XXXIX (1942), 265-278; Muir (1957); Bullough (1957–), II, 3-58.

CRITICISM   There are essentially two divisions of critical thought—and emotion. Some take the play for the farce it seems to be; others find it impossible to accept the "degradation" of Falstaff. Dr. Johnson wrote sensibly that "Falstaff could not love but by ceasing to be Falstaff."

His insight has often been ignored, and critics persistently blame *MWW* for not being *H4.* The following represent both camps.

E. Dowden's *Sh: A Critical Study* (1875) called *MWW* "a play written expressly for the barbarian aristocrats with their hatred of ideas, their insensibility to beauty, their hard, efficient manners, and their demand for impropriety." A. C. Bradley in the famous "The Rejection of Falstaff," *Oxford Lectures* (1909), saw a Falstaff "beaten, burnt, pricked, mocked, insulted, and, worst of all, repentant and didactic." The original character, he added, "is to be found alive in the two parts of *H4,* dead in *H5,* and nowhere else." He summed up with monumental chagrin, "it is horrible." The editors of the Camb edition (1921) grant its imperfections but fall back, as one well may, on its history of eminently successful staging. One of the rare positive responses is that of E. K. Chambers in *Sh: A Survey* (1925). The play, Chambers notes sensibly, has no great pretensions but is admirably constructed, has great vitality, and is an invariable success on the boards. It is both farce and fabliau and quite fulfills the demands of both genres. There is a short essay on the language of *MWW* in G. W. Knight's *The Shakespearian Tempest* (1932). O. J. Campbell, *Essays and Studies in English and Comp. Lit.* (1932), 81-117, reviewed the sources and theorized that Falstaff is modeled after the wicked and lascivious hypocrite of the *commedia dell'arte.* He was satisfied that role dominated character in this play and found its primary virtue in the evident vitality.

E. J. Haller, "The Realism of *MWW,*" *West Virginia Univ. St.,* III (1937), 32-38, studies the play's realism. Haller wrote that "Mistress Ford and Mistress Page are typical Elizabethan *haute bourgeoisie*" and that the play on the whole centers on the great comic (and middle-class) issues of dowry and dominance. H. B. Charlton's essay in *Shakespearian Comedy* (1938) marks a return to the worship of Falstaff. M. Van Doren's *Sh* (1939) sees the wives as "coarse-grained," "monotonous," and "broad-hipped in their comic dialect." The play exhibits, he states, a good deal of craft but very little love on the part of its author. J. S. Schell, "Shakspere's Gulls," *SAB,* XV (1940), 23-33, agrees with Hazlitt that Slender is "a very potent piece of imbecility . . . the only first-rate character in the play." S. Sewell, "The Relation Between *MWW* and Jonson's *Every Man in His Humour,*" *SAB,* XVI (1941), 175-189, applies the "humours" and deceptions of Jonson to *MWW.* A similar treatment is that of O. J. Campbell in *Shakespeare's Satire* (1943). D. Boughner, "Traditional Elements in Falstaff," *JEGP,* XLIII (1944), 417-428, learnedly describes the innumerable *Pantoloni* of the Italian Renaissance. Falstaff resembles them in being a "braggart warrior" who carries to laughable excess the military and courtly accomplishments.

H. Craig, *An Interpretation of Sh* (1948), strongly denies that Falstaff

undergoes a degeneration: he is simply engaged in a comedy of situation. In *Shakespearean Comedy* (1949) T. M. Parrott has a competent
review of the play in which he suggests that Falstaff must play in love
the same illicit part he plays in the affairs of the *H4* plays. D. Stauffer,
Shakespeare's World of Images (1949), notes that the customary story
of comic cuckoldry is reversed; the escapades of *MWW* prove loyalty
and not lust in women. There are two Falstaffs, says S. Sen Gupta in
Shakespearian Comedy (1950). They have little in common "except
the name, a bloated body and a few tricks of phrase." Sen Gupta
dodges the critical task by simply refusing to discuss the Falstaff of
MWW. T. Reik's *The Secret Self* (1952) proposes that *MWW* reveals the
author's rebellion against the authority of women, especially his hostility to Elizabeth I. It reveals also Falstaff's childhood fears of the loss of
maternal love. If this nonsense is not enough, the reader may look over
Reik on the "transvestitism" of Falstaff.

In *The Development of English Humour* (1952) L. Cazamian theorizes
that Falstaff is composed of two parts; in *MWW* only that part constituted of greed and carnality is allowed existence. S. B. Hemingway,
"On Behalf of That Falstaff," *ShQ,* III (1952), 307-311, reasserts the
position of Dr. Johnson. Bullough (1957–) has a worthwhile essay, as
does T. W. Baldwin in his *On the Literary Genetics of Shakspere's Plays
1592-1594* (1959). The latter writes at great length of the structure of
MWW. B. Evans, *Shakespeare's Comedies* (1960), notes that this play
marks the height of Shakespeare's interest in "practices." According to
Evans "no moment is quiet: while one intrigue is starting, another has
reached a peak of exploitation, and another is ending." There are, he
tallies, eleven plots and counterplots. Falstaff is at the mercy of many
of these, and the reason for his unsatisfactory showing is perhaps
accounted for by words taken from Parolles in *AWW*: "who cannot be
crush'd with a plot?" Some essays on Falstaff as an Elizabethan comic
type are in J. Draper's collection, *Stratford to Dogberry* (1961). A.
Gilbert's *The Principles and Practice of Criticism* (1962) examines
MWW as a comedy of manners: it is useful for its summarizing power.
In *Sh and the Idea of the Play* (1962) Anne Righter discusses comic
deceit and disguise: "*MWW* is filled with affirmations of the power of
illusion." There are remarks on the language in Brian Vickers, *The
Artistry of Shakespeare's Prose* (1968).

Further reading: J. R. Brown, "The Interpretation of Shakespeare's
Comedies: 1900-1953," *ShS,* VIII (1955), 1-13; Brown, *Sh and His
Comedies* (1957); J. Dover Wilson, *Shakespeare's Happy Comedies*
(1962).

STAGING Camb 135-138; Craig 560; Odell *passim;* Sprague 45-49;
Trewin *passim.*

See also H. Spencer, *The Art and Life of William Sh* (1940); H. Hunt, *Old Vic Prefaces* (1954); M. Webster, *Sh Without Tears* (1955). See the useful pictorial essay in *The Stratford Scene 1958-1968* (1968), ed. Peter Raby.

BIBLIOGRAPHY   W. Bracy, *MWW: The History and Transmission of Shakespeare's Text* (1952); W. Green, *Shakespeare's MWW* (1962).

TROILUS AND CRESSIDA

TEXT Alexander 193-197; Camb xxxi-xxxviii, 122-134; Chambers 438-449; Greg 338-350; Sisson II, 107-121.

See also J. Q. Adams, "*Tim* and the Irregularities in the First Folio," *JEGP,* VII (1908), 53-63; A. Pollard, *Sh Folios and Quartos* (1909); P. Alexander, "*TrC,* 1609," *Lib,* IX (1928), 267-286; S. A. Tannenbaum, "A Critique of the Text of *TrC,*" *SAB,* IX (1934), 55-74, 125-144, and 198-214; A. Sewell, "Notes on the Integrity of *TrC,*" *RES,* XIX (1943), 120-127; P. Williams, "The 'Second Issue' of Shakespeare's *TrC,* 1609," *SB,* II (1949), 25-33, and "Shakespeare's *TrC*: The Relationship of Quarto and Folio," *ibid.,* III (1950), 131-143; McManaway, 29; A. Walker, "The Textual Problems of *TrC,*" *MLR,* XLV (1950), 459-464, and *Textual Problems of the First Folio* (1953); W. W. Greg, "The Printing of Shakespeare's *TrC* in the First Folio," *Papers Bibl. Soc. Amer.,* XLV (1951), 273-282; M. Shaaber, "*A NV Edition of Sh,*" *ShQ,* IV (1953), 171-181; H. Craig, *A New Look at Shakespeare's Quartos* (1961); J. M. Nosworthy, *Shakespeare's Occasional Plays: Their Origin and Transmission* (1965); E. A. J. Honigmann, *The Stability of Shakespeare's Text* (1965); J. Ramsey, "The Provenance of *TrC,*" *ShQ,* XXI (1970), 223-240.

EDITIONS Arden, ed. K. Deighton (1906); *NV,* ed. H. Hillebrand and T. W. Baldwin (1953); Yale, ed. J. Campbell (1956); Camb, ed. J. Dover Wilson and A. Walker (1957); Pelican, ed. V. K. Whitaker (1958).

SOURCES K. Eitner, "Die Troilus-Fabel," *ShJ,* III (1868), 252-300; W. Hertzberg, "Die Quellen der Troilus-Sage," *ShJ,* VI (1871), 169-225; R. A. Small, *The Stage-Quarrel* (1899); J. S. Tatlock, "The Siege of Troy in Elizabethan Literature," *PMLA,* XXX (1915), 673-770; H. E. Rollins, "The Troilus-Cressida Story from Chaucer to Sh," *PMLA,* XXXII (1917), 383-429; V. K. Whitaker, *Shakespeare's Use of Learning* (1953); R. Presson, *Shakespeare's TrC and the Legends of Troy* (1953); A. Arnold, "The Hector-Andromache Scene in Shakespeare's *TrC,*" *MLQ,* XIV (1953), 335-340; Muir (1957); Bullough (1957–), VI, 83-221; R. Kimbrough, "The Origins of *TrC,*" *PMLA,* LXXVII (1962), 194-199.

CRITICISM Some, like J. Q. Adams (*A Life of William Sh,* 1923), have thought that *TrC* offers no problem beyond the workings of action and plot. Others have ranged widely and have been satisfied that the play reveals a myriad of possible meanings. The proposed "real" meanings have been as various as a satire on Elizabethan playwrights, a reflection of Shakespeare's despair, a parable of the spirit and the flesh.

J. S. Tatlock, "The Chief Problem in Sh," *Sew,* XXIV (1916), 129-147, early expressed the view that there is no special mystery to the play. G. C. Taylor later raised the uncomfortable question, "Why does one put the play down with revulsion of feeling towards it stronger than towards any other Elizabethan treatment of the same theme?" His essay appeared in *PMLA,* XLV (1930), 781-786. An influential essay appeared in G. W. Knight's *The Wheel of Fire* (1930). The play was seen as a conflict of love and war: another overriding conflict was that between intuition and intellect. According to Knight, "the Trojan party stands for human beauty and worth, the Greek party for the bestial and stupid elements of man, the barren stagnancy of intellect divorced from action." The oppositions are perhaps too strict and too simple.

One of the most important essays on *TrC* appeared in W. W. Lawrence's *Shakespeare's Problem Comedies* (1931). Its subject is the limitations imposed on the play by the source materials it depends on. Lawrence believes that the times and the nature of production demanded "an intellectual and rhetorical piece, with a strong flavour of indecorum." O. J. Campbell, *Comicall Satyre and Shakespeare's TrC* (1938), finds the tone a consequence of Juvenalian influence, to which he attributes also the interest in sexual abnormality and excess. He connects the play to the satire of Jonson and Marston. Campbell's thesis is considered by the *NV* editors, pp. 382-385. Campbell's work and that of Knight (above) formulated the critical polarities of *TrC.* M. Van Doren, *Sh* (1939), is intensely subjective, but that is often the characteristic of the good critic. He finds the style of *TrC* "loud, brassy, and abandoned." The characters are conceived in disgust and manifest only moral degradation. W. W. Lawrence's "Troilus, Cressida and Thersites," *MLR,* XXXVII (1942), 422-437, lists *caveats* for the critic and attempts to redeem the play from disgust, of either author or critic. T. Spencer, *Sh and the Nature of Man* (1942), sees the play as a tragedy of the destruction of values, the triumph of passions over ideals.

In *Sh and the Popular Dramatic Tradition* (1944), S. L. Bethell dismissed the dramatic business and called the play simply "an excuse for thought." The drama may be that of Greek and Trojan, but the allegory works out the mysteries of time and value. An exceptionally able defense of *TrC* is Una Ellis-Fermor's "Discord in the Spheres" in *The Frontiers of Drama* (1945). That the play is difficult she grants, but only as it is an experiment in tragedy. She suggests that the play is the working out of the discovery that man is unable to imagine absolute value in either imaginative or objective terms. I. A. Richards, *"TrC and Plato," HR,* I (1948), 632-676, finds in *The Republic* the theme of this play: "our souls at any one time are attacked by endless opposite views." The Platonic ideal is that of constancy; reality affords only valuations that are temporary and irreconcilable. *The Dream of Learning*

(1951) by D. G. James discovers in *TrC* signs of the "new doubt" which rejected Baconian optimism. O. J. Campbell summed up Troilus as a sensual gourmet; W. Dunkel in "Shakespeare's Troilus," *ShQ,* II (1951), 331-334, characterizes the hero as the man who "thinks on the basis of what he sees and hears" alone. In L. C. Knights' *"TrC* Again," *Scrutiny,* XVIII (1951), 144-157, men are seen as creatures of time and appearance. The play exemplifies irrationality in control of human affairs. It is split between those who see the world only through the limitations of reason and those who see it without even that useful constraint.

The verdict of V. K. Whitaker in *The Seventeenth Century* (1951) is, I think, open to doubt: *TrC* he judges to be the same kind of failure as *MM.* In both he finds philosophy unassimilated by drama. R. Presson (above) has detailed and useful comparisons of plot and underplot with the sources. A. F. Potts, *"Cynthia's Revels, Poetaster,* and *TrC,"* *ShQ,* V (1954), 297-302, affirms the position of Campbell on satire and suggests that the Ovidian surrender of intellect to love came to Sh through Ben Jonson. The best summary of criticism is K. Muir's *"TrC,"* *ShS,* VIII (1955), 28-39. Muir himself finds the play a paradigm of "the world and the flesh" making "the best the victims of the worst." The defeated political vision of *TrC* and *Cor* is the subject of M. MacLure, "Sh and the Lonely Dragon," *UTQ,* XXIV (1955), 109-120. For P. Dickey, *Not Wisely But Too Well* (1957), love turned to lust in action furnishes the play's tragic content. W. R. Bowden, "The Human Sh and *TrC,"* *ShQ,* VIII (1957), 167-177, attempts to compromise between critics who see the play as a conflict of reason and passion and those who follow G. W. Knight in seeing it as the opposition of intellect and intuition.

M. C. Bradbrook, "What Sh Did to Chaucer's *Troilus and Criseyde,"* *ShQ,* IX (1958), 311-319, is a determined assault on those who find the play a satire. Her scene-by-scene analysis is convincing, as is her summation: *TrC* is a "vision not of the grandeur but the pettiness of evil; the squalor and meanness and triviality of betrayal." B. Morris, "The Tragic Structure of *TrC,"* *ShQ,* X (1959), 481-491, attempts to define the play as a tragedy and elevates Troilus to the status of tragic hero. The play is described as a paradigm of suffering, futility, and destruction, which may disregard its comic content. A. S. Knowland, *"TrC,"* *ShQ,* X (1959), 353-365, attacks the subjectivists and attempts to criticize the play in terms of neither "key" speeches nor themes but by its total dramatic impact. L. C. Knights, *Some Shakespearean Themes* (1959), returns to the appearance-reality dichotomy and sees in the play bewilderment and ambiguity both in private and public experience. A rewarding essay is in R. Ornstein's *The Moral Vision of Jacobean Tragedy* (1960). While Ornstein judges the characters as too evidently part of a dialectic, he has an eye for the drama and its elements of decadence. W. Main suggests in "Character Amalgams in Shakespeare's *TrC*," *SP*, LVIII (1961), 170-178, that in different scenes the dramatic agents become different Jacobean emotional stereotypes. F. W. Sternfeld's *Music in Shakespearean Tragedy* (1963) affords unusual insight into the play's sensual euphony.

Nevill Coghill reviews the critical problems in *Shakespeare's Professional Skills* (1964) and concludes that this is "a straight tragedy of the traditionally anti-Homeric, anti-Greek kind, based on Caxton, Lydgate, and Chaucer." He finds in it the collapse of medieval values when faced with the new individualism of the Renaissance: "Chaucer and Malory are out and Machiavelli is in." Robert Kimbrough, *Shakespeare's TrC and Its Setting* (1964), covers the literary and theatrical background. The notes and bibliography are good; Kimbrough's answers to the problems raised by the play are interesting but not definitive. His exposition, however, is valuable. See also Willard Farnham, "Troilus in Shapes of Infinite Desire," *ShQ*, XV (1964), 257-264. See also N. Frye, *Fools of Time* (1967) and "Old and New Comedy," *ShS*, XXII (1969), 1-5; Arnold Stein, "*TrC*: The Disjunctive Imagination," *ELH*, XXXVI (1969), 145-167. For many years it has been assumed that this play is a *locus classicus* for the articulation of Elizabethan ideals on order. A corrective to this is offered by Herbert Howarth in *The Tiger's Heart* (1970).

The following study the play's language: W. Empson, *Some Versions of Pastoral* (1935); D. Traversi, *An Approach to Sh* (1938); A. Yoder, *Animal Analogy in Shakespeare's Character Portrayal* (1947); W. Nowottny, " 'Opinion' and 'Value' in *TrC*," *EC*, IV (1954), 282-296; F. Kermode, "Opinion, Truth and Value," *ibid.*, V (1955), 181-187; K. Schmidt di Simoni, *Shakespeare's TrC* (1959); F. Daniels, "Order and Confusion in *TrC* I, iii," *ShQ*, XII (1961), 285-291; Brian Vickers, *The Artistry of Shakespeare's Prose* (1968).

Further reading: C. Williams, *The English Poetic Mind* (1932); W. Henderson, "Shakespeare's *TrC*," *Parrott Presentation Volume* (1935); E. M. W. Tillyard, *The Elizabethan World Picture* (1943); S. Merton, "*Tem* and *TrC*," *CE*, VII (1945), 143-150; A. Harbage, *As They Liked It* (1947); W. Elton, "Shakespeare's Portrait of Ajax," *PMLA*, LXIII (1948), 744-748; L. Hotson, *Shakespeare's Sonnets Dated* (1949); E. M. W. Tillyard, *Shakespeare's Problem Plays* (1949); T. W. Baldwin, "Structural Analysis of *TrC*," *Sh-Studien* (1951), 5-18; P. Kendall, "Inaction and Ambivalence in *TrC*," *J. S. Wilson Festschrift* (1952); H. Fluchère, *Sh* (1953); H. Heuer, "*TrC* in neuerer Sicht," *ShJ*, LXXXIX (1953), 106-127; J. R. Brown, "The Interpretation of Shakespeare's Comedies: 1900-1953," *ShS*, VII (1955), 1-13; M. T. Herrick, *Tragicomedy* (1955); P. Siegel, *Sh and the Elizabethan Compromise* (1957); H. Swanston, "The Baroque Element in *TrC*," *DUJ*, XIX (1957), 14-23;

A. Gérard, "Meaning and Structure in *TrC," ES,* XL (1959), 144-157; A. Kernan, *The Cankered Muse* (1959); B. Evans, *Shakespeare's Comedies* (1960); R. Ornstein, *Discussions of Shakespeare's Problem Comedies* (1961); D. Kaula, "Will and Reason in *TrC," ShQ,* XII (1961), 271-283; J. Enck, "The Peace of the Poetomachia," *PMLA,* LXXXVII (1962), 386-396; R. Kaufmann, "Ceremonies for Chaos," *ELH,* XXXII (1965), 139-159.

STAGING Camb xlvii-lvi; Craig 864; Odell *passim;* Trewin *passim.*

See also H. Spencer, *The Art and Life of William Sh* (1940); G. F. Reynolds, "*TrC* on the Elizabethan Stage," *AMS* (1948); Enck (above). There is a remarkably thorough stage history in the *NV.* See also Gareth L. Evans, "The Reason Why: The Royal Shakespeare Season 1968 Reviewed," *ShS,* XXII (1969), 142-144.

BIBLIOGRAPHY S. A. Tannenbaum, *Shakespeare's TrC: A Concise Bibliography* (1943); Kimbrough (above).

ALL'S WELL THAT ENDS WELL

TEXT Alexander 191-193; Camb xxxi-xxxiii, 101-113; Chambers 449-452; Greg 351-353; New Arden xi-xviii; Sisson I, 168-183.

See also A. Thiselton, *Some Textual Notes on AWW* (1900); A. H. Tolman, *What Has Become of . . . 'Love's Labour's Won'?* (1902); W. T. Hastings, "Notes on *AWW*," *SAB*, X (1935), 232-244; McManaway 29; T. W. Baldwin, *Shakspere's Love's Labor's Won* (1957); review of Baldwin by R. C. Bald, *MP*, LV (1957), 276-278.

EDITIONS Camb, ed. A. Quiller-Couch and J. Dover Wilson (1929); New Arden, ed. G. K. Hunter (1959); Pelican, ed. Jonas Barish (1964).

SOURCES N. Delius, "Shakespeares *AWW* and Paynter's *Giletta of Narbonne*," *ShJ*, XXII (1887), 26-44; H. G. Wright, "How Did Sh Come to Know the *Decameron*?" *MLR*, L (1955), 45-48, and *Boccaccio in England* (1957); Muir (1957); Bullough (1957—), II, 375-396.

CRITICISM Most modern critics have found Helena too deceptive and Bertram too ignoble for their tastes. There are, I think, really two issues. Are they in fact as bad as they seem? If so, is the play a "failure"? What I consider the best essays answer both queries in the negative.

E. Dowden in his *Sh: A Critical Study* (1875) anticipated modern symbolic and thematic criticism. He found Helena "the providence of the play" in healing the king and redeeming her husband. Dowden disregarded the vexed issue of probability and found the *raison d'être* of the play in "the energy, the leap-up, the direct advance of the *will* of Helena." W. W. Lawrence's "The Meaning of *AWW*," *PMLA*, XXXVII (1922), 418-469, is the basis for his chapter in *Shakespeare's Problem Comedies* (1931). After a review of critics from Johnson to Lounsbury, he attempts to evaluate *AWW* on the basis of its sources. These are the folk tales of the "healing of the king" and "fulfilment of the tasks," both of which involve the poor, weak, and innocent maiden who accomplishes the impossible. Lawrence urges that dramatic probabilities do not matter so much as the simple opposition of good and evil, to which the audience is expected to respond. Character, he admits, makes this difficult in *AWW*, but what is central is the progress from affliction to happiness. G. Vogt's article on medieval analogues is in *JEGP*, XXIV (1925), 102-124. E. K. Chambers has a hostile essay in *Sh: A Survey* (1925). He contends that masculine intellect is discredited in *Ham* and idealism in *JC*; *AWW*, he believes, demonstrates the degradation of love by the "imperious instinct" of sex. The Camb edition (1929) finds the play inept and worse; the essay is based on assumptions with which not everyone may agree. In *Sh* (1939) M. Van Doren has a balanced essay; his conclusion is that the folk tale depends for effect on simplicity and that character and atmosphere in *AWW* are too dark and complex to fulfill that simplicity. H. Spencer, *The Art and Life of William Sh* (1940), attempts to moderate the passion felt by Coleridge, Hazlitt, and their followers for Helena and the contempt felt by many moderns for Bertram.

E. E. Stoll, *From Sh to Joyce* (1944), has an extensive review of the critics of *AWW*. Stoll finds no particular problem in the play—he differs from those who defend the play in terms of its sources by pointing out that Sh and his audience were not much interested in medieval *virtue* but were very much taken with *romance*. It is probably the last, he thinks, that nullifies the play's inconsistencies. E. M. W. Tillyard in *Shakespeare's Problem Plays* (1949) finds *AWW* deficient in execution rather than substance. His criticism of the poetry (no "imaginative warmth") is not convincing since his terms indicate anachronistic standards of judgment. He notes the heavy burden of the Morality in *AWW*. The main problems for H. S. Wilson in his "Dramatic Emphasis in *AWW*," *HLQ*, XIII (1950), 222-240, are the "improbabilities of the action, the inconsistency of the heroine and the moral baseness of the hero, the coarseness of the dialogue and the poor quality of the verse." Wilson offers no easy solution: the play's virtues for him are its complexities of character and the seriousness of its study of love.

M. C. Bradbrook, "Virtue Is the True Nobility," *RES*, I (1950), 289-301, states that the "symbolic and extrapersonal significance" of the characters is unsuccessfully portrayed. The play is interpreted allegorically: Helena (true nobility and Truth herself) and Parolles (false nobility and Lies personified) contend, as in a Morality, for the being of Bertram. Bradbrook's *Sh and Elizabethan Poetry* (1951) adds that the moral problem is mixed (for the worse) with the evident social and sexual problems. C. Leech, "The Theme of Ambition in *AWW*," *ELH*, XXI (1954), 17-29, explores the social ambitions of Helena. He finds her driven by these as well as by the power of love. On the whole he thinks the play satirical, a representation of a world that is weak, stupid, and conniving. He perhaps takes the deception of Helena too seriously. A notable defence of the play is J. Arthos, "The Comedy of Generation," *EC*, V (1955), 97-117. Arthos likens *AWW* to the comedy of Molière and asserts that when the limits of understanding are made clear, "when it is necessary to call on hope and faith," only then can the "terrible truths" be accepted. In other words, he interprets the play as a mystery, moving from pain to begetting; its central symbol is the unborn child, which represents the strange commingling of love and lust. The deception, which others have found cynical, he describes as a device necessary to prove innocence; in this case we do not find the amorality of *Le Seigneur Jupiter sait dorer la pilule.*

R. Goldsmith, *Wise Fools in Sh* (1955), judges both the play and its
fool distasteful. The views of the fool on sex, he suggests, implicitly
comment on those of Bertram and Parolles. An important article is
A. H. Carter's "In Defence of Bertram," *ShQ,* VII (1956), 21-31. Carter
discerns duality in all the characters: "if Bertram is guilty of lies and
evasions, so is Helena; if he fails to respect her choice, she will allow
him none; if he rejects her, she drives him from her; if he humiliates her
by refusing her, she humiliates him by choosing him publicly." Carter
observes that the youth and passion of the hero and heroine are themselves positive dramatic and existential qualities in the sterile and cynical world they inhabit. He falls back on Shaw's "Life Force" as an
explanation of the energy and meaning of the play. An evaluation of
this article is F. G. Schoff's "Claudio, Bertram, and a Note on Interpretation," *ShQ,* X (1959), 11-23. G. W. Knight adds an important treatment to the critical history of *AWW* in *The Sovereign Flower* (1958).
He relates the "miraculous" in this play to its operation in *WT.* There is
explanation of the mysteries of healing, virginity, and honor. A fine discussion of language and character makes up for Knight's predictable
obsession with "resurrection."

One of the best introductory essays is that in G. K. Hunter's New Arden
edition (1959). This deals generously and with scholarly complexity
with language, character, sources, and themes. One of Hunter's principal
points is that there is no "central, acceptable, and unified viewpoint"
that operates, as in *TN,* to define the standards which the play exerts.
He finds the play not coherent, for its realism is critical, its story conventional, and its other elements magical. S. Nagarajan, "The Structure
of *AWW,*" *EC,* X (1960), 24-31, has a good review of problems and
critics. Nagarajan commits himself to the belief that whatever the
"actual final cause" of the play is, it is not ethical. It may be, he suggests, the "love-interest." The issue of "true nobility" is at any rate
secondary—a vehicle for creating and solving the central problem of
love. W. N. King, "Shakespeare's Mingled Yarn," *MLQ,* XXI (1960),
33-44, does not think that the play is much concerned with moral solu-
tions. It exists to define character, explore psychology, and assert the
complexity of life. R. Turner, "Dramatic Conventions in *AWW,*" *PMLA,*
LXXV (1960), 497-502, writes that the deceptions are merely the
stock-in-trade of romance. Turner relates the play to the prodigal son
story, whose prime interest is the redemption of its protagonist.
Turner's account of the drama from 1601-1604 is thought-provoking:
many romances produced then were of this type. See also Turner's note
and the response by R. Hapgood in *PMLA,* LXXIX (1964), 177-182.
J. F. Adams, "*AWW*: The Paradox of Procreation," *ShQ,* XII (1961),
261-270, notes that the play is intensely concerned with sexuality, and
he examines this warm impulse with the proper scholarly frigidity. He
sees the "problem" of the play in the taming of sex by civilization.

A. P. Rossiter asserts in *Angel with Horns* (1961) that the medieval myth is used ironically in what is essentially a commentary on harsh human reality. The study emphasizes the moral discords. E. La Guardia's "Chastity, Regeneration and World Order in *AWW," Myth and Symbol* (1963), reduces the play to a system of initiation, purification, and regeneration on the basis of very slender evidence.

James Calderwood offers a reading of the play in "Styles of Knowing in *AWW," MLQ,* XXV (1964), 179-191. Jay Halio discusses the "self-treason" of the play and the paradox of worthy ends and immoral means: *"AWW," ShQ,* XV (1964), 33-43. The play's religious elements are treated by Robert Hunter in *Sh and the Comedy of Forgiveness* (1965). Hunter points out that "the world of comedy is threatened not so much by strife as by mutability." The elegaic tone of the play and its themes of decay and rejuvenation are well handled. A major book covering the play's critical history is Joseph Price's *The Unfortunate Comedy* (1968). There is a good interpretation of the play which takes account of its warring elements and the problem of their evaluation.

Further reading: G. Krapp, "Parolles," *Shakespearian Studies,* ed. B. Mathews and A. Thorndike (1916); J. M. Murry, *Sh* (1936); E. Legouis, "La Comtesse de Roussillon," *English,* I (1937), 399-404; E. Fripp, *Sh, Man and Artist* (1938); H. B. Charlton, *Shakespearian Comedy* (1938); H. Pettigrew, "The Young Count Lucien," *West Virginia Univ. Bulletin,* IV (1943), 23-30; T. M. Parrott, *Shakespearean Comedy* (1949); S. Sen Gupta, *Shakespearian Comedy* (1950); N. Coghill, "The Basis of Shakespearian Comedy," *E&S* (1950), 1-28; E. Sehrt, *Vergebung und Gnade bei Sh* (1952); J. R. Brown, "The Interpretation of Shakespeare's Comedies: 1900-1953," *ShS,* VIII (1955), 1-13, and *Sh and His Comedies* (1957); C. J. Sisson, "Shakespeare's Helena and Dr. William Harvey," *E&S* (1960), 1-20; B. Evans, *Shakespeare's Comedies* (1960); R. Ornstein, *Discussions of Shakespeare's Problem Comedies* (1961). R. Hapgood, "The Life of Shame: Parolles and *AWW," EC,* XV (1965), 269-278; J. W. Bennett, "New Techniques of Comedy in *AWW," ShQ,* XVIII (1967), 337-362; Brian Vickers, *The Artistry of Shakespeare's Prose* (1968); Roger Warren, "Why Does It End Well? Helena, Bertram, and the Sonnets," *ShS,* XXII (1969), 79-92.

STAGING Camb 187-189; Craig 805; Odell *passim;* Sprague 75; Trewin *passim.*

See also M. Clarke and R. Wood, *Sh at the Old Vic* (1954); T. Guthrie, "Sh at Stratford, Ontario," *ShS,* VIII (1955), 128-131; R. David, "Plays Pleasant and Plays Unpleasant," *ShS,* VIII (1955), 134-136; M. St. Clare Byrne, "The Sh Season at the Old Vic, 1958-59, and Stratford-upon-Avon, 1959," *ShQ,* X (1959), 556-567; *Shaw on Sh* (1961). There is an important commentary on staging in Price, above.

MEASURE FOR MEASURE

TEXT Alexander 188-191; Camb 97-111; Chambers 452-457; Greg 354-356; New Arden xi-xxxi; Sisson I, 74-87.

See also A. E. Thiselton, *Some Textual Notes on MM* (1901); R. H. Wilson, "The Mariana Plot of *MM,*" *PQ,* IX (1930), 341-350; *Complete Works of Sh,* ed. G. L. Kittredge (1936), 97-98; J. W. Lever, "The Date of *MM,*" *ShQ,* X (1959), 381-388; S. Musgrove, "Some Composite Scenes in *MM,*" *ShQ,* XV (1964), 67-74.

EDITIONS Camb, ed. A. Quiller-Couch and J. Dover Wilson (1922); Yale, ed. D. Harding (1954); Pelican, ed. R. C. Bald (1956); New Arden, ed. J. W. Lever (1965).

SOURCES W. Smith, "Two Commedie dell'Arte on the *MM* Story," *Romanic Rev.,* XIII (1922), 263-275; F. E. Budd, "Rouillet's *Philanira* and Whetstone's *Promos and Cassandra,*" *RES,* VI (1930), 31-48, and "Material for a Study of . . . *MM,*" *Revue de Littérature Comparée,* XI (1931), 711-736. The latter is a survey of (literary) crimes like that of Angelo before 1604. The conclusions are that the story used in *MM* was both popular and comic and not necessarily to be judged by the standards of real life. See also Thomas Izard, *George Whetstone* (1942), 53-79; R. H. Ball, "Cinthio's *Epitia* and *MM,*" *Elizabethan Studies . . . in Honor of G. F. Reynolds* (1945); Mary Lascelles, *Shakespeare's MM* (1953), 6-42; Muir (1957); Bullough (1957—), II, 399-530; A. F. Potts, *Sh and the Faerie Queene* (1958); Charles Prouty, "George Whetstone and the Sources of *MM,*" *ShQ,* XV (1964), 131-145.

CRITICISM There have been three principal issues studied: character, allegory, and the overriding question of believability. All three have greatly troubled the critics; the inability to interpret the play as either solely a drama or parable is matched only by the critics' inability to tolerate each other. In the words of Ernest Schanzer, no other play has called forth "such violent, eccentric, and mutually opposed responses."

Dr. Johnson stated that *MM* revealed Shakespeare's "knowledge of human nature," but he was the last for a considerable time to be so detached. Coleridge found the play "painful," "disgusting," and "horrible." Mrs. Jameson and a whole school of virginophiles began the adoration of Isabella, whom they endowed with biographical reality. The "melting tenderness" recognized in her by William Winter was exceeded as a critical referent only by the rhapsodies of Hamilton Mabie, who found her "stainless," "incorruptible," and "adorable." It was at

least a change from Mrs. Lennox, who had dusted off Isabella long
before as an affected prude and a "Vixen in her Virtue."

The first modern essay of real moment was the introduction to the
Camb edition by Sir Arthur Quiller-Couch. He found the play unclear
and unattractive; Isabella he dismissed as "something rancid in her
chastity." The essay is impatient and rather acid but exposes if it does
not solve the ambiguities of *MM*. A few years later W. H. Durham outlined the inconsistencies of generations of earlier critics in his "*MM* as
Measure for Critics," *Cal. Essays in Crit.* (1929). This constitutes an
anthology of the kind of opinion mentioned by Schanzer (above). Its
principal value lies in its exposure of the errors involved in applying
morality, sentiment, and even logic to a kind of art that resists them.
G. W. Knight's famous essay, "*MM* and the Gospels" is in *The Wheel of
Fire* (1930). This is the basis for all succeeding essays on the specifically
Christian meaning of the play. To condense Knight's thesis, he found
MM a New Testament parable which opposed love and mercy to justice.

A variety of issues was taken up in the next decade, and some of the
best essays were done then. W. W. Lawrence wrote an essay central to
the understanding of *MM* in his *Shakespeare's Problem Comedies*
(1931). He examines sources, alterations, conventions, and intellectual
history and concludes that the play is about human and not metaphysical issues. That it is improbable he grants, but not on its own terms. An
essay modifying some of Lawrence's views is H. Fairchild's "The Two
Angelo's," *SAB,* VI (1931), 53-59. In *The Mythical Sorrows of Sh*
(1934), C. J. Sisson launched a celebrated attack on the increasingly
common assumption that *MM* and other "dark" plays furnished information on the state of Shakespeare's mental health. J. M. Murry, *Sh*
(1936), has a good analysis of the nature of justice in this play. One of
the most admirable essays is R. W. Chambers' *The Jacobean Sh and MM*
(1937). There is mature consideration of the "problems" and accurate
historical analysis. Sh, Chambers writes, treats the "barbarous old story
of *Promos and Cassandra*" by "removing its morbid details, harmoniz-
ing its crudities, giving humanity and humour to its low characters,
turning it into a consistent tale of intercession for sin, repentance from
and forgiveness of crime." I find Chambers' work satisfying not because
it happens to have a moral conclusion but because it is well reasoned.
M. C. Bradbrook's "Authority, Truth and Justice in *MM*," *RES,* XVIII
(1941), 385-399, sees the play as the eventual union of Truth and
Justice, as in a Morality.

There are three noteworthy articles in *Scrutiny.* The first of these is
L. C. Knights' "The Ambiguity of *MM*," X (1942), 222-233, which
formulates the play's contrasts as those of natural impulse and liberty

versus self-restraint and law. The mainspring of the action is "sexual instinct." The play is viewed as essentially cynical, a vehicle for the author's own disgust. F. R. Leavis replied to this in "The Greatness of *MM*," *ibid.*, 234-247. He maintained that the play was distinguished by a high valuation of life and morality. D. A. Traversi, "*MM*," *ibid.*, XI (1943), 40-58, analyzed the language, which he found characterized by intense concentration on the meaning of simple words. The play was for Traversi a balance between the themes of dissolution and fertility. An extreme theological interpretation is that of R. Battenhouse, "*MM* and Christian Doctrine of the Atonement," *PMLA*, LXI (1946), 1029-1059. Perhaps too much pity is wasted on Angelo—his debates with himself are called the "crucifixion of a soul"—by W. Dodds in "The Character of Angelo in *MM*," *MLR*, XLI (1946), 246-255. Another extreme of religious interpretation is D. J. McGinn's "The Precise Angelo," *AMS* (1948). This claims, wrongly I think, that the play shows "Shakespeare's sympathy with Roman Catholic institutions" and his hostility to Calvinism. E. M. W. Tillyard, *Shakespeare's Problem Plays* (1949), believes that Sh was defeated by his material. The play falls into two halves which do not match: the display of human passions in action and the rather unlikely allegorical solution. A good discussion of "The Renaissance Background of *MM*" is that of E. Pope, *ShS*, II (1949), 66-82.

W. Sypher, "Sh as Casuist," *Sew*, LVIII (1950), 262-280, has a theory of double valences—the characters represent more than one quality. The Duke, for example, seems to stand for both "comic irresponsibility and ethical responsibility." The essay is good on the whole but infiltrated by modish terminology. Sypher believes that the play represents the baroque form of art with its unresolved stresses. An important review of studies is C. Leech's "The 'Meaning' of *MM*," *ShS*, III (1950), 66-73. He summarizes that the play has "a morality-framework, much incidental satire, a deep probing into the springs of action, a passionate sympathy with the unfortunate and hard-pressed." R. M. Smith, "Interpretations of *MM*," *ShQ*, I (1950), 208-218, evaluates the play's critical history and outlines its major problems. W. Empson's "Sense in *MM*," is in *The Structure of Complex Words* (1951). The word "sense" reflects the play's ambiguities: sensuality and sensibility are its alternative meanings. V. K. Whitaker's "Philosophy and Romance" in *The Seventeenth Century* (1951) asserts that the source could not bear the burden of philosophy placed on it by Sh. A thoughtful and somber essay on law and human nature is in A. Sewell's *Character and Society in Sh* (1951). The fullest study of the play is M. Lascelles' *MM* (1953). The book has many virtues, not the least of them its examination of sources and differing interpretations. In a scene-by-scene analysis Lascelles demonstrates the fluctuations of characters who are thoroughly believable and consistent. The play seems to her to be centered on "the self-knowledge which is the basis of integrity." To that point all its actions tend.

N. Coghill, "Comic Form in *MM," ShS,* VIII (1955), 14-26, emphasizes the evident joy of the ending, which triumphs over sexual anguish, treachery, and injustice. D. L. Stevenson's "Design and Structure in *MM," ELH,* XXIII (1956), 256-278, surveys the critics: "Isabella's chastity cannot at once be Griselda-like and archaic to Lawrence, destroy the plot for Tillyard, and rescue it for Battenhouse." He observes that the play is not a homily and argues convincingly that it dramatizes rather than evaluates comic "natural guiltiness." R. Ornstein, "The Human Comedy," *UKCR,* XXIV (1957), 15-22, finds that it is the critics who impose moral dilemmas that the characters refuse to recognize. The play about "a comic world of little men dwarfed by the minor catastrophes their frailties create" ends upon a simple revelation: with a little more suffering, a little more wisdom has been gained. F. Fergusson, *The Human Image in Dramatic Literature* (1957), has an intelligent analysis of "nature" versus "institutions." The essay by E. Schanzer in *The Problem Plays of Sh* (1963) concludes that the public concern of the play is with the nature of justice and the private concern is the nature of Isabella's choice. While the private one is treated problematically the public one is not; both, however, are connected by a hope for something more humane than Law alone.

The New Arden edition of J. W. Lever has the customary apparatus of textual, source, and critical study. It offers in addition a good interpretation of *MM* as a drama of ideas, and should be read as a concise summary of much of the foregoing material. A good piece by Robert Hunter is in his *Sh and the Comedy of Forgiveness* (1965). Hunter joins the anti- ✗ theological school and gives a creditable account of the play as a secular romance. An important book—David L. Stevenson's *The Achievement of Shakespeare's MM* (1966)—goes over the hostile critics pretty thoroughly. There is an intelligent account of the theology and of the play's sexual content. Yet another antitheological essay of importance is Marco Mincoff's "*MM*: A Question of Approach," *ShStud,* II (1966), 141-152. Mincoff describes Shakespeare's deviation from his sources and suggests that our moralization of this play springs not from its actuality but from structural flaws. The occasion of the play is studied by Josephine W. Bennett, *MM as Royal Entertainment* (1966). The thesis, that *MM* is to be seen strictly in relationship to its courtly audience, has won very little assent. For a collection of material on this play see R. Soellner and S. Bertsche, *MM, Text, Source and Criticism* (1966). R. Berman's "Sh and the Law," *ShQ,* XVIII (1967), 141-150, attempts to rebut the sentimentalized Christianity so persistently attributed to this play.

The following study the social issues bearing on the play. D. Harding,

"Elizabethan Betrothals and *MM,*" *JEGP,* XLIX (1950), 139-158; E. Schanzer, "The Marriage-Contracts in *MM,*" *ShS,* XIII (1960), 81-89; W. Dunkel, "Law and Equity in *MM,*" *ShQ,* XIII (1962), 275-285; J. Dickinson, "Renaissance Equity and *MM,*" *ibid.,* 287-297; S. Nagarajan, "*MM* and Elizabethan Betrothals," *ShQ,* XIV (1963), 115-119.

Further reading: C. J. Reimer, *Der Begriff der Gnade in Shakespeares MM* (1937); W. H. Durham, "What Art Thou, Angelo?" *Studies in the Comic* (1941); J. C. Maxwell, "*MM*: A Footnote to Recent Criticism," *Downside Rev.,* LXV (1947), 45-59; T. M. Parrott, *Shakespearean Comedy* (1949); M. Kreiger, "*MM* and Elizabethan Comedy," *PMLA,* LXVI (1951), 775-784; E. Sehrt, *Vergebung und Gnade bei Sh* (1952); H. S. Wilson, "Action and Symbol in *MM* and *Tem,*" *ShQ,* IV (1953), 375-384; P. Siegel, "*MM*: The Significance of the Title," *ShQ,* IV (1953), 317-320; J. R. Brown, "The Interpretation of Shakespeare's Comedies: 1900-1953," *ShS,* VIII (1955), 1-13; W. Sypher, *Four Stages of Renaissance Style* (1956); W. W. Lawrence, "*MM* and Lucio," *ShQ,* IX (1958), 443-453; D. L. Stevenson, "The Role of James I in Shakespeare's *MM,*" *ELH,* XXVI (1959), 188-208; R. Ornstein, *The Moral Vision of Jacobean Tragedy* (1960) and *Discussions of Shakespeare's Problem Comedies* (1961); A. Caputi, "Scenic Design in *MM,*" *JEGP,* LX (1961), 423-434; R. Southall, "*MM* and the Protestant Ethic," *EC,* XI (1961), 11-33.

STAGING Camb 160-165; Craig 834; Odell *passim*; Sprague 64-66; Trewin *passim.*

See also *Hazlitt on Theatre* (1895); R. David, "Shakespeare's Comedies and the Modern Stage," *ShS,* IV (1951), 135-138; M. Webster, *Sh Without Tears* (1955); W. Merchant, *Sh and the Artist* (1959); ed. F. Fergusson and C. J. Sisson (1961); R. Hethmon, "The Theatrical Design of *MM,*" *Drama Survey,* I (1962), 261-277. See also the remarks on staging in Josephine W. Bennett, *MM as Royal Entertainment* (1966).

OTHELLO

TEXT Alexander 162-166; Camb 121-135; Chambers 457-463; Greg 357-374; New Arden xv-xlv, 199-237; Sisson II, 245-258.

See also K. Cameron's two articles on the text in *PMLA,* XLVII (1932), 671-683, and XLIX (1934), 762-796; C. Hinman, "Principles Governing the Use of Variant Spellings as Evidence of Alternate Setting by Two Compositors," *Lib,* XXI (1940), 78-94, and "The 'Copy' for the Second Quarto of *Oth,*" *AMS* (1948); A. Walker, "The 1622 Quarto and the First Folio Texts of *Oth,*" *ShS,* V (1952), 16-24, and *Textual Problems of the First Folio* (1953). See also Laurence Ross, "Three Readings in the Text of *Oth,*" *ShQ,* XIV (1963), 121-126; Nevill Coghill, *Shakespeare's Professional Skills* (1964); E. A. J. Honigmann, *The Stability of Shakespeare's Text* (1965); K. Muir, "The Text of *Oth,*" *ShStud,* I (1965), 227-239.

EDITIONS *NV,* ed. H. H. Furness (1886); ed. G. L. Kittredge (1941); Camb, ed. J. Dover Wilson and A. Walker (1957); Yale, ed. T. Brooke and L. Mason (1957); New Arden, ed. M. R. Ridley (1958); Pelican, ed. G. E. Bentley (1958).

SOURCES A. Krappe, "A Byzantine Source of Shakespeare's *Oth,*" *MLN,* XXXIX (1924), 156-161; W. Bullock, "The Sources of *Oth,*" *MLN,* XL (1925), 226-228; M. Praz, *Machiavelli and the Elizabethans* (1928); W. Wokatsch, "Zur Quelle des *Oth* und zu Shakespeares Kenntnis des Italienischen," *Archiv,* CLX (1932), 118-119; J. M. French, "Othello Among the Anthropophagi," *PMLA,* XLIX (1934), 807-809; T. W. Baldwin, "A Note upon Shakespeare's Use of Pliny," *Parrott Presentation Volume* (1935); T. Stroup, "Shakespeare's Use of a Travel-Book Commonplace," *PQ,* XVII (1938), 351-358; E. E. Stoll, "Source and Motive in *Mac* and *Oth,*" *RES,* XIX (1943), 25-32; J. Draper, "Sh and the Doge of Venice," *JEGP,* XLVI (1947), 75-81; N. Allen, "The Source of *Oth,*" *Delaware Notes,* XXI (1948), 71-96; C. Camden, "Iago on Women," *JEGP,* XLVIII (1949), 57-71; K. Muir, "Sh and Florio," *NQ,* CXCVII (1952), 494-495, and "Holland's Pliny and *Oth,*" *ibid.,* CXCVIII (1953), 513-514; Muir (1957); Bullough (1957–), forthcoming volume; B. Spivack, *Sh and the Allegory of Evil* (1958).

CRITICISM The *NV* offers a selection of early criticism. The following important books survey more recent work: R. Heilman, *Magic in the Web* (1956); M. Rosenberg, *The Masks of Oth* (1961); L. Dean, *A Casebook on Oth* (1961).

In 1693 Thomas Rymer published *A Short View of Tragedy.* This is an

angry, amusing, and interesting piece which claims that *Oth* is a bloody
farce. Perhaps it tells us more about neoclassical criticism than about
Sh, but the reader will want to see a full-scale application—one might
say a remorseless one—of the laws of probability and morality to art.
Dr. Johnson and Coleridge have valuable essays. Among the most famous of the latter's critiques is that of the "motiveless" Iago, the man
whose hatred requires only an object and not a reason. Some distinguished nineteenth-century opinion on *Oth* may be found in R.
Moulton, *Sh as a Dramatic Artist* (1892), and in Swinburne's *Three
Plays of Sh* (1909).

One of the best studies of character is in A. C. Bradley's *Shakespearean
Tragedy* (1904). Bradley's remarks on intrigue and accident, on the
theme of sexual jealousy, and on the fall of a great nature are all worth
reading. E. E. Stoll, *Oth* (1915), sets forth the principle elaborated by
his later studies: the play is built around paradoxes of character and
structure that are logically unsatisfactory. A distinguished essay is in
Granville-Barker (1946). This long study covers character, dialogue,
staging, and sources. It is the author's contention that the play is a
"conflict of being"—what he calls the "fortress of good" is attacked
and brought down stone by stone. Perhaps most valuable is the scene-
by-scene analysis. H. B. Charlton's *Shakespearian Tragedy* (1948) is
valuable for its comparisons of *Oth* and the story of Cinthio from
which it derives. R. Flatter, *The Moor of Venice* (1950), interprets the
play with perhaps too much emphasis on the passion of Iago and the
very dubious joy of the hero at his death. C. Leech, *Shakespeare's
Tragedies* (1950), compares this tragedy of sexual jealousy with other
seventeenth-century tragedies. Three books devoted entirely to this
play are G. R. Elliott, *Flaming Minister* (1953), R. Heilman, *Magic in
the Web* (1956), and M. Rosenberg, *The Masks of Oth* (1961). The first
of these examines the play very nearly line-by-line and has the advan-
tages which accrue to this kind of study. It tends, however, to impose
the single-minded idea that pride is the only motivating force. Heilman's
book is the best introductory study. There is a good account of character revealed in language, of theme, and of character itself. Heilman suggests that symbolic oppositions like those of harmony and chaos, darkness and light reinforce the conflict of characters. Rosenberg has an
illuminating study of staging and criticism and some pertinent remarks
on the principals.

B. Stirling, *Unity in Shakespearian Tragedy* (1956), studies "Reputation" and finds it dominant in the play. It has two forms: an objective
regard for esteem and honor and an "inverted, egoistic" form which
leads eventually to the ritual murder of Desdemona. H. S. Wilson, *On
the Design of Shakespearian Tragedy* (1957), finds *Oth* the most painful of the tragedies. Wilson suggests that "the Christian significance of

the action" is the cause of the play's greatness, for Othello, in his inadequacy, "typifies the human situation, as the Christian sees it." Many critics, including myself, disagree. Two worthwhile essays are in the Camb (1957) and New Arden (1958) editions. The latter has a helpful section on "double-time."

Othello himself has been the subject of interpretation so divergent as to make the common reader despair. E. E. Stoll in *Oth* (1915) attempted to demolish the nineteenth-century opinion of the tragic grandeur and spirituality of the hero. He advanced the idea that Othello has in fact no psychology to speak of; the play is a system of dramatic illusions which account for those violent and inconsistent changes in character that no psychology can clarify. Stoll's reassertions of his position are in *Art and Artifice in Sh* (1933); "An *Oth* All-too Modern," *ELH*, XIII (1946), 46-58; and "Another *Oth* Too Modern," *AMS* (1948). A notable attack on the hero was T. S. Eliot's "Sh and the Stoicism of Seneca" (1927). Eliot accused Othello of *Bovarysme* before his suicide: self-dramatization and self-pity. His essay sometimes goes under the heading of "the hero cheering himself up." The weak Othello was replaced by the sensual Othello in D. A. Traversi's *An Approach to Sh* (1938). Traversi was countered by the "magnificent human being" conception of the hero of T. Spencer in *Sh and the Nature of Man* (1942). B. Stirling, "Psychology in *Oth*," *SAB*, XIX (1944), 135-144, defended the mind of the Moor, arguing that he clearly showed emotional collapse, spiritual chaos, and a believable state of passionate irrationality. L. Kirschbaum, "The Modern Othello," *ELH*, II (1944), 283-296, attacks Stoll's condemnation and points out that the question of the hero's character involves the "close interweaving of great man, mere man, and base man that makes of Othello the peculiarly powerful and mysterious figure he is." H. B. Charlton, *Shakespearian Tragedy* (1948), sets forth the "primitive" theory: "the elements of moral manhood are simple and unadulterated in him, and they exhibit themselves in their primitive purity and strength." He is simpler than civilized man in his responses. A summation of the hero's weaknesses is in Heilman (above): "the unripeness of his sense of his own past, the flair for the picturesque and the histrionic, the stoicism of the flesh unmatched by an endurance of spirit, the capacity for occasional self-deception, the hypersensitivity to challenge, the inexperience in giving. . . ."

A famous attack is that of F. R. Leavis, "Diabolic Intellect and the Noble Hero," *The Common Pursuit* (1952). Leavis' position is that Othello is an egotist whose nature was not shaped by Iago but merely stimulated by him. H. Gardner, *The Noble Moor* (1955), reviews critics hostile to the hero and suggests that they are so because of modern distaste for the heroic. This is a first-rate study of the play as a whole. A. Gerard, " 'Egregiously an Ass': the Dark Side of the Moor," *ShS*, X

(1957), 98-106, has a good analysis of the schools of criticism. He
supplies his own answer to the matter—Othello is a pagan and barbarian
easily aroused to wrath. J. Holloway, *The Story of the Night* (1961),
attempts to refute conceptions of the "weak" Othello.

Iago has been the subject of much exploration. Many of the studies
cited have a good deal to say about him, and those by Rosenberg,
Traversi, and Granville-Barker might be noted. Coleridge's proposal that
he was a form of the Satanic incarnate has convinced an army of readers. Others, like Leavis, believe that he is only an adjunct to the thoroughly human failings of the Moor. A. C. Bradley, *Shakespearean
Tragedy* (1904), argued, I think with reason, that Iago was an artist of
evil: "his action is a plot . . . and in the conception and execution of it
he experiences the tension and joy of artistic creation." J. Draper,
"Honest Iago," *PMLA*, XLVI (1931), 724-737, argued, not very fruit-
fully, that Iago did indeed have a motive: he takes seriously Iago's fears
of cuckoldry. S. Tannenbaum, "The Wronged Iago," *SAB*, XII (1937),
57-62, notes that illicit sexuality permeates the play and that it is
always a possibility in the human relationships suggested. Iago is himself jealous, and possibly with reason. Worth examining are J.
McCloskey, "The Motivation of Iago," *CE*, III (1941), 25-30, and the
more general "The Elizabethan Malcontent" by T. Spencer in *AMS*
(1948). B. Spivack's *Sh and the Allegory of Evil* (1958) is a thorough
study of Iago and his antecedents on the Tudor stage. Rosenberg takes
account of past criticisms.

For collections on this play see Leonard Dean, *A Casebook on Oth*
(1961); Laurence Lerner, *Shakespeare's Tragedies* (1963); *ShS*, XXI
(1968) which is largely devoted to *Oth*. An important review of
research is Helen Gardner's retrospective of twentieth-century criticism
in the latter. In that same volume see also Ned Allen's valuable piece on
composition and "double time."

Some critics believe that Othello suffers damnation, and urge us to
interpret the text as a Christian rather than as a secular drama. A series
of essays hostile to this view is Robert West's *Sh and the Outer Mystery*
(1968). West does a good job of separating the supernatural from the
theatrical.

There are a number of valuable studies of language and theme. G. W.
Knight, *The Wheel of Fire* (1930), contains a famous essay on "The
Oth Music." Knight analyzes the transformation of Othello as it is
revealed in his rhetoric. There is perhaps too much of the metaphysical
in this essay, but its remarks on style and meaning are seminal. Spurgeon (1935) discusses the imagery of "animals in action, preying upon
one another." See also M. Morozov, "The Individualization of Shake-

speare's Characters Through Imagery," *ShS,* II (1949), 83-90; P.
Jorgensen, *"Honesty* in *Oth," SP,* XLVII (1950), 557-567; W. Empson,
The Structure of Complex Words (1951); Clemen (1951); Evans (1952);
S. L. Bethell, "Shakespeare's Imagery: The Diabolic Images in *Oth,"*
ShS, V (1952), 62-80; W. Nowottny, "Justice and Love in *Oth," UTQ,*
XXI (1952), 330-344; Brian Vickers, *The Artistry of Shakespeare's
Prose* (1968).

Further reading: M. Prior, "Character in Relation to Action in *Oth,"*
MP, XLIV (1947), 225-237; G. Bonnard, "Are Othello and Desdemona
Innocent or Guilty?" *ES,* XXX (1949), 175-184; J. I. M. Stewart, *Character and Motive in Sh* (1949); D. A. Traversi, "Othello," *The Wind and
the Rain,* VI (1950), 248-269; K. Burke, *"Oth*: An Essay to Illustrate
a Method," *HR,* IV (1951), 165-203; K. Muir, "The Jealousy of Iago,"
English Misc., II (1951), 65-83; J. Draper, *The Oth of Shakespeare's
Audience* (1952); J. Moore, "Othello, Iago, and Cassio as Soldiers," *PQ,*
XXXI (1952), 189-194; J. Money, "Othello's 'It is the cause . . .' " *ShS,*
VI (1953), 94-105; P. Siegel, "The Damnation of Othello," *PMLA,*
LXVIII (1953), 1068-1078; S. Barnet, "Some Limitations of a Christian Approach to Sh," *ELH,* XXII (1955), 81-92; F. Dickey, *Not Wisely
But Too Well* (1957); R. Langbaum, *The Poetry of Experience* (1957);
P. Alexander, "Under Which King, Bezonian," *Elizabethan and Jacobean
Studies Presented to F. P. Wilson* (1959); W. Rosen, *Sh and the Craft of
Tragedy* (1960); M. Mack, "The Jacobean Sh," *Jacobean Theatre*
(1960); J. Lawlor, *The Tragic Sense in Sh* (1960); J. K. Walton,
"Strength's Abundance," *RES,* XI (1960), 8-17; J. Bayley, *The Characters of Love* (1960); M. Mack, "Engagement and Detachment in Shakespeare's Plays," *Essays on Sh . . . in Honor of Hardin Craig* (1962);
Eldred Jones, *Othello's Countrymen* (1965).

STAGING   Camb lvii-lxix; Craig 946; Odell *passim;* Sprague 185-223;
Trewin *passim.*

See also W. Winter, *Sh on the Stage* (1911); *Stanislavsky Produces Oth*
(1948); R. De Smet, *"Oth* in Paris and Brussels," *ShS,* III (1950), 98-
106; A. C. Sprague, *Shakespearian Players and Performances* (1953);
M. Webster, *Sh Without Tears* (1955); B. Alden, "Edwin Forrest's
Othello," *Theatre Annual,* XIV (1956), 3-18; R. David, "Drams of Eale,"
ShS, X (1957), 131-134; D. Seltzer, "Elizabethan Acting in *Oth," ShQ,*
X (1959), 201-210. There are good essays on staging in Granville-Barker,
Rosenberg, and Dean (above). See also G. Wilson Knight, *Sh in Production* (1964); Kenneth Tynan, *Oth: The National Theatre Production*
(1967); Carol Carlisle, *Sh from the Greenroom* (1969). There are valuable plates, reviews, and criticism in Tynan's edition.

BIBLIOGRAPHY   S. A. Tannenbaum, *Shakespeare's Oth: A Concise
Bibliography* (1943).

KING LEAR

TEXT Alexander 166-169; Camb vii-xiv, 122-139; Chambers 463-470; Greg 375-388; New Arden xv-xx; Sisson II, 230-244.

See also M. Doran, *The Text of Lear* (1931); J. Q. Adams, "The Quarto of *Lear* and Shorthand," *MP*, XXXI (1933), 135-163; B. A. P. Van Dam, *The Text of Shakespeare's Lear* (1935); W. W. Greg, *The Variants in the First Quarto of Lear* (1940); L. Kirschbaum, *The True Text of Lear* (1945); S. A. Small, "The *Lear* Quarto," *SAB,* XXI (1946), 177-180; F. Bowers, "An Examination of the Method of Proof Correction in *Lear,*" *Lib,* II (1947), 20-44, and "*Lear* (New Arden Sh)," *ShQ,* IV (1953), 471-477; A. Walker, *Textual Problems of the First Folio* (1953); P. Williams, "Two Problems in the Folio Text of *Lear,*" *ShQ,* IV (1953), 451-460; A. S. Cairncross, "The Quartos and the Folio Text of *Lear,*" *RES,* VI (1955), 252-258; H. Craig, *A New Look at Shakespeare's Quartos* (1961); E. A. J. Honigmann, *The Stability of Shakespeare's Text* (1965).

EDITIONS *NV,* ed. H. H. Furness (1880); ed. G. L. Kittredge (1940); ed. G. I. Duthie (1949); New Arden, ed. K. Muir (1952); Pelican, ed. A. Harbage (1958); Camb, ed. J. Dover Wilson and G. I. Duthie (1960); ed. G. B. Harrison and R. McDonnell (1962).

SOURCES W. Perrett, *The Story of King Lear from Geoffrey of Monmouth to Sh* (1904); W. B. Henderson, "Montaigne's *Apologie of Raymond Sebond,* and *Lear,*" *SAB,* XIV (1939), 209-225, and *ibid.,* XV (1940), 40-54; W. W. Greg, "The Date of *Lear* and Shakespeare's Use of Earlier Versions of the Story," *Lib,* XX (1940), 377-400; R. Perkinson, "Shakespeare's Revision of the Lear Story," *PQ,* XXII (1943), 315-329; F. Pyle, "*TN, Lear* and *Arcadia,*" *MLR,* XLIII (1948), 449-455; R. A. Law, "Holinshed's Leir Story and Shakespeare's," *SP,* XLVII (1950), 42-50, and "*King Leir* and *Lear,*" *Studies in Honor of T. W. Baldwin* (1958); I. Ribner, "Sidney's *Arcadia* and the Structure of *Lear,*" *Studia Neophilologica,* XXIV (1952), 63-68, and "Sh and Legendary History," *ShQ,* VII (1956), 47-52; Muir (1957); Bullough (1957–), forthcoming volume.

CRITICISM The general criticism of this play depends heavily on the gifted critics of earlier times, and the reader can do no better than go directly to them. Dr. Johnson's admirable *Notes* are fundamental. See also Hazlitt, Coleridge, Charles Lamb's "On Shakespeare's Tragedies," *Complete Works* (1875), and Swinburne's *A Study of Sh* (1880). Other worthwhile studies of the nineteenth century are H. N. Hudson's *Lectures on Sh* (1848), E. Dowden's *Sh: A Critical Study* (1875), and R.

Moulton's *Sh as a Dramatic Artist* (1885). A deservedly familiar study
is A. C. Bradley, *Shakespearean Tragedy* (1904), which sets a high standard in the interpretation of character. Leo Tolstoy's famous attack on
Lear was printed in *The Fortnightly Review* (1906).

The *NV* has a long collection of critical opinion of the eighteenth and
nineteenth centuries. *ShS* for 1960 is devoted to *Lear*. A collection of
critical excerpts is H. Bonheim's *The Lear Perplex* (1960). The essays in
the latter cover linguistic, psychological, and political matters; many of
them are, in their complete form, quite important. This sampler, however, is wider than it is deep and does not furnish a coherent sense of
each thesis. See also *KL: Text, Sources, Criticisms,* ed. G. B. Harrison
and R. McDonnell (1962).

H. Craig, "The Ethics of *Lear,*" *PQ,* IV (1925), 97-109, suggests that
the play shares the ethical views of *The Republic* and the *Nichomachean
Ethics.* One of the first studies of the symbolism of *Lear* was G. W.
Knight's *The Wheel of Fire* (1930). The concept of the comedy of the
grotesque is important; of equal value is Knight's study of the "inscru-
table, enigmatic" atmosphere. He suggests that *Lear* is a play of "creative suffering," a kind of purgation for its participants. His opinion that
the play is regenerative has been highly influential and, I think, pernicious. It gives too easy a solution for the problems the play raises—and
it has been abused by the critics who accept it.

The essays of M. Van Doren in *Sh* (1939), T. Spencer in *Sh and the
Nature of Man* (1942), and Granville-Barker (1946) are valuable.
Spencer writes of *Lear* as a study of relationship between children and
parents, men and the state, man and the gods. Granville-Barker is particularly strong on dialogue, staging, and minor characters. G. Bickersteth,
The Golden World of Lear (1946), discusses Nature in its material,
human, and divine aspects. A full study of language and themes is R.
Heilman's *This Great Stage* (1948). Heilman considers such topics as
Age, Law, Justice, and Reason in Madness; there is an excellent analysis
of "Nature" and its operation. It is essential to compare this book with
the essay it provoked by W. Keast, "Imagery and Meaning in the Interpretation of *Lear,*" *MP,* XLVII (1949), 45-64. H. B. Charlton, *Shakespearian Tragedy* (1948), has an unusual insight into the primitiveness
of the realm and its inhabitants. It is this, he claims, that maintains a
sense of the nearness of man and beast. The line dividing them is thin;
it exists within man's own consciousness. J. Danby, *Shakespeare's
Doctrine of Nature* (1949), distinguishes the elements of reasonable and
irrational "Nature." He is especially concerned with the conflict of
communal values and the anarchic individual will. There is a very good
chapter on Edmund, who represents the latter. Christianity and pagan-
ism are considered by J. C. Maxwell in "The Technique of Invocation in

Lear," MLR, XLV (1950), 142-147. C. Leech, *Shakespeare's Tragedies*
(1950), examines *Lear* in the context of other plays by Sh and his contemporaries. George Orwell's "Lear, Tolstoy and the Fool" is reprinted
in *Shooting an Elephant* (1950). The "brutal reality" of life in *Lear* is
the subject of D. G. James, *The Dream of Learning* (1951). James declares that the play gives the initiative to evil but finally allows it to be
overcome by the power of endurance of the good.

J. V. Cunningham, *Woe and Wonder* (1951), writes of the metaphor of
ripeness and death. *Lear* as a tragedy of old age is treated by L. Campbell in *Shakespeare's Tragic Heroes* (1952). In a series of influential
essays in *Scrutiny,* D. A. Traversi covered character, symbol, and
themes. His three articles—XIX (1953), 43-64, 126-142, and 206-230—
center on the symbolism of the storm, which is a metaphor for the
force of tragic insight in the mind of the king. W. Nowottny, "Lear's
Questions," *ShS,* X (1957), 90-97, discusses the exploitation of ambiv-
alent terms; they reveal the "subtle interplay between the flesh as mere
flesh and the qualities the flesh embodies." All the questions, it is suggested, lead up to the great query of the Renaissance, "What is Man?"

H. S. Wilson, *On the Design of Shakespearian Tragedy* (1957), finds the
ultimate value of *Lear* to be the power of human love. He likens the
king to Oedipus, who is also brought from human weakness, through
suffering, to a state of unearthly insight. Perhaps Wilson underestimates
the power of hatred in this play and the limitations of Lear's insights.
Some Shakespearean Themes (1959) by L. C. Knights considers *Lear*
"a stage in the emergence of the modern European consciousness"—it
opposes the view of the orderly disposition of "Nature" with the concept of impersonal forces. The work on *Lear* and the other great tragedies that has been most visible recently is J. Holloway's *The Story of
the Night* (1961). This play is connected to Shakespeare's general concern with the special class of the alienated. Holloway finds that *Lear* is
an exemplar of the power of chaos, a power as natural to the Elizabethan world picture as that of order. The examination of the text is
good, but the study is based on anthropological assumptions which do
not fully convince. R. Fraser's *Shakespeare's Poetics in Relation to Lear*
(1962) interprets the play in the light of Elizabethan emblems and
offers a good deal of information on the ethical background.

Jan Kott's *Shakespeare Our Contemporary* (1964) persuaded many
readers of the resemblance of *KL* and Beckett's *Endgame.* Kott saw in
this play many of the philosophical predicaments and absurdities of the
twentieth century, and modernized it accordingly. I am generally hostile to this interpretation and have found some justification in the review by Frank Kermode in *New York Review of Books,* September 24,
1964: as he puts it, Kott shows principally "a weakness for striking but

improbable historical parallels." Another negative review by a responsible critic is Harry Levin's "Reducing Sh," *YR,* LIV (Winter 1965),
261-265 which deplores the ruthless working of this play into fake
existentialism. See Alfred Harbage, *Conceptions of Sh* (1966). Maynard
Mack's *KL in Our Time* (1965) is an important study of structure and
psychology. Especially to be noted is the chapter on "Archetype,
Parable, and Vision." There are valuable remarks on staging. Mack's
central issue is the importance this play has achieved for moderns. See
also L. C. Knights, *Further Explorations* (1965). Simply as a caution I
list Grigori Kozintsev's *Sh: Time and Conscience* (1966). This is a piece
betraying the customary dishonesty of Communist literary criticism. It
attempts to convert *KL* into propaganda against scholasticism and
feudal capitalism.

The number of special studies is large; the following have proved their
importance, one hopes, by attracting good critical minds and will lead
the reader to awareness of the play's complexity. R. W. Chambers,
"Lear," Glasgow Univ. Pub., LIV (1940), 20-52, is a luminous study of
the play and its analogues. The difficult issue of the Christian content
of *Lear* was treated by O. J. Campbell, "The Salvation of Lear," *ELH,*
XV (1948), 93-109. He claimed, as many critics do still, that the play is
purgatorial and that the king dies "at peace" with his condition. There
is an important article on this matter by S. Barnet, "Some Limitations
of a Christian Approach to Sh," *ELH,* XXII (1955), 81-92. Barnet
argued that Christianity must not be forced on this or any other Shakespearean play. Campbell's view was reiterated by I. Ribner, "The Gods
Are Just," *TDR,* II (1958), 34-54. R. Sewall's *The Vision of Tragedy*
(1959) takes the view that while the king undergoes a purgatorial suffering he is by no means redeemed by any form of Grace. He grows in
knowledge and ends in death—in that judgment both good and evil are
assimilated. This view appears to me a very sensible one. B. Everett's
"The New *Lear,*" *CQ,* II (1960), 325-339, is dead set against the Christian interpretations; it set off a debate in succeeding pages of *CQ.*
William Elton's *KL and the Gods* (1966) should conclude the war of
religion. He intelligently attacks the Christian interpretation of the play
and, I think, defeats it. He finds Providence to be inoperative, and
denies that the play is a paradigm of religious enlightenment and
regeneration.

R. C. Bald, " 'Thou, Nature, Art My Goddess': Edmund and Renaissance Free-Thought," *AMS* (1948), studies rationalism in *Lear.* Freud's
"The Theme of the Three Caskets," *Complete Works,* XII (1958), adds
to our knowledge of the play's mythic background. A. Sewell, *Character and Society in Sh* (1951), determines that tragic conflict is seen in
this play as inherent in society itself. Nowhere else is man "so certainly
exhibited as a member of all organic creation, and of the elemental

powers." An indispensable volume of essays is *Tragedy: Modern Essays in Criticism* (1963), ed. L. Michel and R. Sewall.

A good deal of critical energy has been applied to studies of the fool and folly in *Lear,* and there is no better place to begin than in E. Welsford's *The Fool* (1935). This historical and critical analysis of the fool in Western life and art offers some sound and very influential ideas about the identity of folly and innocence, madness and actual reason. Wisdom clothed in folly is the subject of R. Goldsmith, *Wise Fools in Sh* (1955). W. Empson's *The Structure of Complex Words* (1951) is an excellent study of word and metaphor. The chapter "Fool in Lear" studies the surprisingly manifold connotations of the term. C. French, "Shakespeare's 'Folly': *Lear," ShQ,* X (1959), 523-529, discusses the conception of Christian innocence in folly. The related subject of madness has been often treated; it is discussed in passing in many of the works noted above. Some special studies include A. Pauncz, "Psychopathology of Shakespeare's *Lear," Amer. Imago,* IX (1952), 57-78; S. Kahn, " 'Enter Lear Mad,' " *ShQ,* VIII (1957), 311-329; N. MacLean, "Episode, Scene, Speech and Word: the Madness of Lear," *Critics and Criticism* (1952); J. Donnelly, "Incest, Ingratitude, and Insanity: Aspects of the Psychopathology of *Lear," Psycho-Analytic Rev.,* XL (1953), 149-155. There is a good deal more Freud than fact in the studies of Pauncz and Donnelly.

The language is studied in the following: G. W. Knight, *The Wheel of Fire* (1930); Knight, *The Shakespearian Tempest* (1932); P. Kreider, "Gloucester's Eyes," *SAB,* VIII (1933), 121-132; Spurgeon (1935); G. Kernodle, "The Symphonic Form of *Lear," Elizabethan Studies . . . in Honor of G. F. Reynolds* (1945); J. C. Ransom, "On Shakespeare's Language," *Sew,* LV (1947), 181-198; R. Heilman, *This Great Stage* (1948); Keast (above); Clemen (1951); Empson (above); Evans (1952); Traversi (above); P. Jorgensen, "Much Ado About *Nothing," ShQ,* V (1954), 287-295; T. Greenfield, "The Clothing Motif in *Lear," ShQ,* V (1954), 281-286; Brian Vickers, *The Artistry of Shakespeare's Prose* (1968).

Further reading: J. Bransom, *The Tragedy of Lear* (1934); W. Farnham, *The Medieval Heritage of Elizabethan Tragedy* (1936); J. M. Murry, *Sh* (1936); J. Draper, "The Old Age of King Lear," *JEGP,* XXXIX (1940), 527-540; J. Stewart, "The Blinding of Gloster," *RES,* XXI (1945), 264-270; E. Muir, "The Politics of *Lear," Essays on Literature and Society* (1949); J. Lothian, *Lear: A Tragic Reading of Life* (1949); G. Williams, "The Poetry of the Storm in *Lear," ShQ,* II (1951), 57-71; L. C. Knights, *Shakespeare's Politics* (1957); H. Jaffa, "The Limits of Politics," *Amer. Political Science Rev.,* LI (1957), 405-427; J. Barish and M. Waingrow, " 'Service' in *Lear," ShQ,* IX (1958), 347-355; B. Spivack,

Sh and the Allegory of Evil (1958); W. Frost, "Shakespeare's Rituals and the Opening of *Lear,*" *HR,* X (1958), 577-585; H. MacLean, "Disguise in *Lear,*" *ShQ,* XI (1960), 49-54; R. West, "Sex and Pessimism in *Lear,*" *ShQ,* XI (1960), 55-60; I. Ribner, *Patterns in Shakespearian Tragedy* (1960); M. Mack, "The Jacobean Sh," *Jacobean Theatre* (1960); Alfred Harbage, "The Fierce Dispute," *Conceptions of Sh* (1966); M. Rosenberg, *The Masks of Lear* (1972).

STAGING Camb lvi-lxix; Craig 982; Odell *passim*; Sprague 281-297; Trewin *passim.*

See also H. Spencer, *Sh Improved* (1927); J. C. Adams, "The Original Staging of *Lear,*" *AMS* (1948); A. C. Sprague, *Shakespearian Players and Performances* (1953); F. E. Halliday, *The Cult of Sh* (1957); B. Joseph, *The Tragic Actor* (1959); A. Szyfman, "*Lear* on the Stage," *ShS,* XIII (1960), 69-71; M. St. Clare Byrne, "*Lear* at Stratford-on-Avon, 1959," *ShQ,* XI (1960), 189-206; G. Wilson Knight, *Sh in Production* (1964); M. Mack, *KL in Our Time* (1965); Esther Jackson, "*KL:* The Grammar of Tragedy," *ShQ,* XVII (1966), 25-40; Carol Carlisle, *Sh from the Greenroom* (1969).

BIBLIOGRAPHY S. A. Tannenbaum, *Shakespeare's Lear: A Concise Bibliography* (1940); H. Bonheim, *The King Lear Perplex* (1960).

MACBETH

TEXT Alexander 170-173; Camb vii-xlii, 87-91; Chambers 471-476; Greg 389-397; New Arden xiii-xxxviii; Sisson II, 192-205.

See also R. C. Bald, *"Mac* and the 'Short' Plays," *RES,* IV (1928), 429-431; A. Thaler, *Sh and Democracy* (1941); A. Stunz, "The Date of *Mac," ELH,* IX (1942), 95-105; J. M. Nosworthy, "The Bleeding Captain Scene in *Mac," RES,* XXII (1946), 126-130, and *"Mac* at the Globe," *Lib,* II (1947), 108-118; Nosworthy, "The Hecate Scenes in *Mac," RES,* XXIV (1948), 138-139; R. Flatter, *Shakespeare's Producing Hand* (1948); J. G. McManaway, "Textual Studies," *ShS,* II (1949), 145-149; W. Empson, "Dover Wilson on *Mac," KR,* XIV (1952), 83-102; K. Danks, "Is F₁ *Mac* a Reconstructed Text?" *NQ,* ns, IV (1957), 516-519; J. M. Nosworthy, *Shakespeare's Occasional Plays* (1965).

EDITIONS Ed. E. K. Chambers (1893); *NV,* ed. H. H. Furness, Jr. (1903); ed. J. Q. Adams (1931); ed. G. L. Kittredge (1939); Camb, ed. J. Dover Wilson (1947); New Arden, ed. K. Muir (1951); Yale, ed. E. Waith (1954); Pelican, ed. A. Harbage (1956).

SOURCES W. G. Boswell-Stone, *Shakespere's Holinshed* (1896); L. Winstanley, *Mac, Lear, and Contemporary History* (1922); A. and J. Nicoll, *Holinshed's Chronicle as Used in Shakespeare's Plays* (1927); L. Hotson, *I, William Sh* (1937), 172-202; E. E. Stoll, "Source and Motive in *Mac* and *Oth," RES,* XIX (1943), 25-32; H. Paul, *The Royal Play of Macbeth* (1950); M. C. Bradbrook, "The Sources of *Mac," ShS,* IV (1951), 35-47; L. Campbell, "Political Ideas in *Mac* IV.iii," *ShQ,* II (1951), 281-286; R. A. Law, "The Composition of *Mac* with Reference to Holinshed," *TxSE,* XXXI (1952), 35-41; J. Jack, *"Mac,* King James, and the Bible," *ELH,* XXII (1955), 173-193; Muir (1957); Bullough (1957—), forthcoming volume; R. Barker, *Thomas Middleton* (1958).

CRITICISM K. Muir's New Arden edition (1951), xlvi ff., has a useful summary of nineteenth-century criticism. In addition to Coleridge and Hazlitt, Muir comments on the critical responses to *Mac* of Mrs. Siddons, Whately, Fletcher, and other minor figures. Thomas De Quincy's famous "On the Knocking at the Gate in *Mac"* (1823) is widely reprinted. This fine essay explains how the murderers are cut off from the world by their crime and suddenly united with it by the knocking, which "makes known audibly that the reaction has commenced; the human has made its reflux upon the fiendish." J. Hales, *Notes and Essays on Sh* (1884), also examined the porter scene and pointed out that it suggests the porter at the gate of Hell in the Morality plays. In this way the castle has come to represent Hell itself.

A. C. Bradley's great essays on *Mac* are in his *Shakespearean Tragedy* (1904). His remarks on the atmosphere and dramatic concentration of action are summaries of nineteenth-century insights—and quite certainly the seeds of modern criticism. There has been no better study of the character of the principals. The nature of the dramatic universe was outlined by W. Raleigh in his *Sh* (1907); it is a world of force and suffering, a world without divinity. M. Maeterlinck, *"Mac," Fortnightly Rev.*, XCIII (1910), 696-699, has a good appreciation of the poetry. A scornful dismissal of the romantic critics is in G. L. Kittredge's *Shakspere* (1916). A. Quiller-Couch, *Shakespeare's Workmanship* (1918), discusses the difficulty of making a murderer and traitor into a great tragic hero. He concludes that the operation of the supernatural in *Mac* is absolutely essential: far from being a theatrical frill, it accounts fully for the involuntary change from nobility to degradation in Macbeth. G. W. Knight's two books on the tragedies, *The Wheel of Fire* (1930) and *The Imperial Theme* (1931), contain important essays on language and theme. The first of these emphasizes the mystery and doubt in the play's atmosphere—its moral darkness. The major essay in the latter book is on "life-themes." Knight writes here of the symbols which express honor, magnificence, creation, and innocence.

E. E. Stoll's essays in three books—*Sh Studies* (1927), *Art and Artifice in Sh* (1933), and *From Sh to Joyce* (1944)—deprive Macbeth of any justifiable motives for his crime. Stoll attempts to expose a conflict of character that is at the heart of the meaning of the play. The psychological improbabilities are treated, I think far too literally, in L. Schücking's *The Baroque Character of the Elizabethan Tragic Hero* (1938). A very good study is in D. A. Traversi's *An Approach to Sh* (1938). Traversi notes that "degree" is talked about in other plays, particularly *TrC*, but that only in *Mac* is it apprehended in terms of immediate experience. Although M. Van Doren's essay on *Mac* in *Sh* (1939) is derivative, it has some very good things to say about time and atmosphere. There is ample discussion of the destroyed and inverted human relationships in S. Spender's important study of "Time, Violence and *Mac*," *Penguin New Writing*, III (1946), 115-126.

A celebrated essay is L. C. Knights' "How Many Children Had Lady Macbeth" in *Explorations* (1946). Knights begins by annihilating the vast shoal of critics who see *Mac* and other plays as stories of living beings. More interested in the total poetic qualities of the play, Knights writes about character as only one of its components. For him the play is simply a "statement of evil" which tells, in images of passion and confusion, a story of unnatural disorder. The milieu of *Mac* and its relationship to Elizabethan history is well treated by H. B. Charlton in *Shakespearian Tragedy* (1948). R. Walker's *The Time Is Free* (1949) is devoted entirely to *Mac.* It is of value for its scene-by-scene analysis and its attention to textual matters. But it too bogs down in religion: John Wain has described this as "a passionately engagé piece of criticism, offering a full-scale Christian interpretation." A. Sewell notes in *Character and Society in Sh* (1951) that "we lose the sense of that ethical and political order which is expressed in social institutions" because the central imagery of the play has no social referents.

R. Speaight, *Nature in Shakespearian Tragedy* (1955), writes of the universal schism reflected in Macbeth's anarchic character. His sin is against both man and Nature, for "the state is the ritual expression" of the unwritten laws that make it possible. A well-known study of G. Santayana is reprinted in *Essays in Literary Criticism* (1956). This drama, he writes, like the other tragedies, does not have a genuine Christian content; the invocation of doctrine is purely dramatic and suffers in comparison with its integral status in Dante. I believe the answer to this is straightforward: Sh is not writing a medieval poem about religion but the story of characters to whom knowledge itself is problematical. The four themes of "darkness, sleep, raptness, and contradiction" are the substance of B. Stirling's *Unity in Shakespearian Tragedy* (1956). One could wish for a fuller working-out of these in structural terms.

F. Fergusson's *The Human Image in Dramatic Literature* (1957) includes the earlier *"Mac* as the Imitation of an Action." There is a good account of how the imagery confirms action, centering on the striving beyond reason and nature that informs the entire play. Fergusson pitches his argument on Aristotelian tragic theory. L. Kirschbaum, "Banquo and Edgar: Character or Function?" *EC,* VII (1957), 1-21, suggests that Banquo serves a purely instrumental purpose; he exists to respond to Macbeth, to comment on his fortune, to symbolize the humanity that is the victim of ambition. W. H. Auden writes of Macbeth and Oedipus in "The Dyer's Hand," *Anchor Rev.,* II (1957), 255-301. Oedipus illustrates "spectacular misfortune," but "every member of the audience knows that the possibility of becoming a Macbeth exists in his nature." Freud's essay on those wrecked by success—he takes Lady Macbeth as his example—is in *The Complete Works,* XIV (1957), 318-324.

The most extended study of language and theme is G. R. Elliott's *Dramatic Providence in Mac* (1958). The method is close examination of the text; the intention is to prove the play broadly Christian in meaning. This seems unlikely to me; a fair review is in *ShQ,* X (1959), 234-236. L. C. Knights, *Some Shakespearean Themes* (1959), reiterates that the meaning is the poetry, which expresses continually a sense of Nature outraged. The images of "life delighting in life" with which the play begins serve to define the exact dimensions of Macbeth's guilt, to show how much more than political is his crime. A useful essay on the concept of time and its representational qualities is in T. Driver's *The Sense of History in Greek and Shakespearean Drama* (1960). *Mac* and the theory of tragedy are the subjects of W. Booth's "Shakespeare's Tragic Villain," *Shakespeare's Tragedies,* ed. L. Lerner (1963). *ShS,* XIX (1966) is devoted entirely to this play. Of special value is G. K. Hunter's review of *Mac* in the twentieth century. See also the essays of R. B. Heilman, "The Criminal as Tragic Hero"; W. A. Murray, "Why Was Duncan's Blood Golden?"; Kenneth Muir, "Image and Symbol in *Mac*"; Arthur McGee, "*Mac* and the Furies." Another and extremely useful collection is John Wain's *Shakespeare: Macbeth* (1968). There is a good sampling of eighteenth- and nineteenth-century criticism.

The supernatural in *Mac* has attracted much research. What I judge to be the best book on the subject is W. C. Curry's *Shakespeare's Philosophical Patterns* (1937). Its subject is Renaissance theology and demonology; there is an excellent application of these to the change in character of the principals. Curry concludes that Macbeth, by reason of his inalienable freedom of the will, determines his own spiritual transformation. Other useful works include J. Masefield's *Sh and Spiritual Life* (1924); M. Doran's "That Undiscovered Country," *PQ,* XX (1941), 413-427; W. Farnham, *Shakespeare's Tragic Frontier* (1950); R. M. Frye, "*Mac* and the Powers of Darkness," *Emory Univ. Quar.,* VIII (1952), 164-174. See also the piece by Robert West on demonology in *Sh and the Outer Mystery* (1968).

Language: Spurgeon (1935); C. Brooks, *The Well-Wrought Urn* (1947); M. Morozov, "The Individualization of Shakespeare's Characters Through Imagery," *ShS,* II (1949), 83-106; A. Stein, "*Mac* and Word-Magic," *Sew,* LIX (1951), 271-284; Evans (1952); M. Burrell, "*Mac*: A Study in Paradox," *ShJ,* XC (1954), 167-190; M. Mahood, *Shakespeare's Wordplay* (1956); J. Lawlor, "Mind and Hand," *ShQ,* VIII (1957), 179-193. Brooks' essay is noteworthy.

Further reading: J. M. Murry, *Sh* (1936); T. Spencer, *Sh and the Nature of Man* (1942); S. L. Bethell, *Sh and the Popular Dramatic Tradition* (1944); W. A. Armstrong, "The Elizabethan Conception of the Tyrant," *RES,* XXII (1946), 161-181, and "The Influence of Seneca and Machiavelli on the Elizabethan Tyrant," *ibid.,* XXIV (1948), 19-35; J. Arthos, "The Naive Imagination and the Destruction of Macbeth," *ELH,* XIV (1947), 114-126; H. Gardner, "Milton's 'Satan' and the Theme of Damnation in Elizabethan Tragedy," *E&S* (1948), 46-66; J. Spargo, "The Knocking at the Gate in *Mac*," *AMS* (1948); E. Waith, "Manhood and Valor in Two Shakespearean Tragedies," *ELH,* XVII (1950), 262-272; C. Leech, *Shakespeare's Tragedies* (1950); R. Crane, *The Languages of Criticism* (1953); L. C. Knights, "On the Background

of Shakespeare's Use of Nature in *Mac," Sew,* LXIV (1956), 207-217;
H. S. Wilson, *On the Design of Shakespearian Tragedy* (1957); L. Dean,
"Mac and Modern Criticism," *Eng. Jour.,* XLVII (1958), 57-67; W.
Rosen, *Sh and the Craft of Tragedy* (1960); M. Mack, "The Jacobean
Sh," *Jacobean Theatre* (1960); I. Hyde, *"Mac:* A Problem," *English,*
XIII (1960), 91-94; A. Rossiter, *Angel with Horns* (1961); V. Kantak,
"An Approach to Shakespearian Tragedy," *ShS,* XVI (1963), 42-52;
John Brown, *Mac* (1963); Terence Hawkes, *Sh and the Reason* (1964).

STAGING   Camb lxix-lxxxii; Craig 1045-1046; Odell *passim*; Sprague
224-280; Trewin *passim.*

See also S. Siddons, "Remarks on the Character of Lady Macbeth," in
T. Campbell's *Life of Mrs. Siddons* (1834); W. Winter, *Sh on the Stage*
(1911); J. C. Adams, *The Globe Playhouse* (1942); J. Masefield, *A Mac
Production* (1945); A. Downer, "The Life of Our Design," *HR,* II
(1949), 242- 263; G. W. Knight, *Principles of Shakespearian Production*
(1949); F. Neilson, *A Study of Mac for the Stage* (1952); A. C. Sprague,
Shakespearian Players and Performances (1953); E. Waith, *"Mac:* Inter-
pretation vs. Adaptation," *Sh: Of an Age and for All Time* (1954); R.
David, "The Tragic Curve," *ShS,* IX (1956), 122-131; G. B. Evans,
Shakespearean Prompt-Books of the Seventeenth Century, I (1960); W.
Appleton, *Charles Macklin: An Actor's Life* (1960). G. Wilson Knight,
Sh in Production (1964); John Russell Brown, *Shakespeare's Plays in
Performance* (1966); Dennis Bartholomeusz, *Mac and the Players*
(1969); Glynne Wickham, *Shakespeare's Dramatic Heritage* (1969);
Carol Carlisle, *Sh from the Greenroom* (1969). The Bartholomeusz
book has an interesting theatre history and is full of illuminating and
enjoyable historical material.

BIBLIOGRAPHY   S. A. Tannenbaum, *Shakespeare's Mac: A Concise
Bibliography* (1939).

129

ANTONY AND CLEOPATRA

TEXT Alexander 174-178; Camb vii-x, 124-130; Chambers 476-478; Greg 398-403; New Arden vii-xxiii; Sisson II, 259-275.

See also K. Elze, "Notes and Conjectural Emendations on *AC* and *Per*," *Englische Studien*, IX (1886), 267-290; A. Thiselton, *Textual Notes on AC* (1899); M. Bayfield, *A Study of Shakespeare's Versification* (1920); J. C. Maxwell, "Shakespeare's Manuscript of *AC*," *NQ*, CXCVI (1951), 337; M. Thomas, "The Repetitions in Antony's Death Scene," *ShQ*, IX (1958), 153-157; D. Galloway, " 'I am Dying, Egypt, Dying': Folio Repetitions and the Editors," *NQ*, ns, V (1958), 330-335; A. Norman, "*The Tragedie of Cleopatra* and the Date of *AC*," *MLR*, LIV (1959), 1-9.

EDITIONS *NV*, ed. H. H. Furness, Jr. (1907); ed. G. L. Kittredge (1941); Camb, ed. J. Dover Wilson (1950); New Arden, ed. M. R. Ridley (1954); Yale, ed. P. Phialas (1955); Pelican, ed. M. Mack (1960).

SOURCES C. T. Brooke, *Shakespeare's Plutarch* (1909); H. Mac-Callum, *Shakespeare's Roman Plays* (1910); M. Shackford, *Plutarch in Renaissance England* (1929); J. Schütze, "Daniels *Cleopatra* und Sh," *Englische Studien*, LXXI (1936), 58-72; P. Westbrook, "Horace's Influence on Shakespeare's *AC*," *PMLA*, LXII (1947), 392-398; I. Ribner, "Sh and Peele," *NQ*, CXCVII (1952), 244-246; J. Rees, "An Elizabethan Eyewitness of *AC*," *ShS*, VI (1953), 91-93; L. Michel and C. Seronsy, "Shakespeare's History Plays and Daniel," *SP*, LII (1955), 549-577; A. Norman, "Source Material in *AC*," *NQ*, ns, III (1956), 59-61, and "Daniel's *The Tragedie of Cleopatra* and *AC*," *ShQ*, IX (1958), 11-18; E. Schanzer, *Shakespeare's Appian* (1956), and "Daniel's Revision of his *Cleopatra*," *RES*, VIII (1957), 375-381; Muir (1957); Bullough (1957—), V, 215-449; J. L. Barroll, "Sh and Roman History," *MLR*, LIII (1958), 327-343.

CRITICISM Dryden's *Preface* to *All for Love* (1678) stated that the "excellency of the Moral" of *AC* was that "the chief persons represented, were famous patterns of unlawful love; and their end accordingly was unfortunate." The critical history of the play has been away from this position and toward that outlined by Hazlitt: the appreciation of the great conflict of "Roman pride and Eastern magnificence." It has often been agreed that Coleridge was right in assigning this play equal station with the four other great tragedies.

The first sustained modern study was that of A. C. Bradley in *Oxford Lectures* (1909). His essay on Cleopatra is memorable: from a "Doll

Tearsheet sublimated" to a "most sovereign creature," he traced her
infinite variety. M. MacCallum, *Shakespeare's Roman Plays* (1910),
may be read on this play, it has been said, with much respect but
scarcely with exhiliration. A very interesting essay is in B. Croce's
Ariosto, Sh and Corneille (1920). Croce saw *AC* as a tragedy of the will;
it couples "the violent sense of pleasure" and "a shudder at its abject
effects of dissolution and death." There is a good analysis of the grand
versus the great style in J. M. Murry's *The Problem of Style* (1921).
G. W. Knight's *The Imperial Theme* (1931) is preeminently concerned
with imagery, but much is said of the "impregnating atmosphere of
wealth, power, military strength, and material magnificence." One of
the first studies of the dualism of love in *AC,* Knight's work is extraor-
dinarily sensitive to the great bursts and delicate foliations of emotion.

An early gun in the cannonade of background studies was J. Draper's
"Political Themes in Shakespeare's Later Plays," *JEGP,* XXXV (1936),
61-93. There is heavy analysis of Elizabethan opinion on politics and
duty but not a great deal that connects all this to Sh. J. M. Murry's *Sh*
(1936) has valuable comments on Antony "incorporate with Nature."
A close reading of the poetry is in F. R. Leavis' *"AC and All for Love,"*
Scrutiny, V (1936), 158-169. D. A. Traversi's *An Approach to Sh*
(1938) makes an intelligent effort to unite varieties of criticism. Instead
of seeing the play as either a story of senseless passion or of triumphant
spiritual love, he attempts to reconcile spirit and sensation. M. Van
Doren, *Sh* (1939), has a thoughtful essay on the extent and meaning of
the universe continually alluded to by the poetry. It lends to the play
an atmosphere beyond space and time, suffused with sensation. T.
Spencer, *Sh and the Nature of Man* (1942), comments on the realism.
There is, Spencer believes, really no tragic metaphysic; because of this
the play assimilates sorrow and simply obviates disillusion. S. L. Bethell,
Sh and the Popular Dramatic Tradition (1944), explores the dialectic of
Rome and Egypt, which stand respectively for morality and pleasure,
intellect and intuition. The sources are touched upon in T. W. Baldwin's
lengthy *William Shakspere's Small Latine and Lesse Greeke* (1944).

Granville-Barker (1946) begins his study with some valuable comments
on the stagecraft of *AC.* There is then a full investigation of character,
construction, and minor matters. The most notable part deals with
Cleopatra's scepticism and amorality. E. Seaton, *"AC and the Book of
Revelation," RES,* XXII (1946), 219-224, traces the splendid and
apocalyptic imagery of the play. An excellent essay on "Poetry and
Morals" by W. K. Wimsatt is in *Thought,* XXIII (1948), 281-299.
Wimsatt forcefully points out that art is a revelation and not a criticism
of life; he dismisses once and for all the red herring of the immorality
of the protagonists. A worthwhile study of "Shakespeare's Enobarbus"
by E. C. Wilson is in *AMS* (1948). Lord David Cecil's *Poets and Story-*

tellers (1948) does a good job of relating the private to the public aspects of the play. He writes of love as part of a great historical process which, because it is itself infinite, allows for every inconsistency the play seems to express. J. Danby, "The Shakespearian Dialectic," *Scrutiny*, XVI (1949), 196-213, concentrates on the ambiguousness of the play and the isolation of the lovers. He formulates the opposition of Rome and Egypt as that of the political and mythical, the mind versus the flesh. A good many critics have disagreed with Danby's assertion that the play's ending is sensually overripe and rotten. J. Dover Wilson's Camb introduction (1950) offers what I think is a good alternative to political interpretations. One of the best long studies is in W. Farnham's *Shakespeare's Tragic Frontier* (1950). This begins with a long study of Plutarch, the principal source. The Renaissance versions and Shakespeare's alterations are examined. A good psychological study follows. Farnham believes that in this case tragedy is a consequence of character, not of the Creation.

N. Pearson, "*AC,*" *Sh: Of an Age and For All Time* (1954), has an interesting appreciation, which sometimes is sentimental. B. Stirling, *Unity in Shakespearian Tragedy* (1956), takes issue with G. B. Shaw's objection to "making sexual infatuation a tragic theme." Stirling finds a large satirical content in *AC*, which constantly brings to bear "moral realism" on the sensual life depicted. H. S. Wilson, *On the Design of Shakespearian Tragedy* (1957), is worth looking over. F. Dickey, *Not Wisely But Too Well* (1957), compares classical, medieval, and the Shakespearean view of the lovers. He has a good, if academic, account of the tragedy of excessive passion. J. Barroll, "Antony and Pleasure," *JEGP*, LVII (1958), 708-720, writes of the play as allegory of Lust, Gluttony, and Sloth. L. C. Knights, *Some Shakespearean Themes* (1959), has valuable comments on the self-consuming nature of love in *AC*. In his edition (1960) M. Mack writes of the mixed response of laughter and sympathy; the characters are both magnificent and tawdry. Cleopatra is both an old campaigner in love and "a force like the Lucretian Venus." E. Waith, *The Herculean Hero* (1962), goes into the mythical origins of Antony: his archetype's "exploits are strange mixtures of beneficence and crime, of fabulous quests and shameful betrayals, of triumph over wicked enemies and insensate slaughter of the innocent, yet the career is always a testimony to the greatness of a man who is almost a god." One of the best studies is in D. A. Traversi's *Sh: The Roman Plays* (1963). Traversi elaborates his earlier thesis (above) and suggests that the play emphasizes decay and dissolution at least as much as it does sensual pleasure. From the fertility of the Nile to the decay of love and life it offers a range of experience which itself contains the meaning of tragedy.

Ernest Schanzer, in *The Problem Plays of Sh* (1963), asserts that this play is best interpreted by comparison to those other "problem" plays, *MM* and *JC.* Robert Ornstein discusses "Love and Art in *AC*" in *Later Sh*, ed. Bernard Harris and John Russell Brown (1966). Brown's *Shakespeare: AC* (1968) is a collection of essays with an especially good section on staging. A recent book devoted entirely to this play is Julian Markels' *The Pillar of the World* (1968).

Cleopatra has drawn to herself as many critics as she once did lovers. A. Symons, *Studies in the Elizabethan Drama* (1920), offered a romantic and sensitive account of her passion. L. Schücking's *Character Problems* (1922) asserted that she was inherently improbable—a whore at the beginning and a goddess at the end of the play. He was attacked for years afterward with great passion by those who saw more to Cleopatra than inconsistency. E. E. Stoll, "Cleopatra," *MLR,* XXIII (1928), 145-163, found another phrase for it: *la donna è mobile.* A less rapturous but more solid essay was E. Buck's "Cleopatra, eine Charakterdeutung," *ShJ,* LXXIV (1938), 101-122. This centered not on her attractive flaws but on her function as destroyer of masculinity. L. Kirschbaum, "Shakespere's Cleopatra," *SAB,* XIX (1944), 161-171, found her consistently portrayed as a harlot and endowed with the psychology of voluptuousness even in her death. A fine discussion is in J. I. M. Stewart's *Character and Motive in Sh* (1949). There is a list of nineteenth-century finger-waggling at the sensual queen. Stewart's is the best interpretation of her sexuality and mysteriousness. Other works of value on Cleopatra are D. Stempel, "The transmigration of the Crocodile," *ShQ,* VII (1956), 59-72; E. Donno, "Cleopatra Again," *ShQ,* VII (1956), 227-233; M. Lloyd, "Cleopatra as Isis," *ShS,* XII (1959), 88-94.

The best study of the language is in M. Charney's brilliant *Shakespeare's Roman Plays* (1961). Other works of note are Spurgeon (1935); Clemen (1951); Evans (1952); B. Spencer, "*AC* and the Paradoxical Metaphor," *ShQ,* IX (1958), 373-378; M. Lloyd, "The Roman Tongue," *ShQ,* X (1959), 461-468; A. Bonjour, "From Shakespeare's Venus to Cleopatra's Cupids," *ShS,* XV (1962), 73-80. See also Markels (above).

Further reading: E. K. Chambers, *Sh: A Survey* (1925); J. Wilcox, "Love in *AC*," *Papers Mich. Acad. Science, Arts and Letters,* XXI (1935), 531-544; R. Binder, *Der Dramatische Rhythmus in Shakespeares AC* (1939); D. Lyman, "Janus in Alexandria," *Sew,* XLVIII (1940), 86-104; J. Phillips, *The State in Shakespeare's Greek and Roman Plays* (1940); R. Walker, "The Northern Star," *ShQ,* II (1951), 287-293; H. Brown, "Enter the Shakespearean Tragic Hero," *EC,* III (1953), 285-302; V. K. Whitaker, *Shakespeare's Use of Learning* (1953); J. C. Maxwell, "Shakespeare's Roman Plays: 1900-1956," *ShS,* X (1957), 1-11; T. J. B. Spencer, "Sh and the Elizabethan Romans," *ShS,* X (1957), 27-38; J. Leeds Barroll, "Antony and Pleasure," *JEGP,*

LVII (1958), 708-720; A. Stein, "The Image of Antony," *KR,* XXI
(1959), 586-606; M. Mack, "The Jacobean Sh," *Jacobean Theatre*
(1960); G. Couchman, "*AC* and the Subjective Convention," *PMLA,*
LXXVI (1961), 420-425; Michael Lloyd, "Antony and the Game of
Chance," *JEGP,* LXI (1962), 548-554; Harold Fisch, "*AC*: The Limits
of Mythology," *ShS,* XXIII (1970), 59-67.

STAGING   Camb xxxvii-xlvi; Craig 1073; Odell *passim*; Sprague 330-
333; Trewin *passim.*

See also *NV;* G. W. Stone, "Garrick's Presentation of *AC,*" *RES,* XIII
(1937), 20-38; J. M. Brown, "Miss Bankhead Tries Cleopatra," *Two on
the Aisle* (1938); H. Spencer, *The Art and Life of William Sh* (1940);
B. Jenkin, "*AC*: Some Suggestions on the Monument Scenes," *RES,*
XXI (1945), 1-14; Granville-Barker (1946); Folio Society edition
(1952); M. Webster, *Sh Without Tears* (1955); *Shaw on Sh* (1961); *The
Stratford Scene 1958-1968,* ed. Peter Raby (1968); John Russell
Brown, *Sh:AC* (1968).

CORIOLANUS

TEXT Alexander 178-182; Camb 130-137; Chambers 478-480; Greg 404-407; Sisson II, 122-133.

See also C. Hayhurst, *A History of the Text of Cor* (1924); A. King, "Notes on *Cor*," *ES*, XIX (1937), 13-20, and XX (1938), 18-25; G. B. Harrison, "A Note on *Cor*," *AMS* (1948).

EDITIONS Ed. E. K. Chambers (1898); Arden, ed. W. Craig and R. Case (1922); *NV*, ed. H. H. Furness, Jr. (1928); Pelican, ed. H. Levin (1956); Camb, ed. J. Dover Wilson (1960); ed. A. Walker (1964).

SOURCES R. Büttner, "Zu *Cor* und seiner Quelle," *ShJ*, XLI (1905), 45-53; C. T. Brooke, *Shakespeare's Plutarch* (1909); M. MacCallum, *Shakespeare's Roman Plays* (1910); M. Shackford, *Plutarch in Renaissance England* (1929); H. Heuer, "Sh und Plutarch," *Anglia*, LXII (1938); 321-346; F. Lees, "*Cor*, Aristotle, and Bacon," *RES*, I (1950), 114-125; J. A. K. Thomson, *Sh and the Classics* (1952); K. Muir, "Menenius's Fable," *NQ*, CXCVIII (1953), 240-242; H. Heuer, "From Plutarch to Sh," *ShS*, X (1957), 50-59; Muir (1957); Bullough (1957−), V, 453-563; J. L. Barroll, "Sh and Roman History," *MLR*, LIII (1958), 327-343; E. Honigmann, "Shakespeare's Plutarch," *ShQ*, X (1959), 25-33.

CRITICISM The extra-literary meaning of *Cor* was asserted by Hazlitt, who believed that "any one who studies it may save himself the trouble of reading Burke's *Reflections,* or Paine's *Rights of Man,* or the Debates in both Houses of Parliament since the French Revolution." He saw it as the conflict of aristocracy and democracy; Swinburne saw it instead as a "match of passions played out for life and death between a mother and a son." The mainstream of criticism flows between these headlands. It may be noted that, among the earlier writers, Johnson, Coleridge, and Taine have written well on this play.

Among his other distinguished contributions to Shakespearean scholarship, A. C. Bradley opened modern criticism on this play. His *Cor* (1912) remains one of the most intelligent discussions of its namesake. J. M. Murry's essay on Virgilia in *Countries of the Mind* (1922) followed Ruskin, who had admired the sensibility she brought to the drama. For Murry she mediated the "pride of arms and the pride of race which are the theme of this play." A fine study by R. W. Chambers is in *Shakespeare's Hand in the Play of Sir Thomas More* (1923). There is a summary of past criticism and an excellent study of the problem of power as seen by Elizabethans. M. St. Clare Byrne, "Classical Coriolanus,"

National Rev., XCVI (1931), 426-430, wrote a fine essay on the qualities *not* to be found in *Cor*: tragic atmosphere and psychological
romanticism. G. W. Knight, *The Imperial Theme* (1931), has an influential essay on style and meaning. He is especially revealing on the imagery
of violence both in war and Nature. He demonstrates the concentrated
emotion that informs this play. D. A. Traversi, *"Cor," Scrutiny,* VI
(1937), 43-58, emphasizes the iron social framework of the play. He
finds its central irony in the contrast between this framework and the
"natural humanity" of the hero, which is perverted by the forces that
oppose it. H. Heuer, "Sh und Plutarch," *Anglia,* LXII (1938), 321-346,
lists the differences between *Cor* and its sources; its irrational passions
culminate, Heuer thinks, in a form of "Unnatur" which dominates the
political conflict. One of the most influential of essays has been O. J.
Campbell's interpretation in *Shakespeare's Satire* (1943). For Campbell,
the hero is ridiculous and the story is full of "the spirit of derision." It
is essentially about political chaos caused by a degenerate mob and a
leader who is a slave of passion. Its intention—and here Campbell seems
to overstate—is to inculcate the idea of a sound polity.

J. Palmer, *Political Characters of Sh* (1945), refuses to see a conflict of
political ideologies; he interprets the play instead as the conflict of
pride and love. There is a good running commentary and review of
criticism—all in all, a valuable introduction. A very competent theatrical
discussion is in Granville-Barker (1946). There is a fine analysis of the
character of the hero in relation to his culture. The play's elements of
brutality are underscored by L. Kirschbaum in "Shakespeare's Stage
Blood," *PMLA,* LXIV (1949), 517-529. The dialectic of arrogance on
the part of the hero and stupidity on the part of his opposition is the
subject of B. Stirling's *The Populace in Sh* (1949). His comments on
the topical allusions to mob disorder are helpful—although only a due
weight can be given to such evidence. A well-known essay is in J. M.
Murry's *John Clare and Other Studies* (1950). It repeats much of the
earlier study on Virgilia (above) and adds some thoughts on the tragedy
as purely a consequence of attitude and action rather than fate and
nature. The symbolic status of the hero is explored by F. Lees in *"Cor,
Aristotle, and Bacon," RES,* I (1950), 114-125. Coriolanus partakes of
the extremes stated by Bacon of the man of solitude: either a "wild
beast or a god."

W. Farnham, *Shakespeare's Tragic Frontier* (1950), suggests that the
hero is in fact the tragedy; for good and evil, his character is his fate.
His tragic flaw and chief excellence is pride. There is a solid comparison
with Plutarch's version. Possible topical allusions are the subject of E. C.
Pettet, *"Cor* and the Midlands Insurrection of 1607," *ShS,* III (1950),
34-42. A contrast with Jonson concerns E. Honig in *"Sejanus* and *Cor*:
A Study in Alienation," *MLQ,* XII (1951), 407-421. Campbell's theory

of tragic satire is accepted, and Coriolanus is viewed by Honig as a moral primitive filled with psychopathic hatred of his opponents. I doubt whether he in fact fills this description or whether he attains "sensual, mystical happiness" in killing. H. Goddard, *The Meaning of Sh* (1951), believes that Coriolanus finds the mob hateful because he projects upon it his own unconscious hatreds. One would think the text establishes beyond doubt its nature and his motives. Quite unlike Hazlitt, L. C. Knights finds in "Sh and Political Wisdom," *Sew,* LXI (1953), 43-55, that politics is only a framework for the workings of character. The public crisis assumes importance only insofar as it is reflected in the personal and habitual. A literal interpretation of the action as an allegory of the fall of pride is the substance of I. Ribner's "The Tragedy of *Cor,*" *ES,* XXXIV (1953), 1-9.

D. J. Enright, "*Cor*: Tragedy or Debate?" *EC,* IV (1954), 1-19, concludes in favor of the latter. The hero exists principally as he is described by others; the actual man is a disappointment since very little goes on within him. The play is an exercise in logic: a figure with a particular set of qualities meets a particular fate. I. Browning's article in the next issue of *EC,* V (1955), 18-31, differs strongly. There is a good argument for conflict and consciousness in Coriolanus. M. Mac-Lure, "Sh and the Lonely Dragon," *UTQ,* XXIV (1955), 109-120, writes of the failure of the great Renaissance idea of rational and moral politics. Coriolanus cannot accommodate himself to history because he is lost in the contemplation of his own virtues. The hero as soldier is treated in P. Jorgensen's *Shakespeare's Military World* (1956). H. Levin's introduction to his Pelican edition (1956) stresses the likeness of Coriolanus to Ahab. A résumé of the hero's self-defeating tendencies is in H. S. Wilson's *On the Design of Shakespearian Tragedy* (1957). Coriolanus as a "phallic-narcissistic" type is the invention of C. Hofling in *Amer. Imago,* XIV (1957), 407-435. The hero is endowed with a biography of childhood frustration that the text, evidently due to Shakespeare's carelessness, does not supply. There is the usual dash from the play to the life that enthusiasts seem unable to resist. Absolute twaddle.

A well-written study of the unfathomable element of character is H. Heuer's "From Plutarch to Sh," *ShS,* X (1957), 50-59. S. Sen, "What Happens in *Cor,*" *ShQ,* IX (1958), 331-345, has a very good account of psychological conflicts. Some other important articles in *ShQ* are H. Oliver, "Coriolanus as a Tragic Hero," X (1959), 53-60; K. Muir, "The Background of *Cor,*" *ibid.,* 137-145; F. Rouda, "*Cor*—a Tragedy of Youth," XII (1961), 103-106. A. P. Rossiter, *Angel with Horns* (1961), is very good on the politics. A subtle and brilliant essay is that of Una Ellis-Fermor in *Sh the Dramatist* (1961). There are, she points out, two images of Rome in this play. Coriolanus once dedicated himself to its ideal aspect. He then became estranged from the real Rome, corrupt from his mother on down. The passion of Coriolanus is that of a felt loss of integrity in being between corrupt alternatives, in losing the ideal. E. Waith, *The Herculean Hero* (1962), describes the figure of *virtus heroica,* which unleashes energy both terrible and beautiful. Endowed with a measure of greatness, he is inevitably in conflict with his milieu. There is an illuminating account of the myths underlying the story. D. A. Traversi's *Sh: The Roman Plays* (1963) has an excellent commentary on the "destruction of heroism."

For the contrast between real honor and its mere articulation see D. J. Gordon, "Name and Fame," *Papers Mainly Shakespearian,* ed. G. I. Duthie (1964), 40-56. R. F. Hill discusses linguistic and personal oppositions in *"Cor*: Violentest Contrariety," *Essays and Studies,* XVII (1964), 12-23. Kenneth Burke writes of the hero's pride and his social context in *"Cor*—and the Delights of Faction," *Hudson Review,* XIX (1966), 185-202.

M. Charney's *Shakespeare's Roman Plays* (1961) dominates the study of the poetry of *Cor.* See also Spurgeon (1935); J. C. Maxwell, "Animal Imagery in *Cor,*" *MLR,* XLII (1947), 417-421; Clemen (1951); Evans (1952); U. Ellis-Fermor, "Some Functions of Verbal Music in Drama," *ShJ,* XC (1954), 37-48; L. Dean, "Voice and Deed in *Cor,*" *UKCR,* XXI (1955), 177-184; G. Thomas Tanselle and Florence Dunbar, "Legal Language in *Cor,*" *ShQ,* XIII (1962), 231-238; James Calderwood, *"Cor*: Wordless Meanings and Meaningless Words," *SEL,* VI (1966), 211-224; Brian Vickers, *The Artistry of Shakespeare's Prose* (1968).

Further reading: W. Münch, "Aufidius," *ShJ,* XLII (1906), 127-147; A. Tolman, "The Structure of Shakespeare's Tragedies," *MLN,* XXXVII (1922), 449-458; E. K. Chambers, *Sh: A Survey* (1925); F. T. Wood, "Sh and the Plebs," *E&S* (1932), 53-73; E. Baumgarten, "Gemeinschaft und Gewissen in Shakespeares *Cor,*" *NS,* XLIII (1935), 363-384 and 413-425; J. Draper, "Political Themes in Shakespeare's Later Plays," *JEGP,* XXXV (1936), 61-93, and "Shakespeare's *Cor*: A Study in Renaissance Psychology," *West Virginia Bulletin,* III (1939), 22-36; M. Van Doren, *Sh* (1939); J. Phillips, *The State in Shakespeare's Greek and Roman Plays* (1940); A. Thaler, *Sh and Democracy* (1941); T. W. Baldwin, *William Shakspere's Small Latine and Lesse Greeke* (1944); S. Shanker, "Some Clues for *Cor,*" *SAB,* XXIV (1949), 209-213; T. S. Eliot, "Coriolan," *Complete Poems* (1952); H. Brown, "Enter the Shakespearean Tragic Hero," *EC,* III (1953), 285-302; L. Michel, "Yardsticks for Tragedy," *EC,* V (1955), 81-88; N. Brittin, "Coriolanus, Alceste, and Dramatic Genres," *PMLA,* LXXI (1956), 799-807; J. C. Maxwell, "Shakespeare's Roman Plays: 1900-1956," *ShS,* X (1957), 1-11; *ShS* (1957), *passim;* W. Rosen, *Sh and the Craft of Tragedy*

(1960); M. Mack, "The Jacobean Sh," *Jacobean Theatre* (1960); W. Zeeveld, *"Cor* and Jacobean Politics," *MLR,* LVII (1962), 321-334; M. Charney, *Discussions of Shakespeare's Roman Plays* (1964). M. Proser, *The Heroic Image in Five Shakespearean Tragedies* (1965).

STAGING   Camb xli-liii; Craig IIII; Odell *passim;* Sprague 326-330; Trewin *passim.*

See also *Hazlitt on Theatre* (1895); Granville-Barker (1946); "Macready's *Cor,"* in A. Nagler, *Sources of Theatrical History* (1952); M. Clarke and R. Wood, *Sh at the Old Vic* (1954); M. Webster, *Sh Without Tears* (1955); E. Bentley, *The Dramatic Event* (1956); B. Joseph, *The Tragic Actor* (1959); ed. F. Fergusson and C. J. Sisson (1962); Glynne Wickham, *"Cor:* Shakespeare's Tragedy in Rehearsal and Performance," *Later Sh,* ed. Bernard Harris and John Russell Brown (1966) and *Shakespeare's Dramatic Heritage* (1969).

TIMON OF ATHENS

TEXT Alexander 182-188; Camb ix-xiv, 87-97; Chambers 480-484; Greg 408-411; New Arden xiii-xxxii; Sisson II, 166-180.

See also the following, which consider whether *Tim* is Shakespeare's work alone or the work of another playwright revised (the play is now generally accepted as Shakespeare's): J. Q. Adams, *"Tim* and the Irregularities of the First Folio," *JEGP,* VII (1908), 53-63; E. H. Wright, *The Authorship of Tim* (1910); T. M. Parrott, *The Problem of Tim* (1923); R. Haug, "The Authorship of *Tim," SAB,* XV (1940), 227-248; G. Dawson "A Bibliographical Problem in the First Folio," *Lib,* XXII (1942), 25-33; U. Ellis-Fermor, *"Tim:* An Unfinished Play," *RES,* XVIII (1942), 270-283. There is a useful summary in the New Arden edition, xxii ff.

EDITIONS Camb, ed. J. C. Maxwell (1957); New Arden, ed. H. J. Oliver (1959); Pelican, ed. Charlton Hinman (1964).

SOURCES W. Clemons, "The Sources of *Tim," Princeton Univ. Bulletin,* XV (1904), 208-223; J. Q. Adams, "The Timon Plays," *JEGP,* IX (1910), 506-524; E. H. Wright (above); R. W. Bond, "Lucian and Boiardo in *Tim," MLR,* XXVI (1931), 52-68; R. Haug, "The Authorship of *Tim," SAB,* XV (1940), 227-248; W. Farnham, *Shakespeare's Tragic Frontier* (1950); G. Bonnard, "Note Sur Les Sources De *Tim," Ea,* VII (1954), 59-69; Muir (1957); Bullough (1957–), VI, 225-345; R. Goldsmith, "Did Sh Use the Old Timon Comedy?" *ShQ,* IX (1958), 31-38; E. Honigmann, *"Tim," ShQ,* XII (1961), 3-20.

CRITICISM The interpretation of this play is divided between those who regard it as an unfinished failure and those who attempt to see it as an allegory whose inconsistencies are unimportant. Coleridge called it a *"Lear* of the satirical drama"; E. Dowden in *Sh: A Critical Study* (1875) suggested that Timon represented Shakespeare's own suicidal rage and his response to the "injuries of life." A. C. Bradley's *Shakespearean Tragedy* (1904) takes up these ideas. G. W. Knight's "The Pilgrimage of Hate" is in *The Wheel of Fire* (1930). It is an intensely sympathetic essay; the splendor of the hero's prosperity, his magnanimity, and his love inspire lyrical praise. The weakness of Timon is, I believe, much understated: for Knight, he is "civilization's perfected flower." Much recent criticism has been concerned with Timon's flaws, his hatred as well as his love. J. Draper, "The Theme of *Tim," MLR,* XXIX (1934), 20-31, finds the play an attack on usury. He relates it to Elizabethan economics and to the reversals of fortune that often occurred within the ruling classes. M. Van Doren dusts off "spiritual biographers" who have made the play a revelation of its author's soul in his *Sh* (1939). He sees it as an exercise in schemes and symbols, with very little to recommend it as a mature tragedy. In substantial agreement is H. Spencer, *The Art and Life of William Sh* (1940). Quite another view is supplied by J. Phillips, *The State in Shakespeare's Greek and Roman Plays* (1940): *Tim* depicts a corrupt and materialistic social order. Poor literary criticism is joined in this book by superficial analysis of Elizabethan social doctrine.

J. Draper, "The Psychology of Shakespeare's Timon," *MLR,* XXXV (1940), 521-525, suggests that the namesake turns from the sanguine to the melancholy type. One of the best and most influential of studies is U. Ellis-Fermor's *"Tim*: An Unfinished Play," *RES,* XVIII (1942), 270-283. Ellis-Fermor finds the play a rough draft with structure, character, and theme insufficiently developed. She notes that there is very little that reveals Timon's motives—or, indeed, his non-symbolic being. The essay is well argued. T. Spencer, *Sh and the Nature of Man* (1942), agrees that the structure is unsatisfactory but reminds us of the very effective presentation of "the evil reality in human nature under the good appearance." W. Farnham, "The Beast Theme in Shakespeare's *Tim*," *Essays and Studies, Univ. Cal.,* XIV (1943), 49-56, demonstrates that the language portrays men consistently as animals. The range is from the intimation of simple brutishness to "devouring beastliness in cannibal man." A well-known essay is in O. J. Campbell's *Shakespeare's Satire* (1943). Like Jonson's *Sejanus* this play is a study in moral indignation; its true theme is repulsion from human folly. Campbell asserts that the play images a decaying society in which there is no hope of redemption, not even from the hero.

K. Muir, *"Tim* and the Cash-Nexus," *Mod. Quar, Misc.,* I (1946), 57-76, recalls the comments on this play by Marx in *Political Economy and Philosophy* (pub. 1932). Marx interpreted it as a savage study of the divinity of money and its power to change things to their opposites. It was, he said, the great alienating force in society. Muir adds intelligent comment on the gold symbolism and on love as a commodity. Like Marx, he finds the play to be based on neither love nor hatred but on the terrible power of money. A. S. Collins, *"Tim*: A Reconsideration," *RES,* XXII (1946), 96-108, reviews criticism hostile to the play. He writes well of its theatrical virtues and suggests that it intended to reveal, as in an allegory, all the types and classes of men. It has essentially a Morality structure. There are intelligent comments on the scheme of inverted human relationships and on the ritualistic purgation of Athens. The play as a tract for the times is the subject of E. C. Pettet, *"Tim*: The Disruption of Feudal Morality," *RES,* XXIII (1947), 321-336. It is the story, Pettet thinks, of capitalism shattering the medieval fabric. Timon is not a misanthrope, but a maddened idealist. The play is described as a revelation of Elizabethan attitudes toward money and the middle classes.

J. C. Maxwell, *"Tim," Scrutiny*, XV (1948), 195-208, has a penetrating account of Timon's "bounty," his generosity that, ironically, corrupts the beneficiaries. There is a very good discussion of language and theme in this important essay. The sex nausea and disease are treated briefly by I. Brown, *Sh* (1940). D. Stauffer, *Shakespeare's World of Images* (1949), discusses the play as a series of incarnated ideas: "bounty and parsimony, trust and self-interest." In *Christ and Nietzsche* (1948) G. W. Knight asserts that *Tim* is about the predicament of the West itself between man and money. Between spates of foggy philosophy there is some useful matter on the hero as symbol. One of the best studies is in W. Farnham's *Shakespeare's Tragic Frontier* (1950). *Tim* is connected to the late tragedies. The sources, language, and structure are examined, as well as the flaws of the principal.

An extended discussion of *Tim* and the other late plays will be found in C. Leech's *Shakespeare's Tragedies* (1950). There is an interesting thesis on its relationship to the romances. "Timon's Dog" is in W. Empson's *The Structure of Complex Words* (1951). The essay furnishes specific information on the ambiguousness of language in this play. T. Spencer, "Sh Learns the Value of Money," *ShS*, VI (1953), 75-78, finds evidence for the incomplete nature of the play in its varying allusions to the value of specie. An interesting essay on aesthetics is W. Merchant's *"Tim* and the Conceit of *Art," ShQ*, VI (1955), 249-257. What Merchant calls "the interrelation of character, fortune and mutability" is first intimated by minor characters, the poet and painter, and then developed as a major theme. Art, often mentioned in *Tim,* becomes a vehicle for "deceitful appearance." R. P. Draper, *"Tim," ShQ*, VIII (1957), 195-200, discusses Nature as it is seen by the namesake. While he often uses the concept to express a sense of corruption, it functions also as an agency of restoration and even of purgation. The cure as well as the disease is furnished by Nature. W. Nowottny considers "Acts IV and V of *Tim"* in *ShQ*, X (1959), 493-497. There is a continuous imaginative process in which gold, first the symbol of "the confusion of moral, physical, and social distinctions," becomes the "common whore" of mankind and finally leads to a great, symbolic revelation of human corruption.

A. Gomme, *"Tim," EC*, IX (1959), 107-125, attacks modern romantic critics of the play, especially G. W. Knight. The hero is by no means aristocratic—nor is his prosperity magnanimous—rather, he is drunken, complacent, coarse, and asinine. Gomme points out forcefully that even in his greatness Timon stands only for the equivalent of life and pleasure. When the latter is gone, so is the former. There are good comments on the language. H. J. Oliver's New Arden edition (1959) has a worth-while introduction. J. Lawlor, *The Tragic Sense in Sh* (1960), briefly discusses imagery. An important treatment of source, text, and meaning is E. A. J. Honigmann's *"Tim," ShQ,* XII (1961), 3-20. There is a valuable discussion of the place of the play among the other tragedies: Honigmann concludes that it is a great error to either dismiss it as incomplete or to call it a sketch of *Lear.* It is highly experimental and may have proved very satisfactory both to author and audience. D. Cook, *"Tim," ShS,* XVI (1963), 83-94, finds the play a study of the man who plays first the god and then the beast. He has the sin of pride, like the other tragic heroes of Sh.

This play is viewed as part of a pattern of late Shakespearean tragedy by G. K. Hunter in *Later Sh,* ed. Bernard Harris and John Russell Brown (1966). In none of the "plays of exile" does the hero succeed in creating values within himself which will replace those of the rejected social world. M. C. Bradbrook's *The Tragic Pageant of Tim* (1966) considers the play as a Jacobean mask and show. It is intended to differ from other tragedies and our difficulties with it proceed not from an imperfect text or structure but from our own expectations. There are many virtues in Francelia Butler's *The Strange Critical Fortunes of Shakespeare's Tim* (1966). It reviews a good deal of criticism of this play and has important remarks on staging. But it does not go into sufficient detail and is allusive rather than analytical. See the review by H. J. Oliver in *ShQ,* XXI (1970), 90-91.

Further reading: E. K. Chambers, *Sh: A Survey* (1925); A. Woods, "Syphilis in Shakespeare's Tragedy of *Tim," Amer. Jour. Psychiatry,* XCI (1934), 95-107; R. Anderson, "Excessive Goodness a Tragic Fault," *SAB,* XIX (1944), 85-96; J. Draper, "Patterns of Tempo in Shakespeare's *Tim," SAB,* XXIII (1948), 188-194; H. Craig, *An Interpretation of Sh* (1948); P. Thomson, "The Literature of Patronage," *EC,* II (1952), 267-284; K. Muir, "In Defence of Timon's Poet," *EC,* III (1953), 120-121; W. Rosen, *Sh and the Craft of Tragedy* (1960); R. Elliott, *The Power of Satire* (1960); G. W. Knight, *"Tim* and Its Dramatic Descendants," *REL,* II, 4 (1961), 9-18; A. Lancashire, *"Tim*: Shakespeare's *Dr. Faustus," ShQ,* XXI (1970), 35-44.

STAGING   Camb xliii-liv; Craig 1018; Odell *passim*; Sprague 333-334; Trewin *passim.*

See also W. Ebisch and L. Schücking, *A Sh Bibliography* (1931), 253; H. Spencer, *The Art and Life of William Sh* (1940); G. W. Knight, *Principles of Shakespearian Production* (1949); H. S. Wilson, *On the Design of Shakespearian Tragedy* (1957); R. Walker, "Unto Caesar," *ShS,* XI (1958), 128-132; W. Merchant, *Sh And the Artist* (1959);

K. Tynan, *Curtains* (1961). G. Wilson Knight, *Sh in Production* (1964) and Francelia Butler, *The Strange Critical Fortunes of Shakespeare's Tim* (1966) have detailed and important information on staging.

CYMBELINE

TEXT   Alexander 206-209; Camb vii-xv, 125-128; Chambers 484-487; Greg 412-414; New Arden xii-xiii, xxviii-xxxvii; Sisson II, 276-285.

See also K. Elze, "A Letter . . . on *Cym,*" *Anglia,* VIII (1885), 263-297; E. H. Meyerstein, "The Vision in *Cym,*" *TLS* (15 June 1922), 396; L. Kellner, "*Cym.* Eine textkritische Studie," *Anglica,* II (1925), 150-172; G. W. Knight, "The Vision of Jupiter in *Cym,*" *TLS,* (21 Nov 1936), 958; H. Craig, "Shakespeare's Bad Poetry," *ShS,* I (1948), 55-56; M. E. Prior, "*Cym,*" *ShQ,* VII (1956), 111-113.

EDITIONS   Arden, ed. E. Dowden (1903); *NV,* ed. H. H. Furness, Jr. (1913); New Arden, ed. J. M. Nosworthy (1955); Camb, ed. J. C. Maxwell (1960); Pelican, ed. Robert Heilman (1964).

SOURCES   R. Boodle, "The Original of *Cym,*" *NQ,* VII (1887), 404, and "Die Quelle zu *Cym,*" *ShJ,* XXIII (1888), 344-347; W. G. Boswell-Stone, *Shakespere's Holinshed* (1896); E. Greenlaw, "Shakespeare's Pastorals," *SP,* XIII (1916), 122-154; A. and J. Nicoll, *Holinshed's Chronicle as Used in Shakespeare's Plays* (1927); W. Thrall, "*Cym,* Boccaccio and the Wager Story in England," *SP,* XXVIII (1931), 639-651; D. Evans, "Some Notes on Sh and *The Mirror of Knighthood,*" *SAB,* XXI (1946), 161-167, and XXII (1947), 62-68; H. S. Wilson, "*Philaster* and *Cym,*" *EIE* (1951), 146-167; J. Nosworthy, "The Sources of the Wager Plot in *Cym,*" *NQ,* CXCVII (1952), 93-96; F. D. Hoeniger, "Two Notes on *Cym,*" *ShQ,* VIII (1957), 132-133; H. G. Wright, *Boccaccio in England* (1957); Muir (1957); Bullough (1957–), forthcoming volume; C. Gesner, "*Cym* and the Greek Romance," *Studies in English Renaissance Literature* (1962). The New Arden and Camb editions have especially good studies of sources.

CRITICISM   Dr. Johnson's *Notes* speak loudly for themselves: "to remark the folly of the fiction, the absurdity of the conduct, the confusion of the names and manners of different times, and the impossibility of the events in any system of life, were to waste criticism upon unresisting imbecility, upon faults too evident for detection, and too gross for aggravation." Hazlitt was much more sympathetic and in his *Characters* wrote an excellent essay on the play's structure. Swinburne's rhapsody on Imogen in *A Study of Sh* (1880) is no more than representative of nineteenth-century *aficionados* of female purity: "the very crown and flower of all her father's daughters . . . the immortal godhead of womanhood." Rather different was the reaction of Bernard Shaw in the *Saturday Review* (26 Sept 1896) who used *Cym* as the occasion to make a famous observation about himself and Sh: "With the single

exception of Homer, there is no eminent writer, not even Sir Walter
Scott, whom I can despise so entirely as I despise Sh when I measure
my mind against his. . . . To read *Cym* and to think of Goethe, of
Wagner, of Ibsen is, for me, to imperil the habit of studied moderation
of statement which years of public responsibility as a journalist have
made almost second nature to me." In *Cym Refinished* (1946 edition)
Shaw added a new fifth act to the play—and some more temperate
remarks.

A very good essay on the imaginative virtues of *Cym* is in A. Quiller-
Couch, *Shakespeare's Workmanship* (1918). There are some worthwhile
comments on the incongruities, which are recognized for what they are:
of no great moment. Idyll and tragicomedy are treated by E. K.
Chambers in *Sh: A Survey* (1925). W. W. Lawrence clarifies plot and
character in *Shakespeare's Problem Comedies* (1931) by relating both
to the old story of the wager to prove a woman's purity. Posthumus
may seem jealous and inconsistent, but he fulfills the archaic role of the
husband who discovers his wife's virtue and virtues. There is a sketch of
the patterns of language in G. W. Knight's *The Shakespearian Tempest*
(1932). D. G. James observes in *Scepticism and Poetry* (1937) that *Cym*
expresses "a crude parody of high religious significances." His essay on
all the last plays is hostile: they are attacked as inconsistent myths of
resurrection that are badly executed in dramatic form. Two essays on
Cym in E. M. W. Tillyard's *Shakespeare's Last Plays* (1938) concern
realism and symbolism; there is some interesting if inconclusive comparison with D. H. Lawrence. F. Tinkler, "*Cym,*" *Scrutiny,* VII (1938),
5-19, finds savage ironies where none appear to exist. He sees the play
as satirical and ironic, with overtones of disgust. It is an unproven case.

The structure of romance in *Cym* is, M. Van Doren notes, "fantastically
ornate." His essay in *Sh* (1939) is an adequate introduction to theme
and character. A. Stephenson, "The Significance of *Cym,*" *Scrutiny,* X
(1942), 329-338, criticizes Tinkler (above). The pervading idea is seen
as that of valuation, expressed often by images of honor, faith, and
rarity. The play tries to attain conceptions of absolute value and ideal
perfection: Imogen is the dramatic incarnation of this attempt. The
essay of Granville-Barker (1946) is essential to understanding *Cym.* The
principal matters studied are language, character, and staging. There is
an honest review of the play's weaknesses. G. W. Knight's *The Crown
of Life* (1947) interprets *Cym* as allegory, myth, and even apocalypse.
Imogen and Posthumus are representative figures of patriotism, sexual
purity, and moral reintegration. Their union, like that of Britain and
Rome, combines history and an esoteric vision of its meaning. The
study is full of points well made, but there is often bad metaphysics
and worse theology. I refrain from further comment and recommend
the reader to R. M. Frye's *Sh and Christian Doctrine* (1963). Studies

with varying viewpoints are D. A. Stauffer's *Shakespeare's World of Images* (1949), E. C. Pettet's *Sh and the Romance Tradition* (1949), and T. M. Parrott's *Shakespearean Comedy* (1949). "Truth and semblance" occupy the first, Pettet examines the romances as a group, and Parrott concerns himself with the play's improbabilities and sensationalism.

C. Camden, "The Elizabethan Imogen," *Rice Institute Pamphlet,* XXXVIII (1951), 1-17, explores Elizabethan evaluations of women and concludes that Imogen represents the most prized value of chastity. This may be so; I find it difficult to believe, however, that she is intended also to be a warning to all maidens who disobey their fathers. J. Danby, *Poets on Fortune's Hill* (1952), does not have a specific section on *Cym,* but his remarks on the romances in general are indispensable. F. R. Leavis discusses the romances in *The Common Pursuit* (1952). His essay, which has become well known, points out those deficiencies in *Cym* that prevent it from being considered equal to *WT.* Leavis prefers a conservative, prosaic interpretation: "the romantic theme remains merely romantic. The reunions, resurrections and reconciliations of the close belong to the order of imagination in which 'they all lived happily ever after.' " W. D. Smith, "Cloten with Caius Lucius," *SP,* XLIX (1952), 185-194, reviews the critics of Cloten, the villain of the piece. D. A. Traversi, *Sh: The Last Phase* (1954), displays sensitive understanding of the language as well as some of the platitudes of modern anthropology. There are dilettante excursions into morality and metaphysics; the eventual meaning of the play is held to reside in its contemplation of "nature," "worship," and "fertility."

J. M. Nosworthy offers a very good introduction in his New Arden edition (1955) in which he attempts to tame the winds of doctrine which have howled about this play. The problems raised by the critics are amply considered; his own judgment is that the play exemplifies a "great act of union" between things that seem hopelessly apart. He notes that the play is both realistic and mystical and for the most part avoids a categoric definition of its mythical-cum-religious qualities. In "The Integrity of Sh: Illustrated from *Cym,*" *ShS,* VIII (1955), 52-56, Nosworthy points out that the play may have a "glorious conglomeration of styles," but that is not enough to divide up the authorship. All its styles are related to Shakespeare's work in other plays. I. Ribner, "Sh and Legendary History: *Lear* and *Cym,*" *ShQ,* VII (1956), 47-52, warns against political interpretations; the play remains, he insists, simply a romance. While all of *ShS,* XI (1958) is of value, J. P. Brockbank's "History and Histrionics in *Cym*" is especially noteworthy. He writes of the destiny of Britain; the figure of Imogen, who symbolizes that destiny; and the progress from historical corruption to visionary perfection. C. Leech and P. Edwards have good essays in the same volume. The latter offers a viewpoint profoundly unsympathetic to the mythologizers. B. Evans, *Shakespeare's Comedies* (1960), has a lengthy study of the structure. He states that it surpasses all other Shakespearean plays in its manipulation of the protagonists' mutual ignorance. E. Jones, "Stuart Cymbeline," *EC,* XI (1961), 84-99, theorizes that the dramatic tableau of peace with which the play ends has a double function: it presents the world waiting for the birth of Christ, and it flatters the pacificism of King James I. This supposes a good deal more than the evidence supports; the ending may simply be a melodramatic and fairly routine romantic reconciliation. F. D. Hoeniger, "Irony and Romance in *Cym,*" *SEL,* II (1962), 219-228, suggests that two viewpoints are maintained until the conclusion: the characters are both taken seriously, as in romance, and ironically.

The Recurring Miracle (1962) by D. R. C. Marsh attempts to find in this play a theme if not a message of life's renewal. The reading is diffuse, and the criticism tends to be moralistic. Robert Hunter has a long essay in *Sh and the Comedy of Forgiveness* (1965). Hunter discusses the motif of the ordeal in romantic love and the implicitly Christian drama of reconciliation. Bernard Harris finds many topical references in " 'What's Past Is Prologue': *Cym* and *H8,*" *Later Sh,* ed. Bernard Harris and John Russell Brown (1966). He believes the play is concerned with the monarchy of King James. Other essays of value in this book are Stanley Wells, "Sh and Romance"; Francis Berry, "Word and Picture in the Final Plays"; John Russell Brown, "Laughter in the Last Plays"; Daniel Seltzer, "The Staging of the Last Plays."

Conspicuously free from speculation are the language studies of Spurgeon (1935) and Clemen (1951). They offer a rarity in the critical canon of this play: some hard facts about the patterns and artifices of rhetoric.

Further reading: A. H. Thorndike, *The Influence of Beaumont and Fletcher upon Sh* (1901); W. Raleigh, *Sh* (1907); F. Ristine, *English Tragicomedy* (1910); L. Strachey, *Books and Characters* (1922); E. Welsford, *The Court Masque* (1927); K. M. Lea, *Italian Popular Comedy* (1934); U. Ellis-Fermor, *The Jacobean Drama* (1936); R. W. Bond, *Studia Otiosa* (1938); D. M. McKeithan, *The Debt to Sh in the Beaumont and Fletcher Plays* (1938); E. Armstrong, *Shakespeare's Imagination* (1946); J. Dover Wilson and R. W. Hunt, "The Authenticity of Simon Forman's *Bocke of Plaies,*" *RES,* XXIII (1947), 193-200; G. E. Bentley, "Sh and the Blackfriars Theatre," *ShS,* I (1948), 38-50; *EIE* (1948), 27-119; C. Leech, *Shakespeare's Tragedies* (1950); A. Harbage, *Sh and the Rival Traditions* (1952); P. Cruttwell, *The Shakespearean Moment* (1954); W. Fischer, "Shakespeares Späte Romanzen," *ShJ,* XCI (1955), 7-24; M. C. Bradbrook, *The Growth and Structure of*

Elizabethan Comedy (1955); R. Behrens, "On Possible Inconsistencies in Two Character Portrayals in *Cym*," *NQ*, ns, III (1956), 379-380; C. Wright, "The Queen's Husband: Some Renaissance Views," *Studies in English*, III (1957), 133-138; N. Woodruff, "*Cym*," *Sh: Lectures on Five Plays* (1958); A. F. Potts, *Sh and the Faerie Queene* (1958); G. Stolzenberg, "Shakespeares *Cym*: Versuch zur Deutung," *Germanisch-Romanische Monatsschrift*, VIII (1958), 46-64; K. Muir, *Last Periods of Sh, Ibsen, Racine* (1961); F. D. Hoeniger, "Irony and Romance in *Cym*," *SEL*, II (1962), 219-228; Northrop Frye, *A Natural Perspective* (1965); Homer Swander, "*Cym*: Religious Idea and Dramatic Design," *Pacific Coast Studies in Sh* (1966), ed. Waldo McNeir and T. Greenfield; Arthur Kirsch, "*Cym* and Coterie Dramaturgy," *ELH*, XXXIV (1967), 285-306.

STAGING   Camb xliii-lv; Craig 1181; Odell *passim*; Sprague 60-64; Trewin *passim*.

See also Granville-Barker (above); Shaw (above); E. Welsford, *The Court Masque* (1927); E. West, "Shaw, Sh, and *Cym*," *Theatre Annual*, VIII (1950), 7-24; M. Webster, *Sh Without Tears* (1955); M. St. Clare Byrne, "The Sh Season at the Old Vic, 1956-1957, and Stratford-upon-Avon, 1957," *ShQ*, VIII (1957), 463-466; *Shaw on Sh* (1961).

THE WINTER'S TALE

TEXT Alexander 209-211; Camb vii-xii, 109-128; Chambers 487-490; Greg 415-417; New Arden xv-xxvii; Sisson I, 195-203.

See also S. A. Tannenbaum, "Textual and Other Notes on *WT*," *PQ*, VII (1928), 358-367, and *Shaksperian Scraps* (1933); *Works*, ed. G. L. Kittredge (1936), 431-432; J. Bullard and W. Fox, "*WT*," *TLS* (14 March 1952), 189, and ensuing essays, pp. 205, 237, 281, 313. See also J. Pafford, "*WT:* Typographical Peculiarities in the Folio Text," *NQ*, ns, VIII (1961), 172-178; J. Somer, "Ralph Crane and 'an Olde Play Called Winter's Tale,' " *Emporia State Research St.* (1962), 22-28; E. A. J. Honigmann, *The Stability of Shakespeare's Text* (1965).

EDITIONS *NV*, ed. H. H. Furness (1898); Camb, ed. A. Quiller-Couch and J. Dover Wilson (1931); Pelican, ed. B. Maxwell (1956); ed. S. L. Bethell (1956); New Arden, ed. J. H. Pafford (1963).

SOURCES S. Wolff, *The Greek Romances in Elizabethan Prose Fiction* (1912); E. Greenlaw, "Shakespeare's Pastorals," *SP*, XIII (1916), 122-154; H. Lancaster, "Hermione's Statue," *SP*, XXIX (1932), 233-238; A. Thaler, "Shakspere and Spenser," *SAB*, X (1935), 192-211; V. K. Whitaker, *Shakespeare's Use of Learning* (1953); P. Simpson, *Studies in Elizabethan Drama* (1955); E. Honigmann, "Secondary Sources of *WT*," *PQ*, XXXIV (1955), 27-38; E. Künstler, "Julio Romano im Wintermärchen," *ShJ*, XCII (1956), 291-298; Muir (1957); Bullough (1957—), forthcoming volume; A. F. Potts, *Sh and the Faerie Queene* (1958); J. Lawlor, "*Pandosto* and the Nature of Dramatic Romance," *PQ*, XLI (1962), 96-113; S. R. Maveety, "What Sh Did with *Pandosto*," *Pacific Coast Studies in Sh,* ed. Waldo McNeir and T. Greenfield (1966), 263-279.

CRITICISM A. Quiller-Couch, *Shakespeare's Workmanship* (1918), acknowledges the mixed or tragicomic nature of *WT* and claims for it unique dramatic effectiveness. Structural weakness and anachronism, he suggests, supply an atmosphere in which dream and vision dominate worldly logic. Romance, E. K. Chambers observes in his *Sh: A Survey* (1925), "will not have you apply too searching a psychology." He discusses the play's structure and suggests that it may be a deliberate flouting of the "unities" defended by Sidney and other rhetoricians. There are some cautious comments on the symbolism, a subject much oppressed by later critics. D. G. James, *Scepticism and Poetry* (1937), dismissed all the last plays as inconsistent myths of resurrection and dramatic failures. He found *WT* not as silly as *Per* but thought its recognitions and resurrections inadequate from the point of view of realism.

One of the first close studies, F. Tinkler's *"WT," Scrutiny,* V (1937),
344-364, found the play an expression of mature sensibility. While its
theme was "Grace and Graciousness," it manifested at the same time
"a continuous tone of irony." Tinkler found in the play varieties of
dialectic: reason versus intuition; the individual versus the state; nature
versus civilization. It is perhaps extreme to view the play as such a dis-
sertation upon culture.

E. M. W. Tillyard's *Shakespeare's Last Plays* (1938) stated that "not to
take the fertility symbolism as intended would be a perverse act of
caution. Perdita should be associated with them, as symbol both of the
creative powers of nature, physical fertility, and of healing and re-creation of the mind." The "abstract symbols" of winter and spring are
noted by M. Van Doren in *Sh* (1939); he emphasizes, however, that its
"concrete symbols" are human beings. There are interesting comments
on the sensuality and "heavy richness" of style and milieu. A complex
relationship is only half-clarified by H. S. Wilson's " 'Nature and Art' in
WT," SAB, XVIII (1943), 114-120. The substance of this popular Renaissance opposition is stated, but it is not fully applied to the text.
G. W. Knight's *The Crown of Life* (1947) has a justly famous essay on
"Great Creating Nature." This essay, indispensable for realizing the
complexity of language and theme, establishes a "sense of mighty
powers, working through both the natural order and man's religious
consciousness, that preserve, in spite of all appearance, the good." The
myth of Proserpina receives particular attention. The critique of P.
Edwards, *ShS,* XI (1958), 8-9, should accompany the reading of Knight.

The most elaborate study is the book of S. L. Bethell, *WT* (1947).
Bethell's is an explicitly Christian interpretation of the play: he invokes
sin, innocence, and grace as its controlling concepts. There is, however,
a great amount of rather more factual matter in this book. If redemption and resurrection seem to dominate, there is also valuable explication and analysis of Elizabethan ideas on the natural and supernatural.
Like Knight's study, this will enlighten where it does not convince. The
general studies in *EIE* (1948), 27-119, should be read in this connection. E. C. Pettet, *Sh and the Romance Tradition* (1949), attacks the
symbolists, especially Tillyard (above). He comes out flatly against the
notions of ritual purgation, suggesting that *WT* and the other romances
are more nearly business propositions for an aging playwright than
explorations of the different planes of reality. F. Hoeniger, "The Meaning of *WT," UTQ,* XX (1950), 11-26, sees the play as more intricate
than a literal interpretation would reveal and claims that it must be
interpreted allegorically. The famous discussion of art and nature is for
him central to this allegory: it raises issues of identity between parents
and children; the rebirth of nature from winter to summer; the rebirth
of human innocence; the place of creative imagination. It is concerned

overall with the great contradictions so often expressed in myth, those of life and death. A. Sewell, *Character and Society in Sh* (1951), is more literal and less easily satisfied. He is concerned with character and finds its delineation a *pastiche*. Repentance, far from having symbolic dimensions, seems to him externally applied.

J. Danby, *Poets on Fortune's Hill* (1952), does not have a specific section on *WT*; his commentary on the romances as a group, however, is valuable. For F. R. Leavis, *The Common Pursuit* (1952), *WT* is a masterpiece. He finds great and rich significance in the "concrete presence of time in its rhythmic processes, and . . . the association of human growth, decay and rebirth with the vital rhythms of nature at large." A conservative and sceptical estimate is that of A. Bonjour in "The Final Scene of *WT*," *ES*, XXXIII (1952), 193-208. He has some strictures against resurrection and myth in *WT* and attacks the school of Knight for its arbitrary assumption that the play reveals "the poet's intuition of immortality." I note that if Knight's ideas have validity, this is the play that tends most to demonstrate it. Given the nature of the play there is no reason not to apply the process of myth study. D. A. Traversi, *Sh: The Last Phase* (1954), deals principally with symbols. He thinks the play concerns "the divisions created in love and friendship by the passage of time and the action of 'blood' and of the final healing of these divisions." Like Tillyard and Knight (above) he interprets it as a kind of parable of resurrection, healing, and unity. This can be carried to extremes, and it is by J. Bryant in "Shakespeare's Allegory: *WT*," *Sew*, LXIII (1955), 202-222. Leontes and his son stand for Judaism, Perdita for the "true Church," Polixenes for the Gentiles, and Paulina for St. Paul. Hermione, quite naturally, stands for Christ. The interpretation does not invite rational discussion.

An important collection of essays on the last plays is in *ShS*, XI (1958). Of special note is N. Coghill's "Six Points of Stage-Craft in *WT*," 31-41, which makes it clear that the dramatic composition is better than generally supposed. The firmness of structure and its relation to theme is the subject of C. Leech's "The Structure of the Last Plays" in the same volume. J. H. Pafford explores "Music, and the Songs in WT" in *ShQ*, X (1950), 161-175. T. Driver's *The Sense of History in Greek and Shakespearean Drama* (1960) treats time and cosmology: "time in *WT* is the means within which reconciliation and fulfillment take place. Reconciliation depends upon repentance, a time of purgation, and the activity of memory, drawing the past into the present." Perhaps too much is made by Driver of the play's representing developments in human history.

B. Evans, *Shakespeare's Comedies* (1960), analyzes the deceptions and concludes that they reveal a good deal about the nature of the play's dramatic universe. We first share the protagonists' sense of disorder in nature and then their overpowering conviction of its essential benefi- cence. The point is slightly strained. K. Muir's *Last Periods of Sh, Racine, Ibsen* (1961) summarizes the last plays and discusses the rela- tionship of romance and symbolic content. N. Frye's essay on "Recog- nition in *WT*," *Essays on Sh . . . In Honor of Hardin Craig* (1962) ex- plains the use of the incredible as a dramatic agency. The strange events and recognitions of the romance supply a "sense of an irresistible power, whether of divine or human agency, making for a providential resolution." Frye's framework is the cosmology of the romances, a scheme in which, intentionally he thinks, much is presented and little explained. The most notorious stage direction in Sh is the subject of D. Biggins' "Exit pursued by a Beare," *ShQ*, XIII (1962), 3-13. The death of Antigonus is explained as thematic if not realistic—a presenta- tion of "destruction, broken integrity, Heavenly vengeance." An ex- tremely able essay accompanies J. H. Pafford's New Arden edition (1963). There is a thorough review of criticism, a good essay on sources, and important remarks on the interpretation. While the regenerative aspects of the play are noted, there are intelligent comments on its limi- tations by a natural order to which death is as central a principle as life.

There is an essay on *WT* in Robert G. Hunter's *Sh and the Comedy of Forgiveness* (1965). A book of importance for all of the last plays is Northrop Frye's *A Natural Perspective* (1965). Frye writes that "the mythical or primitive basis of comedy is a movement toward the rebirth and renewal of the powers of nature, this aspect of literary comedy being expressed in the imagery more directly than in the structure." The book is a very imaginative explanation of myth and psychology, and of their relation to comic themes. *Later Sh,* ed. Bernard Harris and John Russell Brown (1966), has these articles bearing on *WT*: Stanley Wells, "Sh and Romance"; Francis Berry, "Word and Picture in the Final Plays"; John Russell Brown, "Laughter in the Last Plays"; Daniel Seltzer, "The Staging of the Last Plays." There is an excellent collection of eighteenth- and nineteenth-century comments on this play in Kenneth Muir's *Sh: WT* (1969). See also Muir's "The Conclusion of *WT*," *The Morality of Art* (1969). A book devoted entirely to this play is Fitzroy Pyle's *WT: A Commentary on the Structure* (1969). This has a good scene-by-scene reading. The emphasis is on the planning and unity of the play rather than on its mythopoeic qualities. There is a good comparison with the source, *Pandosto.*

Some studies of character include M. Hughes, "A Classical vs. a Social Approach to Shakspere's Autolycus," *SAB,* (1940), 219-226; P. Siegel, "Leontes a Jealous Tyrant," *RES,* I (1950), 302-307; R. Trienens, "The Inception of Leontes' Jealousy," *ShQ,* IV (1953), 321-326. The lan- guage of *WT* has been studied in T. R. Price, "Word-play and Puns in

WT," *Shakespeariana* (1889); *WT,* ed. H. B. Charlton (1916); Spurgeon (1935); Clemen (1951); Evans (1952); *WT,* ed. S. L. Bethell (1956); M. Mahood, *Shakespeare's Word Play* (1957); New Arden, ed. J. H. Pafford (1963).

Further reading: E. Dowden, *Sh: A Critical Study* (1875); T. R. Price, "The Construction of *WT,"* *Shakespeareana* (1890); W. Greg, *Pastoral Poetry and Pastoral Drama* (1906); F. Ristine, *English Tragicomedy* (1910); L. Strachey, *Books and Characters* (1922); E. Welsford, *The Court Masque* (1927); U. Ellis-Fermor, *The Jacobean Drama* (1936); A. R. Fairchild, *Sh and the Arts of Design* (1937); T. Spencer, "Appearance and Reality in Shakespeare's Last Plays," *MP,* XXXIX (1942), 265-274; W. H. Auden, "The Sea and the Mirror," *For the Time Being* (1944); G. Bentley, "Sh and the Blackfriars Theatre," *ShS,* I (1948), 38-50; C. Leech, *Shakespeare's Tragedies* (1950); A. Harbage, *Sh and the Rival Traditions* (1952); D. Bland, "The Heroine and the Sea," *EC,* III (1953), 39-44; H. Oppel, *Shakespeares Tragödien und Romanzen: Kontinuität oder Umbruch?* (1954); W. Fischer, "Shakespeares Späte Romanzen," *ShJ,* XCI (1955), 7-24; D. Marsh, *The Recurring Miracle* (1962); Ernest Schanzer, "The Structural Pattern of *WT,"* *REL,* V (1964), 72-82; Inga-Stina Ewbank, "The Triumph of Time in *WT,"* *REL,* V (1964), 83-100; E. W. Taylor, *Nature and Art in Renaissance Literature* (1964); W. H. Matchett, "Some Dramatic Techniques in *WT,"* *ShS,* XXII (1969), 93-107.

STAGING Camb 185-193; Craig 1217; New Arden 175-181; Odell *passim*; Sprague 66-70; Trewin *passim.*

See also E. Welsford, *The Court Masque* (1927); H. Spencer, *The Art and Life of William Sh* (1940); G. Rylands, "Festival Sh in the West End," *ShS,* VI (1953), 142-145; M. Webster, *Sh Without Tears* (1955); N. Coghill, "Six Points of Stage-Craft in *WT,"* *ShS,* XI (1958), 31-41; W. M. Merchant, *Sh and the Artist* (1959); C. Leech, *TN and Shakespearian Comedy* (1965); G. Wickham, *Shakespeare's Dramatic Heritage* (1969); Pyle (above).

THE TEMPEST

TEXT Alexander 211-216; Camb xxix-xliv, 79-85; Chambers 490-494; Greg 418-421; New Arden xi-xxiv; Sisson I, 43-52.

See also H. D. Gray, "Some Indications that *Tem* Was Revised," *SP*, XXVIII (1921), 129-140; E. K. Chambers, "The Integrity of *Tem*," *RES*, I (1925), 129-150; S. A. Tannenbaum, "Textual Difficulties in *Tem*," *SAB*, VI (1931), 148-160, and "How Not to Edit Shakspere," *PQ*, X (1931), 97-137; H. N. Fairchild, "Emending the Text of *Tem*," *SAB*, VII (1932), 186-191; *Works,* ed. G. L. Kittredge (1936), 3-4.

EDITIONS *NV,* ed. H. H. Furness (1892); Arden, ed. M. Luce (1902); Camb, ed. A. Quiller-Couch and J. Dover Wilson (1921); ed. G. L. Kittredge (1939); New Arden, ed. F. Kermode (1954); Yale, ed. D. Horn (1955); Pelican, ed. N. Frye (1958).

SOURCES W. Newell, "Sources of Shakespeare's *Tem*," *Jour. Amer. Folklore,* XVI (1903), 234-257; J. De Perott, *The Probable Source of the Plot of Shakespeare's Tem* (1905); J. D. Rea, "A Source for the Storm in *Tem*," *MP,* XVII (1919), 279-286; R. Cawley, "Shakespeare's Use of the Voyagers in *Tem*," *PMLA,* XLI (1926), 688-726; R. Howarth, *Shakespeare's Tem* (1936); J. Nosworthy, "The Narrative Sources of *Tem*," *RES,* XXIV (1948), 281-294; M. Hodgen, "Montaigne and Sh Again," *HLQ,* XVI (1952), 23-42; Muir (1957); Bullough (1957–), forthcoming volume; C. Gesner, "*Tem* as Pastoral Romance," *ShQ,* X (1959), 531-539; R. Reed, "The Probable Origin of Ariel," *ShQ,* XI (1960), 61-65.

CRITICISM Coleridge wrote that the importance of *Tem* resided in its quality of arousing the "sympathetic imagination," or that faculty removed from senses and logic. His essay established in part the present critical orientation toward vision and romance in *Tem.* Hazlitt wrote an appreciative essay still worth knowing. Nineteenth-century critics often went allegory-hunting with a vengeance: some found Prospero Understanding, others saw him as Science. Caliban was called everything from the Proletariat to the Missing Link. There is a selection of improbable theories listed by Dowden in *Sh: A Critical Study* (1875); Dowden himself was responsible for the view that the play revealed Sh finally out of the depths of despair and spiritually "On the Heights." This was accepted by M. Luce in his Arden edition (1902); he stated that style is a revelation of soul and drew from this play a rather sticky biography of its author.

There has always been a cult of Miranda-worship, and R. G. Moulton's

Sh as a Dramatic Artist (1888 edition) contributes heavily to it. His praise, however, is tempered by some sound remarks on character. Quite free of the sentimentality that marked earlier work is A. Gilbert's "*Tem:* Parallelism in Character and Situation," *JEGP,* XIV (1915), 63-74, which has valuable comments on the dualistic structure. There are several chapters in A. Quiller-Couch's *Shakespeare's Workmanship* (1918) that attempt to formulate a critical and scholarly context. Colin Still in *Shakespeare's Mystery Play* (1921) called *Tem* "a dramatic representation of the Mystery of Redemption" and in a remarkable burst of intellectual euphoria outlined a scheme of ceremonies, rites, initiations, purgations, and ascensions which it is supposedly about. A much more hard-nosed attitude was taken by E. E. Stoll in "*Tem,*" *PMLA,* XLVII (1932), 699-726. He took a strong stand against allegory and symbolism and the notion of the play as a veiled biography. He gives a very stiff overhauling to critics like Still.

Spurgeon (1935) points out the nature of the play's elemental imagery. Its supernatural aspects are outlined by W. C. Curry in *Shakespeare's Philosophical Patterns* (1937). The concept of Nature in the last plays is treated by J. M. Murry in *Sh* (1936). There is an important qualification of the idea of "re-birth of nature"; Murry makes clear the realism that connects Nature as symbol and as human reality. D. G. James attacked the last plays for being dramatically unsatisfactory in *Scepticism and Poetry* (1937). *Tem* is the best of these according to James—a record of Shakespeare's attitude toward reality itself. James is not free from allegorical assumptions of earlier commentators. E. M. W. Tillyard, *Shakespeare's Last Plays* (1938), discusses the tragic overtones and realism. There are some valuable comments on the hierarchy of life in *Tem,* from animal to intellectual, in M. Van Doren's *Sh* (1939) and T. Spencer's *Sh and the Nature of Man* (1942).

The influence of the essays in G. W. Knight's *The Crown of Life* (1947) has been very great. One of these, on "Myth and Miracle," outlines the pattern of loss, restoration, and vision in the last plays. Knight's study of "The Shakespearian Superman" treats Prospero as the personification of powers and virtues hinted at in the tragedies. Prospero as a symbol of intellectual order is more convincing than as a symbol of Christ. E. C. Pettet, *Sh and the Romance Tradition* (1949), exonerates *Tem* from the strictures of T. S. Eliot on Jacobean romance: "the debility of romantic drama does not depend upon extravagant setting, or preposterous events, or inconceivable coincidences. . . . It consists in an internal incoherence of feelings, a concatenation of emotions which signifies nothing." D. A. Traversi, "*Tem,*" *Scrutiny,* XVI (1949), 127-157, writes of the analogies served by character: Caliban is an analogue of "natural anarchism," Prospero and Miranda represent the dialogue of justice and mercy. Traversi's *Sh: The Last Phase* (1954) adds a long study of symbolism. The play is viewed as a study of the breakdown of one order and its spiritual reconstitution by the power of love. An important essay on the puritanic strain in *Tem* is in C. Leech's *Shakespeare's Tragedies* (1950). The play is interpreted as a study in hierarchy—it alludes not only to such relationships as that between individual and state but between spirit and flesh. This seems somewhat Hegelian—but so does the play.

R. Brower, "The Heresy of Plot," *EIE* (1951), 44-69, examines the Aristotelian poetic criteria and suggests that the totality of language and action may be substituted for these in judging *Tem.* The overriding idea of the play is that of transformation. Brower has an excellent study of "The Mirror of Analogy: *Tem,*" in *The Fields of Light* (1951). Principally explained are the metaphors of storm, strangeness, vision, and change. Both studies are much to be commended. A valuable study of the "intense earthy atmosphere" supplied by images is in Clemen (1951). The play is saturated with images that "continually act upon our senses." A strong rejection of mythical and thematic interpretation is in B. Dobrée's chapter in *E&S* (1952), 13-25. Dobrée argues that repentance and forgiveness in *Tem* are simply fossils, not active dramatic principles. He finds the mood far from charming and the tone not at all visionary; instead the play seems to explore the nature of reality in an analytical way. Two general studies of importance are J. Danby, *Poets on Fortune's Hill* (1952), and F. R. Leavis, "The Criticism of Shakespeare's Late Plays," *The Common Pursuit* (1952).

B. Knox has a very useful study of "*Tem* and the Ancient Comic Tradition" in *EIE* (1954), 52-73. He points out that the play is deeply rooted in Plautine drama, which furnishes stock types of master-servant relationships. Far from being improbable, the play in fact relies on ancient and familiar formulas of domestic comedy. The best study yet done on the play will, I hope, be acknowledged to be in F. Kermode's New Arden edition (1954). Kermode addresses himself to five main topics and makes an important contribution to our understanding of their place in the play. These are: the effect of discoveries in the New World; Renaissance concepts of nature and primitivism; natural and supernatural art; true nobility; the character of pastoral tragicomedy. Some of the moral issues involved in *Tem* are treated by R. Speaight in *Nature in Shakespearian Tragedy* (1955).

F. Neilson, *Sh and Tem* (1956), returns to the notion that the play is a covert autobiography. There are other eccentricities. A very interesting critique is that of J. Hart, "Prospero and Faustus," *BUSE,* II (1956), 197-206. It is suggested that the play is an answer to Marlowe's *Faustus,* which opposes white magic (English humanism) to black magic (the quest for unlimited power). *ShS,* XI (1958) has a number of useful

articles. P. Edwards writes of the critical history of the romances; their
structure is the subject of an essay by C. Leech; music is studied by
J. M. Nosworthy; the magic of Prospero is examined by C. J. Sisson.
The last suggests that the figure of the magician, learned, pacific, and
just, would not be displeasing to the ultimate audience, James I. A
learned essay on analogues of voyages and adventures is in D. C. Allen's
Image and Meaning (1960).

There is an essay on this play in Robert Hunter's *Sh and the Comedy
of Forgiveness* (1965). Northrop Frye's *A Natural Perspective* (1965)
has important remarks on such themes as "The Triumph of Time" and
"The Return from the Sea" in the literature of romance and mythology. *Later Sh* (1966), ed. Bernard Harris and John Russell Brown, has
a group of useful essays: Philip Brockbank, "*Tem:* Conventions of Art
and Empire"; Stanley Wells, "Sh and Romance"; Francis Berry, "Word
and Picture in the Final Plays"; John Russell Brown, "Laughter in the
Last Plays"; Daniel Seltzer, "The Staging of the Last Plays." A. D.
Nuttall, *Two Concepts of Allegory* (1967) is learned and highly interesting. It is, however, both difficult and discursive. It deals, as the title
suggests, with allegory and with states of dream and vision. For useful
collections of essays see D. J. Palmer, *Sh: Tem* (1968) and Hallet Smith,
Twentieth Century Interpretations of Tem (1969). Harry Levin's *The
Myth of the Golden Age* (1969) has a great deal of information about
the Utopian aspects of the play. See also Levin's "Two Magian Comedies: *Tem* and *The Alchemist,*" *ShS,* XXII (1969), 47-58.

The criticism of character, particularly that of Caliban, has sometimes
been obsessive, and the pages of *NV* (1892) have many extracts, some
wise and some as fantastic as their subject. Modern essays of note are
J. McPeek, "The Genesis of Caliban," *PQ,* XXV (1946), 378-381; J.
Hankins, "Caliban the Bestial Man," *PMLA,* LXII (1947), 793-801;
R. Goldsmith, "The Wild Man on the English Stage," *MLR,* LII (1958),
481-491. Ariel is the subject of A. Koszul in *ES,* XIX (1937), 200-204.
See also W. Johnson, "The Genesis of Ariel," *ShQ,* II (1951), 205-210;
R. Reed, "The Probable Origin of Ariel," *ShQ,* XI (1960), 61-65. Pros-
pero is treated by Knight (above) and by F. D. Hoeniger, "Prospero's
Storm and Miracle," *ShQ,* VII (1956), 33-38. There is a section on
Miranda in *NV;* many of the studies described above discuss her sym-
bolic status.

Further reading: L. Strachey, *Books and Characters* (1922); E. Welsford, *The Court Masque* (1927); G. W. Knight, *The Shakespearian
Tempest* (1932); H. Craig, *The Enchanted Glass* (1935); U. Ellis-
Fermor, *The Jacobean Drama* (1936); J. Dover Wilson, *The Meaning
of Tem* (1936); E. Knowlton, "Nature and Sh," *PMLA,* LI (1936), 719-
744; L. Hotson, *I, William Sh* (1937); R. H. West, *The Invisible World*

(1939); *EIE* (1948); G. Bentley, "Sh and the Blackfriars Theatre," *ShS,* I (1948), 38-50; D. Stauffer, *Shakespeare's World of Images* (1949); N. Coghill, "The Basis of Shakespearian Comedy," *E&S* (1950), 1-28; A. Harbage, *Sh and the Rival Traditions* (1952); D. S. Bland, "The Heroine and the Sea," *EC,* III (1953), 39-44; H. S. Wilson, "Action and Symbol in *MM* and *Tem,*" *ShQ,* IV (1953), 375-384; H. Heuer, "Traumwelt und Wirklichkeit in der Sprache des *Tem,*" *ShJ,* XC (1954), 210-228; H. Oppel, *Shakespeares Tragödien und Romanzen: Kontinuität oder Umbruch?* (1954); W. Fischer, "Shakespeares Späte Romanzen," *ShJ,* XCI (1955), 7-24; K. Muir, *Last Periods of Sh, Racine, Ibsen* (1961); D. Marsh, *The Recurring Miracle* (1962); Frank Kermode, *Sh: The Final Plays* (1963); David G. James, *The Dream of Prospero* (1967).

STAGING Camb 109-111; Craig 1248-1249; New Arden lxxi-lxxvi; Odell *passim;* Sprague 40-44; Trewin *passim.*

See also E. Welsford, *The Court Masque* (1927); A. Nicoll, *Stuart Masques* (1937); J. C. Adams, "The Staging of *Tem,* III. iii ," *RES,* XIV (1938), 404-419; C. Ward, "*Tem:* A Restoration Opera Problem," *ELH,* XIII (1946), 119-130; O. J. Campbell, "Miss Webster and *Tem,*" *Amer. Scholar,* XIV (1946), 271-281; W. Milton, "*Tem* in a Teapot," *ELH,* XIV (1947), 207-218; G. W. Knight, *Principles of Shakespearian Production* (1949); M. Clarke and R. Wood, *Sh at the Old Vic* (1954); M. St. Clare Byrne, "The Sh Season at the Old Vic, 1956-1957, and Stratford-upon-Avon, 1957," *ShQ,* VIII (1957), 488-492.

HENRY THE EIGHTH

TEXT Alexander 216-221; Camb vii-xxxvii, 113-171; Chambers 495-498; Greg 422-425; New Arden xv-xxvi; Sisson II, 98-104.

In 1850 J. Spedding's "On the Several Shares of Shakspere and Fletcher in the Play of *H8*," *Gentleman's Magazine*, XXXIV, 115-123 and 381-382, claimed double authorship. His view was substantiated by S. Hickson in *NQ* of the same year. Most modern scholarship assumes that these researches were substantially correct. There are notable exceptions, especially Alexander and Foakes (below). Some recent surveys are in the New Arden and Camb editions. See also W. Farnham, "Colloquial Contractions . . . As a Test of Authorship," *PMLA*, XXXI (1916), 326-358; H. Conrad, "*H8*, Fletchers Werk, überarbeitet von Sh," *Englische Studien*, LII (1918), 204-264; Nicolson (below); P. Alexander, "Conjectural History, or Shakespeare's *H8*," *E&S* (1930), 85-120; B. Maxwell, *Studies in Beaumont, Fletcher, and Massinger* (1939); A. C. Partridge, *The Problem of H8 Reopened* (1949); A. Oras, "Extra Monosyllables in *H8* and the Problem of Authorship," *JEGP*, LII (1953), 198-213; R. A. Foakes, "On the First Folio Text of *H8*," *SB*, X (1958), 55-60; R. A. Law, "The Double Authorship of *H8*," *SP*, LVI (1959), 471-488; M. Mincoff, "*H8* and Fletcher," *ShQ*, XII (1961), 239-260. Studies of special importance are those by Partridge and Mincoff. See also Cyrus Hoy, "Fletcher and His Collaborators," *SB*, XV (1962), 71-90.

EDITIONS Arden, ed. C. K. Pooler (1915); New Arden, ed. R. A. Foakes (1957); Camb, ed. J. C. Maxwell (1962); Pelican, ed. F. David Hoeniger (1966).

SOURCES R. Boyle, "*H8*, An Investigation into the Origin and Authorship," *New Sh Soc. Trans.*, XXI (1880-1886); W. Zeitlin, "Shakespeares *H8* und Rowleys *When You See Me*," *Anglia*, IV (1881), 73-96; W. Boswell-Stone, *Shakespere's Holinshed* (1896); A. H. Thorndike, *The Influence of Beaumont and Fletcher upon Sh* (1901); B. Maxwell, "Fletcher and *H8*," *Manly Anniversary Studies* (1923); A. and J. Nicoll, *Holinshed's Chronicle as Used in Shakespeare's Plays* (1927); R. A. Law, "Holinshed and *H8*," *TxSE*, XXXVI (1957), 3-11; Bullough (1957–), IV, 435-510.

CRITICISM Dr. Johnson wrote a short, incisive essay on *H8* commenting on the splendor of its pageantry and the "meek sorrows and virtuous distress" of Katherine. A mixture of much sentimentality and much insight is in Mrs. Jameson's *Characteristics of Women* (1833). She viewed Katherine, as many nineteenth-century critics did, as the center

of the play. There is worthwhile comment on Katherine's sacrificial
status. The editions of A. Wright (1891) and D. N. Smith (1899) have
interesting remarks. H. N. Hudson, *Sh: His Life, Art, and Character*
(1872), saw *H8* as the drama of an evil king and a saintly queen. His
character studies are good but somewhat sentimental. He concludes that
it is a moral tale of suffering borne with dignity, which covers a multi-
tude of sins in the victim. In this he is close to the conclusions of most
recent critics. G. Brandes, *William Sh* (1898), addresses himself to
Katherine, "a character of mingled charm and distinction, a union of
Castilian pride with extreme simplicity, of inflexible resolution with
gentlest resignation, and of a quick temper with a sincere piety."

Lytton Strachey's *Books and Characters* (1922) has a well-known essay
on the last plays. He describes their author as "bored with people,
bored with real life, bored with drama, bored, in fact, with everything
except poetry and poetical dreams." Strachey believes *H8* is tedious, a
proof of this creative surrender. An important article is M. Nicolson's
"The Authorship of *H8*," *PMLA*, XXXVII (1922), 484-502. Nicolson
notes the great differences in handling chronology and sources in different parts of the play and ascribes part of the discrepancy to Fletcher.
She also finds evident Shakespearean repetition of ideas in subplots.
There is a good analysis of what are presumably Shakespeare's scenes,
of contradictions in character, and of Fletcher's padding. P. Alexander
(above) has some critical remarks in addition to discussion of the text.
C. Clark, *A Study of Shakespeare's H8* (1931), has some helpful extracts from the earlier criticism; his own comments are not very intense.
There is a fine study of the language in Spurgeon (1935). She points
out that "there are three aspects of the picture of a body in the mind of
the writer of the play: the whole body and its limbs; the various parts,
tongue, mouth and so on; and—much the most constant—bodily action
of almost every kind . . . especially and repeatedly the picture of the
body or back bent and weighed down under a heavy burden." G. W.
Knight, "A Note on *H8*," *Criterion*, XV (1936), 228-236, first discussed
the theories he was to develop in *The Crown of Life* (1947). The earlier
essay states that the king is not historically conceived and perhaps not
even a true protagonist but a symbolic figure of power and peace.
Knight discussed, perhaps to the exclusion of other things, the themes
of power, religion, and suffering. He remarked that the tragic content
of this play is connected to Catholicism and its more hopeful aspects
to Protestantism. We are never clear, Knight added, on exact moral
meanings—the play shares this uncertainty with the other late plays.

A useful study is in E. Fripp's *Sh, Man and Artist* (1938). Pageantry,
prophecy, and the visionary nature of the play are considered as they
reflect on "peace, prosperity, the settlements of the Reformation."
Fripp defends the structure, unlike the majority of critics. J. Walleser,

"Staging a Tertiary," *Franciscan Studies,* XXV (1944), 63-78, points out that Katherine is pictured as a follower of the Tertiary rules of *Supra Montem*—she is a quasi-religious figure of justice, duty, submission, prayer, and appeal. P. Wiley, "Renaissance Exploitation of Cavendish's *Life of Wolsey,*" *SP,* XLIII (1946), 121-146, has a very good account of the fortunes of Wolsey in sixteenth-century literature. Wiley believes the *Life* furnished later writers with a pattern of ascent, sin, and fall, even though it was distorted and misunderstood. The most famous essay is G. W. Knight's "*H8* and the Poetry of Conversion," *The Crown of Life* (1947). Although Knight's account of the authorship is not to be trusted, his study of the connection to the other late plays is very good. The essay is complex, difficult to summarize, and essential to the understanding of the play.

A. A. Parker, "Henry VIII in Sh and Calderón," *MLR,* XLIII (1948), 327-352, concludes that Calderón's *La cisma de Ingalaterra* is a better play than *H8*. According to Parker the defect of Shakespeare's play lies in its failure to represent the idea of acquiescence to despotism in dramatic action. His attack on the play's lack of unity and coherence does not take sufficient account of research that has pointed out the tripartite structure. F. Kermode, "What Is Shakespeare's *H8* About?" *DUJ,* IX (1947), 48-55, writes of medieval conceptions inherited from *The Mirror for Magistrates:* "the play may be regarded as a late morality, showing the state from which great ones may fall; the manner of their falling . . . and the part played in their falls for good or ill by a King who, though human, is *ex officio* the deputy of God, and the agent of divine punishment and mercy." H. Craig, *An Interpretation of Sh* (1948), offers a corrective to modern views of the king; he points out that the Elizabethans thought of him as a much greater man than we do. Perhaps his greatest glory was the paternity of Elizabeth I. Craig concludes that *H8* is about the "current of eternal beauty and goodness . . . beneath all the ills that history describes."

E. Waith, *The Pattern of Tragicomedy in Beaumont and Fletcher* (1952), invokes medieval tragedy to explain the tripartite structure. The play is constituted of three parts: the falls of Buckingham, Katherine, and Wolsey. Waith has a very helpful analysis of pageantry and masque and of the great vein of pathos which runs through the farewell speeches. Waith notes the contrast between innate nobility and immoral actions in those characters who live badly and die nobly. He suggests that many speeches are not expressions of character, but rather of a general concept of the tragic hero. A study of the amorous and energetic dances is in D. Richey's "The Dance in *H8*," *Furman Univ. Bulletin,* XXXV (1952), 1-11. I. Ribner, *The English History Play in the Age of Sh* (1957), observes that Sh "follows his sources with a greater fidelity than he had ever before observed in an English history play, with a strange unawareness of the basic inconsistencies within his sources, inconsistencies which he carried over into the play and which make his portrait of Wolsey in particular almost incomprehensible." A very good introduction accompanies the New Arden edition of R. A. Foakes (1957). The editor reviews past interpretations and advances his own valuable ideas about the play. He notes the series of contrasts and oppositions in character and event, the "cycle of suffering and joy," and the themes shared with the other late plays.

C. Leech, "The Structure of the Last Plays," *ShS,* XI (1958), 19-30, finds that *H8* brings to full development an attitude toward life inherent in *Per, Cym,* and *Tem.* Its structure is cyclic and deals with the fall of great persons, but nothing is given final, unambiguous moral shape. M. Doran's review of the New Arden edition is in *JEGP,* LIX (1960), 287-291. There is valuable critical commentary on the style and moral ambiguousness. E. M. W. Tillyard, "Why Did Sh Write *H8?*" *CQ,* III (1961), 22-27, concludes that he made the best—which was far from good—of heterogeneous materials. M. Mincoff's article on the text (above) has a discussion of the style and a revealing examination of tests used to establish authorship. Two very good essays that review the critical history and furnish valuable insights of their own are in Bullough and the Camb edition, both noted above.

Northrop Frye's *A Natural Perspective* (1965) is useful for its treatment of romance in the last plays. There is a very good article on the propaganda value of this play by Howard Felperin: "Shakespeare's *H8:* History as Myth," *SEL,* VI (1966), 225-246. Felperin believes that the mythos of redemption is insufficient in this play because of the weight of its political apologetics. There are a number of essays in *Later Sh,* ed. Bernard Harris and John Russell Brown (1966). See especially Harris' "What's Past Is Prologue" and Daniel Seltzer, "The Staging of the Last Plays." Ronald Berman's *"H8:* History and Romance" is in *ES,* XLVIII (1960), 1-10. This article deals with the element of masque and with the transcendence of history.

Further reading: B. Warner, *English History in Shakespeare's Plays* (1894); F. Schelling, *The English Chronicle Play* (1902); C. T. Brooke, *The Tudor Drama* (1912); J. Marriott, *English History in Sh* (1918); W. Raleigh, *Sh and England* (1918); E. K. Chambers, *Sh: A Survey* (1925); W. Lewis, *The Lion and the Fox* (1927); J. W. Allen, *A History of Political Thought in the Sixteenth Century* (1928); W. Clemen, "Sh und das Königtum," *ShJ,* LXVIII (1932), 56-79; C. Oman, "The Personality of Henry VIII," *Quarterly Review,* CCLXIX (1937), 88-104; M. Van Doren, *Sh* (1939); M. Kennedy, *The Oration in Sh* (1942); L. Campbell, *Shakespeare's Histories* (1947); A. Sewell, *Character and Society in Sh* (1951); J. Danby, *Poets on Fortune's Hill* (1952);

H. Mutschmann and K. Wentersdorf, *Sh and Catholicism* (1952);
G. Steiner, "A Note on Cavendish's *Life of Cardinal Wolsey,*" *English,*
IX (1952), 51-54; H. Jenkins, "Shakespeare's History Plays: 1900-
1951," *ShS,* VI (1953), 1-15; L. C. Knights, *Shakespeare's Politics*
(1957); C. Ferguson, *Naked to Mine Enemies* (1957); K. Muir, *Last
Periods of Sh, Racine, Ibsen* (1961); M. M. Reese, *The Cease of Majesty*
(1961); C. Leech, *The John Fletcher Plays* (1962); P. Bertram, "*H8:*
The Conscience of the King," *In Defence of Reading* (1962); H. M.
Richmond, "Shakespeare's *H8:* Romance Redeemed by History," *Sh
Studies,* IV (1968), 334-349; Herbert Howarth, "An Old Man's Method:
H8 and the Late Plays," *The Tiger's Heart* (1970).

STAGING   Camb xxxviii-l; Craig 1273; New Arden lxii-lxv; Odell
passim; Sprague 76-83; Trewin *passim.*

See also W. Winter, *Sh on the Stage* (1911); E. Welsford, *The Court
Masque* (1927); W. J. Lawrence, "The Stage Directions in *H8,*" *TLS*
(18 December 1930), 1085; Clark (above); H. Spencer, *The Art and
Life of William Sh* (1940); G. Bentley, "Sh and the Blackfriars Thea-
tre," *ShS,* I (1948), 38-50; G. W. Knight, *Principles of Shakespearian
Production* (1949); M. St. Clare Byrne, "A Stratford Production: *H8,*"
ShS, III (1950), 120-129; R. Walker, "Theatre Royal," *The Twentieth
Century,* CLIII (1953), 463-470; T. C. Kemp, "Acting Sh: Modern
Tendencies in Playing and Production," *ShS,* VII (1954), 124-125;
R. Walker, "The Whirligig of Time," *ShS,* XII (1959), 122-126. W.
Merchant, *Sh and the Artist* (1959).

PERICLES

TEXT Alexander 221-222; Camb ix-xxv, 88-97; Chambers 518-528; Greg, *Editorial Problem in Sh* (1954), 74-76; New Arden xxii-lxiii; Sisson II, 285-300.

See also K. Elze, "Notes . . . on *AC* and *Per*," *Englische Studien,* IX (1886), 267-290; K. Steinhäuser, *Die neueren Anschauungen über die Echtheit von Shakespeares Pericles* (1918); H. D. Sykes, *Sidelights on Sh* (1919); S. Spiker, "George Wilkins and the Authorship of *Per*," *SP*, XXX (1933), 551-570; H. Craig, "*Per* and *The Painfull Adventures, SP*, XLV (1948), 600-605; K. Muir, "*Per*, II.v," *NQ*, CXCIII (1948), 362; McManaway, 30; P. Edwards, "An Approach to the Problem of *Per*," *ShS*, V (1952), 25-49; H. Craig, "Review of Sh Scholarship in 1952," *ShQ*, IV (1953), 122; J. G. McManaway, "Textual Studies," *ShS*, VI (1953), 164-165; J. Long, "Laying the Ghosts in *Per*," *ShQ*, VII (1956), 39-42; F. D. Hoeniger, "How Significant Are Textual Parallels?" *ShQ*, XI (1960), 27-37; H. Craig, *A New Look at Shakespeare's Quartos* (1961).

EDITIONS Camb, ed. J. C. Maxwell (1956); Pelican, ed. James McManaway (1961); New Arden, ed. F. D. Hoeniger (1963).

SOURCES This play has been the subject of much tangled inquiry into text and sources. The older view of divided authorship exemplified by Sykes (above) has been much modified by Edwards in his important article (above). See also the argument for divided authorship in the New Arden edition. An important study is K. Muir's *Sh as Collaborator* (1960). Other studies: S. Singer, *Apollonius von Tyrus* (1895); E. Klebs, *Die Erzählung von Apollonius aus Tyrus* (1899); W. Hastings, "Exit George Wilkins?", *SAB*, XI (1936), 67-83, and "Shakespeare's Part in *Per*," *SAB*, XIV (1939), 67-85; H. Craig, "Shakespeare's Development as a Dramatist in the Light of His Experience," *SP*, XXXIX (1942), 226-238; T. M. Parrott, "*Per:* the Play and the Novel," *SAB*, XXIII (1948), 105-113; K. Muir, "The Problem of *Per*," *ES*, XXX (1949), 65-83; Muir (ed.), *The Painfull Adventures of Pericles*, by George Wilkins (1953); Muir (1957); Bullough (1957–), VI, 349-564; E. Schanzer, "Heywood's *Ages* and Sh," *RES*, XI (1960), 18-28.

CRITICISM The criticism of *Per* has generally been unsympathetic except when it devolves into praise, often exaggerated, of the play's mythopoeic qualities. Ben Jonson thought the story was "mouldy"; Steevens found it simply a string of unoriginal adventures. A. Quiller-Couch, *Shakespeare's Workmanship* (1918), wrote of the great success of *Per* on the Elizabethan stage and attributed it to the play's deeply felt moments of emotion and to the character of Marina. E. K. Chambers, *Sh: A Survey* (1925), refused to believe that the first two acts could be the work of Sh; he reserved his praise for the dreamlike qualities of the rest. The first of G. W. Knight's influential studies is in *The Shakespearian Tempest* (1932). The storm is in fact the play for Knight: it furnishes the central symbol for a play that must exist symbolically. The language is well studied, but other matters are avoided. D. G. James' "The Failure of the Ballad-Makers" is in his *Scepticism and Poetry* (1937). It is an intelligent and hostile account of *Per* and the other late plays, centering on the failures of mythology. At the heart of each of these plays is the myth of restoration, the finding of what is spiritually lost, but the myth turns out to be inexpressive in dramatic form, and its symbolism is inconsistent. In *Per* especially there is a strain on reality, since the plot is so difficult to believe.

Like most critics, M. Van Doren juggles the *Per* issue by considering *Per* as part of the group of the last plays. He has some worthwhile remarks, however, in his *Sh* (1939) on the common themes of the romances. H. Spencer, *The Art and Life of William Sh* (1940), has a refreshingly literal outlook on the play. He thinks the brothel scenes, which were a great vexation to Victorians, are the most dramatically interesting in the play. They furnish the opportunity for Marina to leave romance and come to terms with reality. In decided contrast is G. W. Knight's *The Crown of Life* (1947). In this book are two essays which have endowed us, for better or worse, with the view that *Per* is one of a group of plays which are really parables, visions, and myths. *Per* exemplifies the loss of childlike innocence and its resurrection: its characters have principally allegorical status. As ever, Knight's study of language is acute—and, as ever, he subordinates all other matters to thematic mysteries. The group of essays on Sh and myth in *EIE* (1948) might be read in conjunction with Knight.

There is a very useful critical summary in H. Craig's *An Interpretation of Sh* (1948). Somewhat more impressionistic but also of general value is D. A. Stauffer's study in *Shakespeare's World of Images* (1949). Stauffer clarifies the ethical issues, particularly the exemplification of Patience. A book of some value on the last plays is E. C. Pettet's *Sh and the Romance Tradition* (1949). Pettet comments on the problem of evil in *Per,* which is continually intimated by crimes actual and impending. The brothel business is found "as dull as it is dirty" by T. M. Parrott in *Shakespearean Comedy* (1949). C. Leech, *Shakespeare's Tragedies* (1950), goes over the "botched" poetry and characterization. Perhaps the weakest point is that "the good are incorruptible." J. Tompkins, "Why *Per?*" *RES,* III (1952), 315-324, writes of the spectacle and stage-marvels, ranging from a show of severed heads to apparitions of the divine. The major themes, he states, are loss and restoration, womanly purity, corruption of the flesh, sea and storm, and cosmic harmony expressed in music. There are worthwhile comments on the hero's more-than-stoical virtue.

J. Danby, *Poets on Fortune's Hill* (1952), takes up the relation of *Per* to the romances of Sidney and others. There is an intelligent discussion of the "parasitic" nature of the first two acts, which substitute moralizing for dramatic execution. Their inertia is contrasted to the evident success of the remainder of the play. On the whole, a very good introduction to the play. "The Criticism of Shakespeare's Late Plays" is reprinted by F. R. Leavis in *The Common Pursuit* (1952). While *Per* is not considered specifically, the general orientation of the essay is helpful. Another study of general use is D. S. Bland's "The Heroine and the Sea," *EC,* III (1953), 39-44. A study of episodic action and narrative method is J. Arthos' "Pericles, Prince of Tyre," *ShQ,* IV (1953), 257-270. The value of this study resides in its willingness to remain free of the stereotypes of myth. Arthos argues convincingly for the "logic of events" being coherent.

The romances as "expanded images" of rebirth and reconciliation are treated by D. A. Traversi, *Sh: The Last Phase* (1954). *Per* is seen as experimental in this respect, a symbolic pattern of love and moral enlightenment. Some adaptations of this view are in M. Parker's *The Slave of Life* (1955); there is what I am afraid is pseudo-theology on Marina as a symbol for Grace. Some provoking nonsense by A. Feldman is mentioned here for the unwary to be warned. His "Imaginary Incest," *Amer. Imago,* XII (1955), 117-155, claims that *Per,* written by the Earl of Oxford, reveals its author's inner life. What that may have been, the title intimates. The introduction to J. C. Maxwell's Camb edition (1956) is helpful. Certainly a major starting point for the investigation of this play is *ShS* for 1958. Some account of the critical history of *Per* is offered by P. Edwards in his "Shakespeare's Romances: 1900-1957," *ShS,* XI (1958), 1-18. C. Leech, "The Structure of the Last Plays," has a valuable discussion of the cycle of dramatic action, its crisis, and the matter of five-phase divisions. This essay might be supplemented by that of B. Evans in *Shakespeare's Comedies* (1960), which takes up the method of construction. A good part of the play's effect, it is suggested, derives from the discrepant awareness of protagonist and audience. J. Cutts writes of *"Pericles'* 'Most Heuenly Musicke' " in *NQ,* ns, VII (1960), 172-174, and points out its metaphorical meaning. Miracle, morality, and the interplay of Fortune and Providence is the subject of K. Muir's *Last Periods of Sh, Racine, Ibsen* (1961). A final critical listing ought decidedly to include F. D. Hoeniger's New Arden edition (1963), which has a wealth of scholarly and critical information. Hoeniger's own interpretation leaves some room for doubt: he concludes that the play is traditionally Christian. Suffering as a preparation for wisdom was, however, a concept already old before our epoch.

Northrop Frye's *A Natural Perspective* (1965) is of particular importance for this play. Frye begins with a discussion of the reputation of romances like *Per* and follows with important chapters on the mythopoeic qualities of the last plays of Sh. See especially his chapter "The Return from the Sea." *Later Sh,* ed. Bernard Harris and John Russell Brown (1966), has a number of useful essays. See especially Francis Berry, "Word and Picture in the Last Plays" and Daniel Seltzer, "The Staging of the Last Plays." An important essay summarizing research on sources is in the sixth volume of Bullough (1966). See also C. L. Barber, " 'Thou That Beget'st Him That Did Thee Beget': Transformation in *Per* and *WT,*" *ShS,* XXII (1969), 59-68.

Further reading: W. Raleigh, *Sh* (1907); T. Graves, "On the Date and Significance of *Per,*" *MP,* XIII (1916), 545-556; L. Strachey, *Books and Characters* (1922); E. Welsford, *The Court Masque* (1927); U. Ellis-Fermor, *The Jacobean Drama* (1936); T. Spencer, *Sh and the Nature of Man* (1942); E. A. Armstrong, *Shakespeare's Imagination* (1946); G. Bentley, "Sh and the Blackfriars Theatre," *ShS,* I (1948), 38-50; A. Harbage, *Sh and the Rival Traditions* (1952); T. S. Eliot, "Marina," *Collected Poems* (1952); P. Cruttwell, *The Shakespearean Moment* (1954); W. Fischer, "Shakespeares Späte Romanzen," *ShJ,* XCI (1955), 7-24; M. C. Bradbrook, *The Growth and Structure of Elizabethan Comedy* (1955); A. F. Potts, *Sh and the Faerie Queene* (1958); John Arthos, *The Art of Sh* (1964); Howard Felperin, "Shakespeare's Miracle Play," *ShQ,* XVIII (1967), 363-374.

STAGING   Camb xxx-xl; Craig 1155; New Arden lxv-lxix; Odell *passim;* Trewin *passim.*

See also "Phelps' *Per,*" *Sources of Theatrical History,* ed. A. Nagler (1952); M. St. Clare Byrne, "The Sh Season at the Old Vic, 1957-58, and Stratford-upon-Avon, 1958," *ShQ,* IX (1958), 520-523. See *Later Sh* and Barber (above).

Othello paper
— mention something about the language of
Sh' plays in this period — Travers

Z2012   Tannenbaum, S.A. Othello: A Concise Bibliography NY 1943
T3

         Davidson "Structure & Theme in Oth" Discourse 12 1969

PR2829   Rosenberg M, The Masks of Othello
R81   Williamson, K. "'Honest' & 'False' in Othello" Studia 35 (1963) Neophilologica
         McCullen : "Iago's use of proverbs" Studies in Eng Lit 4 1964
         Stirling B: "Psychology in Othello"
         Camden : "Iago on Women" JEGP 48 1949
         Rand : "The Over-Garrulous Iago" Sh Quart I 1950
    *   Heilman   "Magic in the Web"... Lex Ky. 1956
         "Changes in Tempo of I's speech" Anglica 1 1946
         "Constructive & Destructive Iago" DAI 33:724A (Stony Brook)
         "Soliloquy in Ham, Oth + Mac. DAI 33:2331A (Md.)
         F43 69-77 Imagistic Motif in Othel

or   ← Wair, John Ed Othello a Casebook
Dean
leonard F Doran, Madeline Sight of Othello F46 : 69-99 Iago's if
         Bethell "Diabolic Images in Oth" Sh S 5 (1952) 62-80

PR2829   Elliott George R Flaming Minister
EC   Wilcot "Othello's Crucial Moment" SAB 24 (1949) 181-92
         Eliot Selected Essays PN 511 E443
                                    80 4 E42 sb